ON FREEDOM

by

Friedrich Schleiermacher

Translated, Annotated, and Introduced by
Albert L. Blackwell

Schleiermacher: Studies-and-Translations
Volume 9

The Edwin Mellen Press
Lewiston/Queenston/Lampeter

Library of Congress Cataloging-in-Publication Data

Schleiermacher, Friedrich, 1768-1834.
 [Über die Freheit. English]
 On freedom / Friedrich Schleiermacher ; translated, annotated, and
introduced by Albert L. Blackwell.
     p. cm. -- (Schleiermacher studies and translations ; v. 9)
   Includes bibliographical references (p.   ) and index.
   ISBN 0-7734-9583-5
   1. Liberty. 2. Ethics, Modern--18th century. I. Blackwell,
Albert L. II. title. III. Series.
B3093.U2413   1992
123' .5--dc20   92-24108
                                                                    CIP

This is volume 9 in the continuing series
Schleiermacher: Studies-and-Translations
Volume 9 ISBN 0-7734-9583-5
SST Series ISBN 0-88946-362-X

A CIP catalog record for this book is available
from The British Library.

Many thanks to Walter de Gruyter publishing company
for their permission to translate *Über die Freiheit*.

The Edwin Mellen Press   The Edwin Mellen Press
P.O. Box 450   Box 67
Lewiston, NY 14092   Queenston, Ontario
USA   CANADA L0S 1L0

                The Edwin Mellen Press, Ltd.
                  Lampeter, Dyfed, Wales
                UNITED KINGDOM SA48 7DY

            Printed in the United States of America

To my mother,
Olive Brown Blackwell,
with love and admiration

TABLE OF CONTENTS

Abbreviations

EDITOR'S INTRODUCTION

ON FREEDOM
by
Friedrich Schleiermacher

ABBREVIATIONS

(For complete data consult the Selected Bibliography.)

Ak	*Akademie-Ausgabe* of Kant's works
KGA	*Kritische Gesamtausgabe* of Schleiermacher's works
KpV	Kant's *Kritik der praktischen Vernunft*, 1788
KrV B	Kant's *Kritik der reinen Vernunft*, 2d ed., 1787

EDITOR'S INTRODUCTION

Introduction

Freedom of the will . . .
was the only thing I could think about.

One of Schleiermacher's students at the University of Halle has left an account of a confrontation between Schleiermacher and Halle's Professor of Jurisprudence, Theodor Schmalz, over the issue of capital punishment:

> In his garrulousness, Schmalz talked a great deal about the necessity of capital punishment, wanting to prove it from the hackneyed juristic proposition, usually declared in a philosophical guise, that it is based in human nature to murder someone who murders. Schleiermacher had soon drawn him into the highest sphere of the spirit, where he showed how weak the fundamental pillars of his natural law were, and when Schmalz tried several evasive maneuvers, Schleiermacher became quite passionate and with animation evinced the sacredness of life and reviled the mechanical procedure of governmental officials.[1]

This vignette from 1805 is but one of many indications that Schleiermacher's treatise *On Freedom* was fundamental to his thinking. In that treatise of 1790-1792, Schleiermacher had articulated the principle underlying his view of capital punishment:

> [I]t is well for those who punish to be as greatly inspired by the mild feeling imparted by necessity as by accountability's severity. If only punitive laws might be written by lawmakers inspired in this way![2]

Schleiermacher's argument in *On Freedom* is that our actions are necessarily grounded in our character, as shaped and constrained by our circumstances. Punishment, therefore, should be aimed at improving an offender's character and circumstances and thereby the offender's consequent actions. Later in the treatise he observes that

---

1. [Adolph Müller], *Aus dem Nachlaß Varnhagens von Ense: Briefe von der Universität in die Heimath* (Leipzig: F. A. Brockhaus, 1874), 176.

2. *Über die Freiheit*, ed. Günter Meckenstock, in *Kritische Gesamtausgabe* I/1 (Berlin/New York: Walter de Gruyter, 1984), 271.

capital punishment . . . was first impugned by advocates of necessity, on the grounds that if it is carried out, it can motivate no further action.[3]

Some three decades later we find Schleiermacher elaborating this same principle at length in his 1822-23 lectures on Christian ethics:

> The proper goal of all punitive legislation is to maintain obedience to the law. That is true. For the offender to whom we apply the death penalty, however, this no longer has any meaning.[4]

Schleiermacher's treatise *On Freedom*, which I have translated below, is a comprehensive treatment of ethical principles based upon a necessitarian or deterministic point of view. It is a seminal work for Schleiermacher's career and a treatise of enduring ethical significance. Wilhelm Dilthey, writing in 1870, described the treatise as representing "for a long time the only consistent investigation into human freedom from the side of determinism (though unfortunately it remained in obscurity). Even today it remains one of the most fundamental."[5] He cites this treatise and Schleiermacher's other early ethical writings relating to freedom as evidence of Schleiermacher's "early maturity."[6] Günter Meckenstock, editor of the German text, calls Schleiermacher's *On Freedom* "the most comprehensive, imposing and in truth also the most difficult work in the corpus of his early writings."[7]

History of the Text

On Freedom is an uncompleted manuscript of one hundred and three pages in Schleiermacher's hand. Without title, it remained in obscurity among Schleiermacher's papers until Dilthey's 1870 publication of an abridged and paraphrased version,[8] to which he gave the title *On Human*

---

3. *Über die Freiheit*, 312n.

4. *Die christliche Sitte*, ed. Ludwig Jonas, *Sämmtliche Werke* I.12, 2d ed. (Berlin: Georg Reimer, 1884), 248. I am indebted to my Furman University colleague Dr. John Shelley for directing me to this passage.

5. *Leben Schleiermachers* (Berlin: Georg Reimer, 1870), the appendix entitled "Denkmale," 19.

6. "Denkmale," 5. As we shall see, Schleiermacher wrote his treatise between the ages of twenty-two and twenty-four.

7. *Deterministische Ethik und kritische Theologie: Die Auseinandersetzung des frühen Schleiermacher mit Kant und Spinoza 1789-1794* (Berlin/New York: Walter de Gruyter, 1988), 52.

8. "Denkmale," 19-46. Dilthey's version reduces the length radically, slights Part IV, Section 2, and neglects the truncated Part IV, Section 3 altogether.

Freedom [*Über die Freiheit des Menschen*]. Not until the 1984 appearance of the first volume of the Schleiermacher *Kritische Gesamtausgabe* [KGA] did the entire text appear in print,[9] under the meticulous editorship of Meckenstock, who entitles the treatise simply *On Freedom* [*Über die Freiheit*].

My translation is from Meckenstock's KGA edition. Comparisons with a facsimile of the original manuscript have resulted in a few corrections that I have noted. I have translated the KGA's substantive notes and cross-references, adapting pagination as necessary. I have omitted the KGA's critical apparatus, as it pertains to details of the German manuscript.

Meckenstock establishes[10] that Schleiermacher wrote *On Freedom* for the most part during his tenure as a tutor in the household of the East Prussian nobleman Count Friedrich Alexander Dohna in Schlobitten (today Slobity, Poland).[11] Schleiermacher arrived in Schlobitten on 22 October 1790, a month away from the age of twenty-two. The original intention was for him to accompany the eldest son, Wilhelm zu Dohna, to Königsberg for his university studies, but in the end Schleiermacher was retained at Schlobitten to tutor the three younger Dohna sons, Louis, Fabian, and Friedrich. As evidence that Schleiermacher had plenty of time for his own pursuits at Schlobitten, Meckenstock cites Schleiermacher's fascinating letter of 17 December 1790 detailing his daily routine.[12] When Schleiermacher left Schlobitten in May 1793 at the age of twenty-four, he likely carried with him an extensive manuscript of his treatise on freedom.

Meckenstock theorizes[13] that the extant manuscript of *On Freedom* cannot have been intended as copy for a publisher as it is in need of further editorial revision and its handwriting steadily diminishes to virtual illegibility. Perhaps so. To me, however, the manuscript seems carefully prepared. It is marred by very few corrections, and I find Schleiermacher's exposition quite exact, though sometimes dense and somewhat less careful toward the end. As for the handwriting, there can be no arguing about its difficulties.[14] Yet his intense prose and microscopic writing were perennial problems for Schleiermacher's publishers, even after he had accumulated experience in

---

9. KGA I/1, *Jugendschriften 1787-1796* (Berlin/New York: Walter de Gruyter, 1984), 217-356.

10. KGA I/1, LIV-LVIII.

11. For photographs and a detailed description of the Dohna palace, see Carl Grommelt and Christine von Mertens, *Das Dohnasche Schloß Schlobitten in Ostpreußen* (Stuttgart: W. Kohlhammer, 1962). See also the extended description by Johann Christoph Wedeke, Schleiermacher's friend from Schlobitten days, in KGA I/1, XXVn.

12. KGA I/1, XXVI.

13. KGA I/1, LVI.

14. For a facsimile of the final page of Schleiermacher's manuscript of *On Freedom*, see KGA I/1, 218.

such matters.[15] The prospect of recopying such an extensive manuscript as that of *On Freedom* would be formidable for anyone, it seems to me – especially for Schleiermacher, who once wrote:

> [N]othing is so odious to me as to read through a piece of writing right after I have done it. I have had to accustom myself, therefore, to write a piece at the first stroke just as it should be . . . .[16]

Whether or not the manuscript was intended as a publisher's copy, the fact remains that Schleiermacher did not complete his treatise on freedom and submit it for publication, and we do not know why not. Meckenstock offers three plausible conjectures:

> Perhaps responsibility lies with Schleiermacher's protracted and then unavailing efforts through the mediation of his friend Heinrich Catel to find a Leipzig publisher. Perhaps Schleiermacher was dissatisfied with the stylistic composition, with the suspension of genre between rhapsodic and systematic treatment. Perhaps it befell him here for a second time – after his translation plans for the *Nicomachean Ethics* of Aristotle – that in the end he found his field of inquiry already cultivated by another author, that he had to see his own efforts already brought to their goal from another side: that is, in 1793 Leonhard Creuzer published the treatise *Skeptical Observations Concerning the Freedom of the Will* [*Skeptische Betrachtungen über die Freyheit des Willens*], in which with reference to the Kantian table of categories Creuzer undertook a comprehensive systematic and historical investigation of the theme of freedom. Schleiermacher was impressed by this treatise.[17]

Another plausible conjecture is that as Schleiermacher was about to become a pastor, and did become one in 1794, he must have realized that publication

---

15. See, for example, Schleiermacher's discussion of his publisher's difficulties with his 1803 manuscript of *Groundwork to a Critique of Previous Ethical Doctrine*: Heinrich Meisner, ed., *Schleiermacher als Mensch. Sein Werden. Familien- und Freundesbriefe 1783 bis 1804* (Stuttgart/Gotha: Friedrich Andreas Perthes, 1922), 318-19.

16. Letter of 19 October 1803 to Carl Gustav von Brinkmann, in Meisner, *Schleiermacher als Mensch*, 319.

17. *Deterministische Ethik*, 126-7. For details of Schleiermacher's effort to find a publisher, Meckenstock cites his letter of 24 May 1792 to Catel, KGA V/1, 249. For Schleiermacher's thwarted plans to publish his translation of Aristotle, see KGA I/1, XXXIX. For his reference to Creuzer's treatise, see "Schleiermachers Briefwechsel mit Friedrich Heinrich Christian Schwarz," eds. Heinrich Meisner and Hermann Mulert, *Zeitschrift für Kirchengeschichte* 53 (Stuttgart, 1934), 265.

of this treatise with its deterministic point of view could have caused him great difficulties.[18]

Philosophical Background

Schleiermacher was educated in the tradition of the Herrnhuters or Moravian Brethren, first at the Moravian school in Niesky (14 June 1783 to 17 September 1785). At Niesky he breathed the atmosphere of Moravian piety and laid a solid foundation in classical education.[19] From there he went to the Brethren seminary at Barby (22 September 1785 to April 1787), where he suffered under a faculty who showed little sympathy for his increasing struggles with religious doubt. Fleeing the seminary's stultifying pietism, Schleiermacher transferred to the University of Halle (April 1787 to May 1789) – in Schleiermacher's own phrase, "to enlarge the space for reason's play."[20] At Halle he studied little theology, concentrating instead on classics, languages, and philosophy. In particular, he studied under the philosopher Johann August Eberhard (1739-1809), who taught metaphysics in the Halle tradition of Christian Freiherr von Wolff (1679-1754) and also taught the new critical philosophy of Immanuel Kant (1724-1804), albeit as Kant's antagonist.

Kant's *Critique of Pure Reason* had appeared in 1781. Schleiermacher had read Kant's *Prolegomena to Any Future Metaphysics* of 1783 in Barby. In 1785 Kant published the *Groundwork of the Metaphysic of Morals*, followed in 1788 by the *Critique of Practical Reason*. At Halle, Schleiermacher was an avid student of these works. His early writings are motivated to a remarkable degree by the tensions between Kant's critical philosophy and Eberhard's more rationalistic metaphysics, and between Kant's emphasis on pure reason in ethics and Eberhard's stress on the role of experience and moral feeling. We shall see that, in the end, Schleiermacher was persuaded against Eberhard by Kant's critique of traditional metaphysics but that against Kant he retained Eberhard's appreciation for the role of feeling alongside reason in our ethical life. Meckenstock concisely summarizes Schleiermacher's indebtedness to Eberhard and to the University of Halle:

---

18. I am indebted to Dr. Terrence Tice for this suggestion.

19. The fundamental study of this period of Schleiermacher's life remains E. R. Meyer, *Schleiermachers und C. G. Brinkmanns Gang durch die Brüdergemeine* (Leipzig: Friedrich Jansa, 1905). See also Heinrich Meisner, *Schleiermachers Lehrjahre*, ed. Hermann Mulert (Berlin/Leipzig: Walter de Gruyter, 1934).

20. *An Cecilie*, KGA I/1, 199. More about this intriguing work below.

Despite its rational organization and presentation, Eberhard's own ethics of perfection [*Vollkommenheitsethik*] has a strong proclivity toward experience, toward self-observation and observation of others, toward accepting and assimilating life's concrete situations, toward reflecting upon the constellations of conflicts and motives in everyday life. Schleiermacher's inclination toward phenomenological observation, toward paradigmatic ethical situations and kinds of conduct was thoroughly stimulated in this way and was intensified by more exact acquaintance with the philosophy of antiquity. With his high evaluation of the authors of antiquity Schleiermacher remained in the Halle tradition his whole life.[21]

From Halle Schleiermacher moved to Drossen,[22] where for two years (May 1789 to April or May 1790) he lived with his uncle, Samuel Ernst Timotheus Stubenrauch, studying on his own and preparing for his first series of ministerial examinations. There he projected a series of "philosophical experiments" [*philosophischen Versuchen*][23] to clarify and develop his understanding, particularly in relation to Kant. We may count his treatise *On Freedom* a result of these experiments.

In June 1790 Schleiermacher took his theological examinations in Berlin, and in July he was authorized by the Reformed Church to preach in Prussia. With the assistance of his church superior Friedrich Samuel Gottfried Sack, Schleiermacher then secured the position of tutor in the Dohna household at Schlobitten (22 October 1790 to May 1793), the setting of his treatise *On Freedom*.[24]

Associated Writings Prior to "On Freedom"

To Cecilie (1790)

One of the most fascinating documents from this early period of Schleiermacher's life is his work *To Cecilie* [*An Cecilie*], virtually unknown until its 1984 publication in the *Kritische Gesamtausgabe*.[25] Editor Mecken-

---

21. *Deterministische Ethik*, 27. See also p.146 on the same theme.

22. Today Osno Lubuskie, Poland.

23. Letter of 22 July 1789 to Carl Gustav von Brinkmann, KGA V/1, 139.

24. For more extensive chronologies of Schleiermacher's career from 1768, the year of his birth, to 1796, see KGA V/1, XXVI-XXXV. For the years 1796 to 1798, see KGA V/2, XIII-XXI.

25. KGA I/1, 189-212.

stock places its composition in Berlin in 1790, immediately following Schleiermacher's successful performance on his theological examination,[26] and describes it as a *roman à clef* in which Schleiermacher recounts and explores the tensions, stresses, and indeed anguish of a religious pilgrimage such as his from naive pietism through critical thinking to mature faith:

> This treatise in epistolary form bears strongly autobiographical strokes. The religious development of the principal character depicted by the author is largely Schleiermacher's own critical development from Herrnhuter religiosity to an ethical-critical piety joining reason and heart.[27]

To Cecilie is a valuable work not only for students of Schleiermacher's life but for anyone who has shared what Schleiermacher calls the "crisis" of religious faith for a person who

> had accepted a certain system of doctrinal opinions, not as universal consequences of simple principles, but rather as a collection of individual propositions, independent but assembled under certain common titles. Such a person, after rejecting the system because these individual propositions no longer appear to be in accord, can easily arrive at the thought that it is impossible to find a few simple viewpoints for so many objects and that there may well be truths, but no Truth . . . .[28]

In addition to *To Cecilie*, ten of Schleiermacher's other extant writings date from the brief period prior to his treatise on freedom.[29] Three pertain to his study and translations of Aristotle. Of the remaining seven writings, six relate directly to the themes of *On Freedom*. Thus we may understand the exclamation that I have used as this Introduction's epigram, taken from a letter of 1801 in which Schleiermacher recalls this period of his early writings: "Freedom of the will . . . was the only thing I could think about."[30] Besides establishing a general context, a survey of these earlier writings can serve to introduce the principal issues of Schleiermacher's treatise *On Freedom*.

---

26. KGA I/1, LII-III.
27. *Deterministische Ethik*, 132.
28. KGA I/1, 209.
29. See KGA I/1, VI.
30. "Schleiermachers Briefwechsel mit Friedrich Heinrich Christian Schwarz," 265. Cited in Meckenstock, *Deterministische Ethik*, 19n.

"On the Highest Good" (1789)

The earliest of these writings is *On the Highest Good* [*Über das höchste Gut*],[31] likely dating from the early months of 1789, during Schleiermacher's student days at Halle.[32] It is the first "rhapsody"[33] of a series Schleiermacher had planned as critical responses to the moral philosophy of Kant. *On Freedom* is another such rhapsody, as we see from the reference of its opening sentence to "a collection of philosophical rhapsodies,"[34] of which Schleiermacher apparently intended *On Freedom* to be the first installment to be published.

On the Highest Good addresses the thesis question of "what the concept of the highest good must include, and what we must exclude from it" (91). Schleiermacher's answer to the second half of his question is that we must exclude the postulation of a necessary connection between virtue and happiness that Kant makes in his *Critique of Practical Reason*: "the Kantian joining of virtue and happiness in a single concept is not feasible" (101). Schleiermacher surveys the philosophical history of concepts of virtue and happiness and arrives at his conclusion:

> What then is the actual result of our investigation? It is the following: We have been thoroughly confirmed in the opinion that if one presumes that happiness is the highest good, one can never attain a scientific ethics that bears practical necessity within it . . . . (123)

To remedy the error of Kantian moral philosophy, Schleiermacher believes, we must

> completely separate . . . the concept of the highest good from the concept of happiness, for we have found that all attempts to join them with each other have utterly failed. . . . Happiness everywhere showed itself to be a concept wholly unsuited to assume a place in pure ethics. (123-24)

Schleiermacher will confirm this conclusion and further elaborate this remedy in his treatise *On Freedom*.

---

31. KGA I/1, 81-125.
32. KGA I/1, XLI.
33. KGA I/1, 106.
34. Below, p. 3. Schleiermacher's work of 1803, *Groundwork to a Critique of Previous Ethical Doctrine* [*Grundlinien einer Kritik der bisherigen Sittenlehre*], sheds light on what he means by a "rhapsody," namely, an inquiry that is neither dogmatic nor systematic (*Sämmtliche Werke* III/1, 333-34). Meckenstock writes of the rhapsody, "This form of account and narrative, with specific strong argumentative development and associated broad perspectives, was common throughout the literary productions of the time . . ." (KGA I/1, XVIII).

Schleiermacher devotes most of his essay *On the Highest Good* to the second half of his thesis question concerning the concept of the highest good, the question of "what we must exclude" – namely, the concept of happiness. He devotes only the three concluding paragraphs to the constructive half of his question, "what the concept of the highest good must include." "Will we have no doctrine of happiness at all," he asks, "or if we obtain one, in what kind of relation with ethics will it stand?" (124)

Schleiermacher's answer to his rhetorical questions appears to combine a Stoic philosophy of detachment with Eberhard's philosophy of moral feeling:

> Through constant attentiveness and extended practice we can take things to the point where, in normal cases, we avoid the excessively gripping influence of pleasant as well as unpleasant sensations, an influence that is the basis of an inner and inescapable unhappiness, and this art stands in a close association with ethics.
>
> That is to say, as soon as we see that the moral law cannot affect our will and determine it in any other way than by means of moral feeling that relates to that law, it becomes an intrinsically urgent task for us to increase the practical influence of this feeling. In order to do so, it is necessary to dispel the opposing obstacles, and nothing contradicts that moral feeling, the object of which lies at a certain distance from our senses and the distinguishing character of which is therefore a dispassionate gentleness rather than the impetuous, turbulent motivations of attraction and repulsion that are related to the direct sensuous interest of the heart. Thus do ethics and a doctrine of happiness flow together. The very same state of the faculties of sensation and desire that protects us from succumbing to misfortune also renders us more highly receptive to the blessed influences of moral sense, the dominion of which can alone satisfy us. (124-25)

In other words, the only kind of happiness that is of ethical value is the "dispassionate gentleness" of moral sense and the sense of satisfaction it brings us. This concept is quite distinct from our usual idea of happiness as a state of pleasurable sensation. In *On Freedom* we shall find Schleiermacher removing considerations of happiness from ethics just as definitively as he does here and being even more cautious about rejoining the two, even under the guise of "the blessed influences" of moral sense.

Schleiermacher's reaction against the moral philosophy of Kant goes still further. Kant's *Critique of Practical Reason* joins virtue and happiness by means of the postulate of eternal life. Virtue entitles us to happiness, Kant argues, but we know that this life guarantees no actual joining of the two. Therefore we must postulate eternal life, in which the union of virtue and happiness may be fulfilled. Schleiermacher rejects Kant's joining of virtue and happiness in the postulate of eternal life. Thus *On the Highest Good* anticipates another theme of Schleiermacher's treatise *On Freedom*, namely that concepts of eternal life are merely speculative and without ethical cogency. Schleiermacher rejects Kant's postulate of eternal life as being metaphysical and untrue to the critical principles of Kant's own *Critique of Pure Reason*. Meckenstock refers to this crucial development as Schleiermacher's "radicalizing" of Kant's critical philosophy:

> With the destruction of the Kantian doctrine of postulates Schleiermacher has destroyed the final pillar of a rational theology in the sense of the traditional metaphysics.[35]

On the Highest Good therefore marks Schleiermacher's break with the Halle metaphysical tradition of Leibniz and Wolff and anticipates his treatise *On Freedom* with its fuller development of ethical understanding without appeal to metaphysical assertions concerning God and eternal life.

Most importantly, *On the Highest Good* introduces a question that we shall find at the heart of *On Freedom*: how exactly is our consciousness of moral law related to our choosing? In this earlier essay, Schleiermacher's answer is that the relationship is not one of immediate or "pure" causality, as Kant argues in the *Critique of Practical Reason*, but is rather mediated by moral sense. That is, our knowledge of moral law is not alone sufficient to determine our decisions. Rather our ethical knowledge must combine with our moral sense to affect us and attract us to moral choices. Whereas Schleiermacher's earlier essay merely invokes the traditional notion of moral sense, however, *On Freedom* analyzes the dynamics of our choosing as one of its major themes, and that analysis constitutes the treatise's most creative contribution.

Finally, *On the Highest Good* touches on the theme of punishment with which I opened this Introduction. Here, as in *On Freedom*, Schleiermacher rejects Kant's notion of punishment as "mere harm in itself,"[36] insisting rather that the final ethical measure of acts of punishment must be their "beneficence." (103)

---

35. *Deterministische Ethik*, 154.

36. Kant, *Kritik der praktischen Vernunft*, in *Kant's gesämmelte Schriften*, ed. Königlich Preußischen Akademie der Wissenschaften, I/5 (Berlin: Georg Reimer, 1908), 37 (standard pagination). The English translation by Lewis White Beck gives the standard pagination in the margin: Immanuel Kant, *Critique of Practical Reason* (Indianapolis/New York: Bobbs-Merrill, 1956).

"Notes on Kant: Critique of Practical Reason" (1789)

KGA I/1 includes a three-page Schleiermacher manuscript, previously neither published nor described. Editor Meckenstock entitles it *Notes on Kant: Critique of Practical Reason* [*Notizen zu Kant: Kritik der praktischen Vernunft*].[37] He dates it from the first half of 1789, shortly after Schleiermacher's composition of *On the Highest Good*, observing that it relates to Kantian themes different from those of that essay but similar to those of the *Dialogues on Freedom* that Schleiermacher was to write still later in that same year (see below). Specifically, these pages focus on Kant's concept of transcendental freedom.

In his treatise *On Freedom* we shall find Schleiermacher adopting Kant's concept of transcendental freedom, only to modify it in such a way as to reverse its Kantian ethical implications. For Kant, transcendental freedom is the ability to make decisions purely upon the rational basis of moral law, independently of all the empirical conditions of our lives. Schleiermacher rejects this Kantian separation of our moral lives into two realms, the rational and the empirical. Indeed, one of the most distinctive marks of Schleiermacher's ethics is his insistence that our reasoning and our experience, while distinguishable, are finally inseparable.

These early *Notes on Kant* suggest a hint of incredulity on Schleiermacher's part as he re-studies Kant's account of transcendental freedom:

> transcendental freedom. Apparently, therefore, a faculty of causality without necessary connection with what has gone before. I have therefore certainly not misunderstood him. (129)

Schleiermacher's notes suggest an observation that will later figure importantly in his treatise *On Freedom*: "Speculative reason's concept of freedom (transcendental) is *unavoidable* only for *one* otherworldly subject."[38] *On Freedom* will make this cryptic entry more clear: only God the Creator can be thought to enjoy transcendental freedom in the sense defined by Kant's *Critique of Pure Reason*: "a faculty of causality without necessary connection with what has gone before." Such freedom can never apply to human beings.

The *Notes on Kant* then return to the issue that closed Schleiermacher's essay *On the Highest Good*: the question of how our consciousness of moral law is related to our choosing. Here as before Schleiermacher rejects Kant's idea that our consciousness of moral law can determine our choosing "immediately," that is, directly and infallibly, despite all our inclinations to the contrary. Kant had attempted to account for this direct determination of

---

37. KGA I/1, 127-34.
38. KGA I/1, 129. Schleiermacher's parentheses and emphases.

our choosing by means of a unique, *a priori* feeling of "respect" [*Achtung*] for the moral law. Schleiermacher was never able to accept Kant's unique concept. He found it logically contrived and psychologically impossible:

> Kant wishes to make it even clearer how we can understand the occurrence of feeling *a priori*, but he appears to me not to have achieved this either. . . . How the positive *a priori* can be understood is just as empty as before, as is also the assertion that this feeling distinguishes itself from all others. (133)

Schleiermacher ends his *Notes on Kant* with the observation that for Kant "there is no feeling for the law (à la Hutcheson)" (134). This reference to Francis Hutcheson (1694-1746), the British philosopher of moral sense, gives rise to the question of philosophical antecedents to Schleiermacher's concept of moral sense and particular influences upon his use of that term. That Schleiermacher calls several of his early writings on ethical themes "rhapsodies" might suggest a connection with that other great British philosopher of moral sense, Anthony Ashley Cooper, Third Earl of Shaftesbury (1671-1713), who entitled one of his essays *The Moralists: A Philosophical Rhapsody* (1709). Yet in all of Schleiermacher's writings and letters up to 1796, the passing reference to Hutcheson at the conclusion of the *Notes on Kant* is his only mention of either of these moral-sense philosophers.[39] Nor in Kant's two great *Critiques* do we find explicit discussion of Shaftesbury or Hutcheson, except in one schematic chart that provides Kant occasion to dismiss Hutcheson's moral philosophy, along with the those of Montaigne, Mandeville, and Epicurus, as "all together empirical and obviously not fit for the general principle of morality."[40] For lack of evidence, therefore, we can draw no conclusions concerning Schleiermacher's specific acquaintance with these antecedent philosophers. The only certain influence in this regard was his Halle teacher Eberhard, the mediator and reinterpreter of the moral sense tradition.

"Dialogues on Freedom" (1789)

To summarize our findings to this point, the question that closes the essay *On the Highest Good* and is taken up again in the *Notes on Kant*, namely, how exactly our consciousness of moral law relates to our choosing, will prove central to Schleiermacher's treatise *On Freedom*. But between these

---

39. Schleiermacher's first mention of Shaftesbury's name appears in some notes of 1797-98, and it too is only in passing: KGA, I/2, 96.

40. *Kritik der praktischen Vernunft*, 40.

earlier works and that monumental treatise stand Schleiermacher's three *Dialogues on Freedom* [*Freiheitsgespräche*]. Only the last of the three is extant.[41] We know there were three, however, from a letter Schleiermacher wrote from Drossen on 10 June 1789 to his friend Carl Gustav von Brinkmann in Halle:

> Of the dialogues on freedom, or, as I prefer to call them, on the nature of moral actions, two are already completely finished and I shall very soon work on the third as well . . . .[42]

Again to Brinkmann on 22 July 1789:

> You have wanted to see my dialogues on freedom, and I am accommodating you insofar as I can. The third is not yet finished, and I have just undertaken a small improvement in the second . . . .
>
> You will furthermore become aware that certain well-known materials are treated at some length – and this I have at least realized and wished. This seemed to me to be unavoidable, moreover, if I wanted to show that we must treat will power just like every other [power], and if the philosophical character of my Kleon is to be a true and ordinary character, for[43] there really are many who content themselves with a certain inadmissible middle way concerning this point, whereupon incorrect and obscure concepts of accountability are unavoidable. Thus you will perhaps acquit me concerning the overall economy of this dialogue. I am very curious about what you will say concerning its last section, and your thoughts would be welcome to me. The second dialogue will concern itself with several practical consequences. The two friends will investigate whether, with this system, regret is an illusion and how regret must be employed. They will see whether, from the side of sensible motivations to morality, we lose if we have to give up the obscure feeling of indeterminable freedom of choice and whether this kind of necessity of our actions leads to moral quietism. The third will be chiefly devoted to the Kantian concept of freedom and respect for the moral law.[44]

We do not know what happened to the first of these dialogues on freedom. We do know that Schleiermacher soon professed to regard it with dis-

---

41. KGA I/1, 135-64.
42. KGA V/1, 121.
43. Reading Schleiermacher's **wenn** here to be a slip of his pen for **denn**, which makes better sense.
44. KGA V/1, 140-141.

dain, referring to it in a letter to Brinkmann of 18 November 1789 as "rubbish."[45] As for the second dialogue, its manuscript is also lost to us, but probably not its contents. Meckenstock follows Dilthey in believing that the dialogue that interrupts Part II of Schleiermacher's treatise *On Freedom* preserves at least portions of the second dialogue of 1789.[46] The circumstantial evidence for this theory is quite strong, not least the abrupt and awkward change of style in *On Freedom* at the point where the dialogue appears, leading Meckenstock to call the dialogue "a stylistic foundling in the great treatise."[47] More decisively, the issues of the second dialogue – moral regret, feelings of indeterminable freedom, and moral quietism – are themes of the dialogue that appears in Part II of *On Freedom.*

Whereas the dialogue in *On Freedom* involves only Schleiermacher and his fictional friend Kleon, the surviving third Dialogue of 1789 involves three figures: Kleon the inquisitive novice, Kritias the Kantian, and Sophron the synthesizer of classical and Kantian ethics, presumably representing Schleiermacher himself. In fact, Schleiermacher assumes a direct role at the end, taking over the dialogue's conclusion in his own voice, as if he has grown impatient with the laboriousness of dialogical procedure:

> It would be too long-winded to impart this entire review, so I
> wish to content myself with presenting a few of its results.
> (160-61)

This, despite the fact that Schleiermacher has already pruned his dialogue once before, when about a fifth of the way through he has Kritias "suddenly called away" (141).

As this third *Dialogue* opens, Sophron is attempting to respond to Kleon's concern that a philosophy of necessity will undermine the concept of moral accountability [*Zurechnung*] – a challenge to which Schleiermacher will devote primary attention in Part II of his treatise *On Freedom.* In order to meet this challenge Sophron is led to replace Kant's notion of an *a priori* feeling of respect for moral law, which in his *Notes on Kant* Schleiermacher had called "empty,"[48] with a clearly defined understanding of moral sense. Once again Schleiermacher's question is how our consciousness of moral law is related to our choosing, or as Sophron puts it: "to what extent our reason has an influence upon our actions" (153).

Sophron's explanation is that our moral sense consists in a certain enjoyment [*Vergnügen*] we gain by making rational or virtuous choices. Except

---

45. KGA V/1, 162. Meckenstock provides further details in KGA I/1, XLV-VI.

46. KGA I/1, XLVI-VII.

47. KGA, I/1, XLVII.

48. See above, p. xi.

for its different object – namely, practical reason's moral law – our moral sense is a pleasure like our other pleasures and enters into competition with them as we deliberate. The outcome of our deliberation depends upon the relative strengths of these various potential pleasures at the moment of our choosing:

> whether in each contested instance we act rightly will depend only upon the liveliness and strength of this moral feeling in comparison with that which stands over against it. (159)

The Kantian position that "we absolutely must be able to do what we should do" (159) is therefore incorrect, as the novice Kleon is quick to point out (Kant's defender Kritias being no longer present!). Sophron agrees. We are never morally perfect or capable of moral perfection:

> we are in a continual middle state between the sheer wonder of an archetype of moral perfection that exists purely in our thoughts and the gratification of the consciousness that we have made this archetype actual in ourselves. (157)

Complete harmony of the ideal and the actual "is unattainable for us" (158). This perspective serves not to undermine our moral accountability, however, but rather to "confirm" it (159). We measure our actions by the standard of the moral law, not expecting congruence but rather determining to grow toward the ideal to which we are accountable.

Not the moral law alone, then, but love for the moral law motivates us. Moral sense joins our consciousness of moral law with our choosing. Writing in his own voice at the close of the dialogue, Schleiermacher summarizes:

> "Respect" (which is nothing other than moral admiration) is indeed connected to this process, but this feeling is never practical as such, but only as love.
>
> Moreover, we cannot stipulate *a priori* that this feeling breaches inclinations. This is so because this feeling appears only with particular circumstances, and no particular action is conceivable that does not favor some natural inclination. Since with various persons, and with any one person at various times, this feeling is so various, extensively as well as intensively, other feelings will sometimes prevail, and at other times it will prevail over them. We therefore cannot maintain that this feeling is determined by pure reason alone (which indeed is always unaltered and the same) but must affirm rather that it is determined by the receptivity of the faculty of sensation [*des Empfindungsvermögens*] to being affected by the representation

of the moral law. This receptivity is dependent upon other conditions each time.

Schleiermacher's concluding words return the dialogue to its opening theme of moral accountability:

> On this same basis it is clear also that accountability has nothing to do with the presupposition that at every moment something must[49] have been *able* to happen because it *should* have happened. Accountability is simply a comparison of the result that the subjective grounds of motivation have given the faculty of desire in a certain action with the result that reason had previously determined through the moral law. The greater the difference between the two, the greater the feeling of contrast and the greater the consciousness of moral offense by which the judgments of conscience are determined. Not for everything that is proposed to us (such as manifesting the moral law in every particular case) can even the possibility of resolution be presupposed. Unceasingly sensibility gives reason the problem of effecting the greatest possible continuing satisfaction of all inclinations taken together within a subject, a problem that reason will never be in a position to solve. (163-64)

In summary, Schleiermacher believes that moral accountability means that we are capable of measuring our choices against the rational standards of moral law and that the moral worth of our choices is a partial measure of the worth of our moral character. Ethical rationality cannot determine our choices directly, however. We are not simply creatures of pure reason but are creatures of desire as well. If the moral law is to determine our choices, then we must love the moral law, or at least hold it in esteem. That love or esteem must compete with all our other loves and desires in determining our choices. Our resulting choices will therefore not always be moral, but it is always at least conceivable that they might be. Thus we are led to strive for growth toward ethical maturity, in which our sense of moral obligation more and more consistently outweighs our other desires, enabling us to make moral decisions more consistently and with less arduous struggle.

This summary of Schleiermacher's argument in his third *Dialogue* of 1789 previews the argument at the heart of his treatise *On Freedom* of 1792-93.

---

49. I have deleted a "not" at this point, which seems to me to reverse Schleiermacher's intended meaning. The KGA text reads: "*Aus eben diesem Grunde erhelle nun auch daß die Zurechnung nichts mit der Voraussezung zu thun habe, daß in einem jeden Augenblick etwas nicht habe müßen geschehen* können *weil es hat geschehen* sollen [Schleiermacher's emphases]."

"Note on the Knowledge Of Freedom" (1790-92)

The final associated writing prior to *On Freedom* is a single sheet with Schleiermacher's writing on both sides, published for the first time in KGA and provided with the title *Note on the Knowledge of Freedom* [*Notiz zur Erkenntnis der Freiheit*]. It is a sketch pertaining directly to Schleiermacher's preparation of *On Freedom*. Specifically, it presents without elaboration the threefold outline that will govern the final three sections of the treatise: "of freedom as a predicate of human actions, of freedom as a predicate of human situations, and of freedom as a predicate of human faculties."[50]

And so we come to the treatise itself. In the pages that follow I have undertaken my own summary of its argument, with an occasional word of commentary along the way. My aim has been to follow the main argument of Schleiermacher's treatise, which is sometimes complex and occasionally obscure. To facilitate comparisons between my summary and Schleiermacher's text, I have adopted the main headings of the translated treatise as the headings for my summary.

---

50. KGA I/1, 215.

ON FREEDOM

Part I
A New Account of Moral
Choice and Obligation

Introduction

Calling freedom a "controversial subject," Schleiermacher argues that, despite its difficulties, the subject must nevertheless be pursued to the point of clarification. To abandon such inquiry would be to abandon all hope of "practical philosophy," by which Schleiermacher, following Kant, means the philosophy of ethical life. The aim of the treatise, Schleiermacher writes, is "a closer elucidation of the Kantian theory of freedom." The key to success is to base the inquiry upon clearly defined terms, and Schleiermacher takes this as the first aim of his treatise.

Preparatory Analysis of the Concept "Faculty of Desire"

Schleiermacher begins with Kant's fundamental concept of "faculty of desire," that is, our capacity for putting our thoughts or "representations" into effect. Finding Kant's concept not basic enough, however, Schleiermacher defines the even more fundamental concept of "impulse" as "the representing subject's activity, grounded in the subject's nature, of bringing forth representations." Exactly how we put these representations into effect then becomes the question. It is the question of how our faculty of desire functions, or of how we translate our thoughts into decisions.

Schleiermacher devotes the first section of his treatise to analyzing our faculty of desire, carefully defining various significant regions along the spectrum of its operations. The first region is "instinct," wherein our faculty of desire is activated by a single representation. To suggest a simpler example than any Schleiermacher offers, we hear a bang and instantly turn our head to seek out the source. Schleiermacher believes that most of our deciding is more complex than instinctive response, however. We reach most of our decisions by comparing various representations, and we call this process "choice."

Our capacity for understanding enters the process of choice when we generalize from our experiences to formulate empirical judgments to guide our future choices. These rational generalizations we call "maxims." When these maxims are involved in the process of choice we call our faculty of desire a "will." Schleiermacher insists, however, that a maxim never determines our decisions directly or absolutely. Rather, a maxim is one representation among many representations always competing for our decision. Our willing always and intrinsically involves choosing. This is the point of Schleiermacher's most fundamental departure from Kant, who defined "will" as the capacity to decide upon the basis of maxims, regardless of our other representations. For Kant, willing and choosing are two separate capacities. For Schleiermacher, they are distinguishable for purposes of analysis but inseparable in fact.

In Schleiermacher's terminology, when we formulate our maxims not merely by generalizing from empirical experience but by applying rational moral principles, we are exercising "practical reason." Together with this exercise of reason we experience the desire to bring all of our maxims into rational harmony, and this quest for unity is practical reason's ultimate task. It is an everlasting task, however, "on account of the infinite multitude of possible maxims," and so the idea of a completed system of practical reason will remain always an ideal.

The Method of Approach

The next logical question would seem to be this: How exactly does our faculty of desire arrive at a decision from among its many and various competing representations – experiential and rational? Before approaching that question, however, Schleiermacher takes pains to make it clear that a satisfactory answer must be based upon clear definitions and analysis, not upon "an appeal to obscure judgments of common human understanding, still less to expressions of an exceedingly indeterminate and confused feeling of freedom." Equally important, he argues, no satisfactory answer to our ethical or "practical" questions can be based upon analysis that is "theoretical" or, we might say, scientific. Schleiermacher is thoroughly Kantian here, accepting and reinforcing Kant's famous distinction between human reasoning in its theoretical mode and in its practical mode. Kant's great *Critique of Pure Reason* had demonstrated to Schleiermacher's satisfaction that the question of human freedom *in principle* cannot be resolved by the methodologies appropriate to the natural sciences.

What does Schleiermacher mean when he insists that we must follow a practical rather than a theoretical approach to the issue of human freedom? I think he means that we do not ask questions such as these: "According to the analyses of the natural sciences, how does our faculty of desire operate?" and "In light of these scientific conclusions, is moral obligation possible?" Rather we ask: "In light of our experiences of moral obligation, how must we think of our faculty of desire?" We experience moral obligation, and our challenge is to reflect upon how our deciding must operate in order for this actuality to be so.

It turns out, then, that the next logical question is not the theoretical question stated above: How exactly does our faculty of desire arrive at a decision from among its many and various competing representations – experiential and rational? Rather, Schleiermacher poses the next logical question in practical terms: What is moral obligation? And then: Since our faculty of desire is capable of fulfilling moral obligation, how are we to think of its process of arriving at a moral decision from among its many and various competing representations?

Moral Obligation and Moral Choice

Schleiermacher describes three conditions of moral obligation. First, in disagreement with Kant's view, he insists that moral reasoning does not determine our choices *absolutely*, as if moral law were an incontrovertible natural law governing the faculty of desire. Or, as Schleiermacher puts it, moral choice is not an "instinct of reason." Second, moral reasoning *may* determine our choices. It is always at least conceivable that the influence of our moral reasoning might be strong enough to govern our choices amidst our many competing representations. Third, moral reasoning *should* govern our choices, and the extent to which it does so is the gauge of our moral worth. Schleiermacher argues that these are conditions of the concept of moral obligation in all systems of ethics, whether they be empirical, based upon the ideas of happiness or perfection, or rational, like the moral philosophy of Kant.

Defined in this way, Schleiermacher argues, moral obligation presupposes three things about our faculty of desire. It presupposes first that our faculty of desire is a *will*, capable of deciding upon the basis of rational maxims, not merely upon the basis of instinct or of choice governed by sensible objects alone. Second, we must think of our moral reasoning as including its own *impulse*, that is, as being capable of bringing forth representations, which may then become objects of our choosing. Schleiermacher points out that in earlier systems of ethics this moral impulse was called "moral sense," whereas Kant calls it "respect" for the moral law. Exactly what Schleiermacher himself thinks we should call this moral impulse is never quite clear from his treatise. It is best then, perhaps, simply to keep to his own term, "moral impulse."

Finally, if we are to account adequately for our experience of moral obligation, we must think of our will as being in itself *neither good nor evil*. If our will were determinable by moral maxims only, as Kant's moral philosophy seems to assert, moral exercises of our will would not be an obligation for us but simply a tautological fact about us. Conversely, if our will could not be determined by moral maxims at all, moral conduct would not oblige us since it would be impossible for us. Schleiermacher calls this characteristic "the natural undeterminedness of the will." It is a third and final presupposition concerning our will necessary in an accounting for our experience of moral obligation.

With this clarification of the concepts of moral obligation and will, Schleiermacher is now prepared to turn to the question: How does our faculty of desire arrive at a particular choice from among its many and various competing representations? Schleiermacher proposes the following answer. Our faculty of desire is not determined by any single representation, whether external to ourselves or internal, composite or simple. Rather, each of our particular decisions is determined by the particular state of our whole "subjective being" or "soul" – the total condition of our individual, complicated, innermost selves – at the moment of our deciding. In Schleiermacher's own words:

> Thus the proposition appears to be established: the preponderance in which every comparison of choice must end in order to pass over into a complete action of the faculty of desire must in every case be grounded in the totality of present representations and in the state and interrelations of all the soul's faculties that have been produced in the progression of representations in our soul.

Schleiermacher refers to this proposition as his treatise's "thesis."

Recapitulation and Reconstruction

We choose, then, according to what we are. And what are we? According to Schleiermacher, we are extremely complex, subtle, and finally inscrutable persons, beyond the grasp of scientific analysis. The process of our choosing "is filled not simply with life but with superabundant life, multifariously active." Our choosing involves an inseparable commingling of our "senses, fantasy, understanding and reason."   Our faculty of desire ceaselessly "craves, selects, desires, decides, and acts in every moment of our existence."

> In short, it is pointless to divide human beings. All is joined in
> us; all is one.

Again we are at the point of Schleiermacher's break with his mentor Kant, who accounted for human freedom by bifurcating human beings into the rational and the experiential. Schleiermacher will not hear of such division.

These, then, according to Schleiermacher, are the practical presuppositions that account for our experience of moral obligation and "warrant" our moral conduct. Scientifically, it is perfectly true that we can never know the soul's state exactly enough to predict actions with anything more than probability. Ethically, however, the causal connection between our decisions and the state of our soul is the necessary, sufficient, and fruitful presupposition at the basis of our moral lives, as Schleiermacher will next attempt to show.

Part II
Moral Accountability and
The Doctrine of Necessity

On the Objection That
Determinism Undermines Moral Accountability

Schleiermacher accepts the label of "determinism" for his ethical point of view, but he insists that his determinism must be defined only by his own account of the subject, not by anyone else's.[51] He then advances his argument by taking up various objections to his "doctrine of necessity," as he prefers to call his view.

The first objection is the claim that determinism undermines our moral accountability. This objection depends on what we mean by "moral accountability," of course, and Schleiermacher formulates a precise definition:

> Accountability is the judgment by which we assign the morality
> of an action to the person who performed it in such a way that
> our judgment of the action constitutes part of our judgment
> concerning the person's worth.

---

51. To judge from some of Schleiermacher's notes of 1797 that are quite critical of the philosophy of Gottfried Wilhelm Leibniz (1646-1716), Schleiermacher may be protecting his concept of ethical determinism here from confusion with Leibniz's metaphysical determinism. For the notes, see Dilthey, *Leben Schleiermachers*, "Denkmale," 71-74. See below, p. 3.

Schleiermacher points out that according to this definition we may make judgments of accountability – attributing actions to the person who acts, and comparing both to standards developed by our moral reasoning – without answering the question of exactly how the actions have arisen. That is, Schleiermacher argues that his definition of accountability is appropriate to both critics and advocates of a doctrine of necessity.

The objection comes from those who argue that if our decisions are rooted in the persons we are, then each of our particular decisions is determined and we enjoy no real options. We cannot be held morally accountable, so the objection goes, for decisions in which no alternative choices are actually possible. We cannot say that a person *should* decide something when in this particular moment the person *cannot* decide it, since the necessary grounds for actuality are not part of the person's state, not within the person's power.

Schleiermacher argues that this objection rests not upon clear definition and analysis of moral choice and accountability but rather upon indistinct "sentiments" or emotions relating to those concepts. His response is twofold. First, he demonstrates in theoretical terms that his doctrine of necessity is both logically and actually possible. Then he shows in practical terms that the doctrine of necessity, far from contradicting the concept of moral accountability, is the presupposition upon which that concept must rest.

Application of the Doctrine of Necessity
To the Concept of Moral Accountability

Schleiermacher argues that our decisions reveal our moral worth precisely because they are rooted in our soul, our "unity of character and sensibility." Our decisions express the persons we are, and by comparing our decisions with the ideals put forward by moral reasoning we may evaluate our degree of moral maturity and our need for moral growth.

> In the end we are compelled to acknowledge that the very first requirements of moral life, which we have honestly believed ourselves to enjoy in spite of necessity, are blessings secretly bestowed by necessity's hand.

As if sensing that critics of a necessitarian view are not yet likely to be satisfied by his argument, Schleiermacher elaborates their objections further, namely, that determinism robs us of such moral sentiments as praise, blame, satisfaction, and regret. He answers with an extended analogy from artistic experience: we praise or blame artists on the basis of their work, at the same time fully recognizing their indebtedness to formative circumstances of birth, social experience, and training. Schleiermacher suggests that the principal difference limiting this analogy between our ethical and artistic spheres is that the moral impulse of ethical law is more universally experienced than aesthetic sense for canons of artistic judgment.

It is not that the critics who charge determinism with contradictions are experiencing false emotions, Schleiermacher explains, but only that "they perhaps have analyzed their sentiments falsely and have thereby come to incorrect associations that confuse this apparent contradiction with other sentiments that are quite natural and right." Even the feeling that we are "the independent originating cause" of the state of our soul is morally legitimate, he concedes, provided that we temper it with clear practical analysis. He trusts the analysis provided by his treatise to set our associations right, so that we may "view persons bedecked with the entire dignity or disgrace of their actions."

In one of the most vigorous sections of the treatise Schleiermacher argues that if sentiments relating to accountability are not mitigated by the doctrine of necessity the result is human alienation, for our decisions will be thought of as thoroughly private and arbitrary, somehow lifted out of the common human characteristics and social settings that unite us. Only with the conjunction of accountability and necessity "does our feeling attain the attunement required not only by the voice of our heart but also by the solidarity of human society . . . ."

This sense of human commonality and solidarity provides the context for Schleiermacher's discussion of punishment. Schleiermacher maintains that through the doctrine of necessity, punishments – at both the personal and civic levels – are mitigated by feelings of equality, sympathy, and concern, yet without engendering false sentimentality that would weaken the rule of law. Since actions are rooted in our character, punishments for criminal actions should aim at benefiting the criminal's character, while at the same time upholding the basic discipline required for social order and justice.

Interlude: A Dialogue On the Question of God's Justice

At this point Schleiermacher shifts his exposition abruptly from human justice to God's justice, under the guise of an ostensible dialogue with "my friend Kleon." Schleiermacher dismisses rather peremptorily Kleon's question as to whether our personal character is given or shaped, presumably on the grounds that such a question solicits a theoretical answer, which

Schleiermacher has already contended to be both inappropriate and impossible. To Kleon's intense questions concerning the union of virtue and happiness in eternity, Schleiermacher answers simply that we cannot know enough about eternity to answer.

Schleiermacher's "theodicy" or defense of God's justice, he says, consists in a syllogism, with God's wisdom and goodness as the major premise, God's omnipotence and providence as the minor premise, and the conclusion that all souls will meet at the common goal of God's purpose. As for the question of relative happiness along the way to this goal, Schleiermacher repeats the assertion of his earlier essay *On the Highest Good*: happiness is a principle without value for ethical guidance. Even the idea of the enjoyment we gain by making virtuous choices, which was so central to Schleiermacher's third *Dialogue* of 1789, virtually disappears from the argument of *On Freedom*.

Issues Concerning Our Feeling of Freedom

Schleiermacher returns from the dialogue to explore further our feeling that we are completely free. He acknowledges the great but deceptive, even beguiling power of this feeling. He enters into a remarkably extensive presentation of his opponents' claim that only a feeling of complete freedom makes moral life possible and that the doctrine of necessity undermines such a feeling. Schleiermacher seems to believe that this objection is the most tenacious that his treatise has to answer.

Restating his opponents' objection leads Schleiermacher to make a fundamental distinction between "necessity" and "constraint." The feeling of complete freedom that we value so highly, he contends, is the altogether justified feeling that we may free ourselves from constraint, that is, from being absolutely compelled or restrained by particular objects of desire. This is but to repeat one of the basic conditions for moral obligation that Schleiermacher has earlier established: our faculty of desire is not confined to instinct or sensible choice alone but is also capable of self-reflection and -direction on the basis of rational judgment. Yet he has also argued, and argues again here, that such self-reflection and -direction are compatible with the doctrine of necessity – indeed, that only the doctrine of necessity can adequately account for these experiences. In summary, our feeling of complete freedom is a feeling arising from awareness of our deliberations issuing in choice, not a feeling stemming from our consciousness of complete independence from the law of causality. We feel freedom from constraint, not freedom from necessity.

Some Ethical Consequences

Having thus separated the misunderstood constituents of our feeling of freedom from the ethically legitimate, Schleiermacher applies the doctrine of necessity to our deliberations concerning the future and our regrets concerning the past. He contrasts these edifying moral experiences with the unwarranted confidence that stems from supposed feelings of isolation from the universal interconnectedness of life. Regret over a decision, for example, is complacent so long as we are convinced that at the next opportunity we can simply choose differently, without any specific alteration of our character in the meantime. In contrast, regret becomes a fruitful moral sentiment when reflection upon a decision leads us to alter our character, with assurance from the doctrine of necessity that in the future improved character will issue in improved decisions.

Thus Schleiermacher contends that the doctrine of necessity engenders an ethical temperament of modesty, discretion, and prudent activity. Far from undermining our sense of self-activity, the doctrine heightens our sense of personality and leads us toward moral maturity.

Part III
Historical Survey: Concepts of Freedom,
Necessity, and Associated Feelings

Introduction

Schleiermacher devotes Part III of his treatise to the question of why, if all objections to the doctrine of necessity involve misunderstanding, that doctrine has never overcome these illusions and met with universal acceptance. The answer, he says, cannot be merely theoretical but must be based upon the actual history of ideas. Thus he is led to survey the historical development of concepts of freedom and necessity together with their associated feelings, showing that sound ideas of practical conduct and a clear understanding of the principle of universal causality have never coincided until Schleiermacher's own day.

Greek Antiquity

As Greek polytheism gradually gave way to a debate over the concept of unified purpose in the world, three main philosophical viewpoints developed. One viewpoint rejected the concept of unity of purpose and affirmed the concept of chance. The second asserted a unity of purpose resulting from the governance of the world by a wise being. The third asserted a unity of the world grounded in the concept of fate. Advocates of these viewpoints debated the idea of a final causality for the world, but all of them alike lacked the principle of universal efficient causality through which all events are interconnected. Thus their concepts of freedom and necessity remained "foreign" to those concepts as we formulate them in the modern age, with our understanding of comprehensive laws of nature.

The ancient Greeks developed valuable ideas concerning the meaning of moral law and human accountability to it, Schleiermacher concludes, but they were too greatly under the sway of teleological ideas or the idea of fate to develop an adequate understanding the causes operative in human motivations and actions.

Medieval Christianity

Augustine's discussions of grace occasioned closer examinations of the way ethical decisions are brought forth in our soul, but a correctly formulated idea of necessity was still lacking. The result was confused arguing on the part of the medieval scholastics, often arbitrary and sophistical. Ethical maxims inherited from antiquity were not studied to discover their foundation in basic moral principles but were rather simply attributed to divine revelation, and there ethical analysis came to an end.

Furthermore, medieval Christianity inextricably joined human accountability with the notion of eternal divine punishment for transgressions. The concept of the necessity of human actions obviously contradicted this notion. If human actions are results that according to the doctrine of necessity could have occurred in only one way, then eternal punishment for these actions would be unwarranted. Thus the majority "stuck stubbornly to the assertion that the doctrine of necessity suspended all morality since it overthrew the legitimacy of divine punishment."

With the doctrine of necessity thus considered completely refuted, the question remained: How, then, do human actions occur? In answer, the only real alternative to the doctrine of necessity was the doctrine of "indifferentism" or "equilibrism": the idea that human actions are completely isolated from all necessitating causes. Advocates of this view, Schleiermacher writes, asserted that "in the moment of a certain act or resolution I could decide in any conceivable way, and nowhere in the preceding course of the world is there a necessitating ground sufficient to have determined this way to the exclusion of every other." Schleiermacher contends that this assertion, arising as it did by default, rested upon no supporting arguments but merely upon the feelings of freedom he has already shown to be illusory and upon anecdotal instances of supposed equilibristic choices that in principle cannot ever amount to proof or disproof. We might note here that when, in the modern period, Kant developed what he thought were rigorous supporting arguments for an equilibristic concept of freedom, Schleiermacher was no better satisfied.

Schleiermacher is convinced that indifferentism, though designed to reconcile ethical conduct and divine punishments, in fact undermines both concepts. "How can I be accountable for an action when we cannot determine the extent to which it belongs to my soul? And yet this is obviously the case with the system of indifferentism." Schleiermacher states his final assessment of indifferentism as follows:

> indifferentism is one of the errors in philosophy arising from the need to preserve the authority of two covertly contradictory presuppositions. It could not possibly prevail, therefore, because it could not achieve this impossible goal. On the other hand, it could not be completely struck down either . . . . For us this is easy, however, because we are long accustomed to the truth that morality is to be thought of as sufficiently established independently of divine commands and punishments.

Thus Schleiermacher boldly declares himself a citizen of the modern age – the now mature student who was once driven from pietistic Barby "to enlarge the space for reason's play."

The Rise of Fatalism

Arising from the conjunction of indifferentism and the Christian doctrine of divine "prescience" or foreknowledge, the "grim issue" of fatalism reappeared in Christian form, according to which every human action is regarded as a mystical decree of divine will according to predetermined divine plan. This idea denies divine wisdom's immanence in the world order, however. It also denies all relation between our actions and ourselves and utterly negates both our obligation to moral law and our accountability for our choices.

More Recent Systems of Ethics

Schleiermacher observes that the modern period's search for moral law that is supposed to be justified by the consequences of human decisions has led to the two ethical systems of "happiness" and "perfection." In both systems, however, practical reasoning has remained subordinated to theoretical, and moral reform was thereby impeded. Further progress became possible only when traditional "moral sense," upon which moral law was thought to be based, was reversed by the (Kantian) concept of a motivating feeling based purely upon moral law and when, in turn, that feeling (unlike the Kantian feeling of "respect") was integrated with all other feelings in our soul. This integration, of course, is the central contribution of Schleiermacher's own treatise.

Thus Schleiermacher brings his historical survey up to, and slightly beyond, the Kantian era. Why does he not discuss Kant's ideas more explicitly? Meckenstock is probably correct:

> Kant's critique of ethics is for Schleiermacher so present and so powerfully at work that it does not allow itself to be included in a historical survey.[52]

Explicit or not, Schleiermacher's thesis is clear: not until the critical philosophy of Kant could a practical ethical determinism be articulated. *On Freedom* is that articulation.

Part IV
On the Distinctive Usage
Of Several Technical Terms in This Doctrine

Introduction: The Importance and Difficulties Of Clear Definition

Having attempted in Parts I through III to respond to objections concerning the doctrine of necessity, Schleiermacher now turns to a constructive elaboration of freedom. He begins by discussing the elusiveness of terminology and the need for clear definitions, formulated in terms of the ideas developed in Parts I and II.

---

52. *Deterministische Ethik*, 116.

Section 1. Preliminary Presentation Of a General Definition for Every Use of the Word Freedom

Schleiermacher explains that his task of defining "freedom" is complicated by the fact that the word is universal in common usage and is elaborated differently in every philosophical system. Still, he wishes to open his process of definition by seeking a feature that is generic or common to all usages. This basic feature of freedom, he suggests, is the absence of constraint – that is, the absence of compulsion or restriction, either temporal or conceptual.

From this most general feature Schleiermacher then advances to a general definition by means of Kant's description of "transcendental freedom" from the *Critique of Pure Reason*: "'transcendental freedom is the faculty of initiating a series of events.'" One important correction – namely, the deletion of Kant's additional stipulation that a free agent possesses the faculty of initiating a series of events "from itself" – then yields the general definition Schleiermacher seeks: freedom consists in the faculty of initiating a series of events. We have already noted that this "corrected" Kantian definition in fact represents Schleiermacher's radical departure from Kant's idea of transcendental freedom, which Schleiermacher seems to regard as a variety of the equilibrism his treatise has attacked so vigorously.

Schleiermacher's task for the remainder of the treatise is to apply this general definition to different kinds of freedom. Specifically, he will "deal with a threefold relationship of our concept: namely, with freedom as predicate of human actions, with freedom as a predicate of human situations, and with freedom as a predicate of human faculties." Schleiermacher completed his treatment of only the first of these three relationships. We shall see that his treatise breaks off after a single page devoted to the second.

Section 2. Concerning Freedom As a Predicate of Human Actions

According to Schleiermacher's analysis, this first kind of freedom is again of three types. Freedom as a predicate of actions may apply either to action in general or to particular actions, and in turn the particular actions may be either "ideal" or mental, or "real" or physical.

Freedom As a Predicate of Action in General

Applying the generic concept of freedom to human action in general leads again to equilibrism – the notion that our actions are absolutely isolated from all causal influences. Once again Schleiermacher takes on the challenge of refuting this chief rival to his doctrine of necessity. If freedom is the faculty of initiating a series of events, and if we are generally free of influence from any series of events, Schleiermacher observes, then no free action of one human being can ever influence the free action of another, and our entire social fabric is destroyed. This can hardly be a solution to the question of how our moral experience is possible.

Schleiermacher acknowledges that the concept of freedom of action in general has a logical place in his systematic exposition of freedom, but as pertaining to human beings it is an empty place. He denies that the category of freedom of action in general has any application in the world of human experience. As Schleiermacher suggested in his 1789 *Notes on Kant*, such absolute freedom can be predicated of the deity alone, and even to the deity only in the role of Creator *ex nihilo*, "the undetermined Cause of all determined things."

Freedom As a Predicate of Particular Determinate Actions

We come then to the heart of Schleiermacher's treatise: his explanation of what it means to call our actions free. At the same time, unfortunately, his clarity begins to cloud as the treatise nears its abrupt termination. Schleiermacher's explanation appears to be the following. In the case of our "real" actions, or our actions that affect the material world, freedom of choice means the unconstrained passage of the psychological succession of thoughts in our minds into the succession of events in the material world. In the case of our "ideal" actions, or the activity within our mental world, freedom of will means the unconstrained passage of a rational principle into a succession of ideas in our minds – and perhaps, though not necessarily, into the succession of events in the material world in turn.

Schleiermacher insists that all of these processes exist within the universal realm of "genial" necessity. Freedom is not isolation from interconnectedness but rather unconstrained passage of certain kinds of interconnectedness into other kinds: rational into psychological, psychological into material. All of these processes, moreover, are reciprocal and continually "intermeshing." Their interactions far exceed our capacity for analysis. Thus

Schleiermacher says nothing theoretical about *how* these interactions take place. He claims only that if we are to account for our experience of moral obligation, we must presuppose *that* these interactions take place.

Schleiermacher concludes this section on freedom as a predicate of human actions by insisting that moral obligation pertains to all of our actions. We may not excuse ourselves by claiming that we freely began a course of actions but that our initial choice now binds us so that we are no longer free. Nor may we excuse ourselves by claiming that we freely chose a goal for our actions but that, once we have made it, that choice constrains us. We might recall again Schleiermacher's assertion from much earlier in the treatise: our faculty of desire "craves, selects, desires, decides and acts in every moment of its existence," not merely at the moment of inaugural decisions. We are accountable for all the decisions of our lives.

Section 3. Concerning Freedom As a Predicate of a Situation

By "situation" here Schleiermacher does not mean primarily a condition imposed upon us by nature. Though such conditions do "influence and very often restrict our actions and set limits to our intentions," our freedom as spiritual beings enables us to transcend purely physical constraints. Schleiermacher's interest is rather "the influence of our will and actions upon the wills and actions of others." The situations pertaining most intimately to our freedom are the conditions of sociality: "the community of people with other people, as choosing, acting beings." He distinguishes for analysis three kinds of sociality: our social, civic, and political situations. And here the treatise breaks off.

Why the treatise breaks off at this point we have touched on above.[53] What Schleiermacher intended to say in the remainder of his treatise is a more substantive question. Our only recourse is to gather suggestions from Schleiermacher's other writings. Concerning freedom as a predicate of social situations, for example, we might consult Schleiermacher's essay of 1799, "Toward a Theory of Social Conduct" [*Versuch einer Theorie des geselligen Betragens*], which opens with the words "free sociality," together with an appositive phrase concerning lack of constraint:

---

53. P. iv.

> Free sociality, bound and determined through no external pur-
> pose, is openly claimed by all cultured persons as one of their
> first and noblest needs.[54]

As to what Schleiermacher might have said in his proposed final section
on freedom as a predicate of human faculties, we might consult his lectures
on psychology, delivered four times during the years 1818 to 1834. They are
filled with materials that echo and augment his early treatise *On Freedom*:

> We presuppose the original unity of body and soul and the
> equally original unity of all we can differentiate within the soul
> itself.[55]

In what might almost amount to an outline for the treatise's missing discussion of freedom as a predicate of human faculties, Schleiermacher's lectures
distinguish three forms of our "self-activity" or "spontaneity": the impulse to
self-preservation, self-acquisition, and self-manifestation.[56] We also find
Schleiermacher repeating yet again his early treatise's attacks on the indif-
ferentist notion of freedom:

> If we wish to posit this indifference, then we must posit it in
> every moment. As a person has today established character, so
> tomorrow it can be annulled. That is, regarded in the whole
> continuity of existence, the individual being appears to us as
> something absolutely fortuitous .... There is simply no basis
> for maintaining that a person will still be the same tomorrow as
> today, but no basis for denying it either. Now it is perfectly
> clear that no one really acts upon this presupposition, for we
> always act as if we believe that in a certain sense we are able to
> count on people ....[57]

Toward Evaluating "On Freedom"

I have translated *On Freedom* in the hope of encouraging others to evaluate the viewpoint and arguments it expresses. Meckenstock suggests a few
specific issues inviting further clarification and exploration. One such issue
concerns Schleiermacher's appeal to our awareness of moral law.[58] He

---

54. Ed. Herman Nohl, *Schleiermachers Werke* II, eds. Otto Braun and D. Joh. Bauer
(Leipzig: Felix Meiner, 1913), 3.

55. *Psychologie*, ed. L. George, *Sämmtliche Werke* III/6 (Berlin: Georg Reimer, 1862),
12.

56. *Psychologie*, 243-61.

57. *Psychologie*, 268-9.

58. See Meckenstock, *Deterministische Ethik*, 50, 74.

seems thoroughly Kantian in his assumption that the requirements of morality are clear and accessible to us:

> we are fully entitled to presuppose in everyone complete
> knowledge of a right and exact feeling for the moral law, which
> resides in the soul itself.[59]

Schleiermacher's treatise nowhere elucidates this "right and exact feeling,"
however. He only alludes to it in the sentences we have already noted: "in
earlier systems of morality this impulse was called the moral sense. In present systems it is called respect for the moral law."[60] The "moral sense" of
pre-Kantian British moral philosophy and the "respect" of Kant's ethical system are quite different if not alien concepts, as we have seen Kant himself insisting.[61] I have suggested that we simply stick to Schleiermacher's own term
"moral impulse." Other interpreters might clarify exactly how Schleiermacher might have wished that phrase to be explained.

Likewise Schleiermacher is vague about the content of the moral law.
Perhaps he simply agreed with Kant that the authority of categorical imperatives such as "Do not lie" and "Do not commit perjury" is rationally self-evident. His treatise nowhere states what our moral imperatives are, however,
or explores the question of how we arrive at moral judgments. In our day, of
course, answers to these questions are far from universally shared or even
acknowledged. Interpreters might shed new light on Schleiermacher's treatise in relation to our current debates over this issue of the content of moral
law.[62]

Another issue inviting exploration is Schleiermacher's insistence that we
may both acknowledge our immersion in "the universal chain of causes and
effects" and at the same time feel ourselves to be "the independent originating cause" of our situation:

> I do not have to depend on the view that the two different sen-
> timents occur at different points of time. Let them intermingle
> completely and alter so often that they appear to be fully si-
> multaneous. There will be nothing in the two that cannot co-
> exist even in a unity of feeling.[63]

Meckenstock thinks it no accident that instead of providing analysis that
might establish his problematic psychological assertion here, Schleiermacher

---

59. Below, p. 45n.
60. Above, p. xx.
61. Above. p. xii.
62. See for example the survey of this issue and the original proposals in Franklin I.
Gamwell, *The Divine Good: Modern Moral Theory and the Necessity of God* (New York:
Harper Collins, 1990).
63. Below, p. 49.

lapses into a series of rhetorical questions.[64] Is Schleiermacher's psychology convincing here or faulty?

Still another deficiency of *On Freedom* is Schleiermacher's lack of specificity in referring to advocates of the various philosophical positions he characterizes. In the sweeping historical survey of Part III, for example, the only philosopher or theologian actually named is Augustine. Meckenstock is right to say that Schleiermacher's philosophical characterizations amount to typology,[65] albeit astute and suggestive typology. The treatise's value will be greater to the degree that interpreters can relate its arguments to specific texts of specific opponents.

Associated Writings
Subsequent to "On Freedom"

Of course *On Freedom* represents a seminal beginning to Schleiermacher's writings on ethics, not an ending. He continues to explore these ethical themes throughout his career, and especially in his writings immediately subsequent to that treatise. Schleiermacher does not call his essay *On the Worth of Life* [*Über den Wert des Lebens*],[66] written in Schlobitten in 1792-93,[67] a "rhapsody," but it is in actuality more rhapsodic in form and tone than *On Freedom* and belongs among the series of writings Schleiermacher projected in response to the moral philosophy of Kant.[68] In this personally revealing essay Schleiermacher returns to the theme of the substance of moral law. As in *To Cecilie*[69] he confesses to struggling against moral skepticism:

> The frightful danger of an irremediable practical skepticism stands before me there, and would I always remain far away from the conviction of possessing truth, which will alone set my mind at rest? (405)

His struggles are vindicated, however, as he attains insight into the goal that can elevate his moral life above the banal activities of sheer existence:

> Indeed, there is such a purpose, and everything leads me forward to the lovely idea I have about it. Knowing and desiring should be one, not two things in me. Complete, constant har-

---

64. *Deterministische Ethik*, 80. See also 129.
65. *Deterministische Ethik*, 116.
66. KGA I/1, 391-471.
67. See KGA I/1, LXII-XIII.
68. See above, p. vi.
69. See above, p. vii.

> mony of the two to the fullest degree to which they are possible
> within me, unity of both in purpose and object – that is hu-
> manity, that is the fine goal that is hidden within human na-
> ture. The first stipulation I assign to life is to deliver objects
> that engage each power individually, objects, moreover,
> wherein even this harmony of knowing and desiring can be re-
> vealed and through which that harmony can be promoted.
> (410)

To discover the balance of virtue and resignation that leads us toward this
goal of accepting all that we understand and comprehending all that we desire: this is the substance of moral life.[70]

The determinism of Schleiermacher's treatise *On Freedom* receives fur-
ther attention in his three subsequent writings relating to the philosophy of
Spinoza: *Spinozism* [*Spinozismus*], *Short Presentation of the Spinozistic System*
[*Kurze Darstellung des Spinozistischen Systems*] and *On Those Things in
Jacobi's "Letters" and "Realism" Not Pertaining to Spinoza, And Especially On
His Own Philosophy* [*Über dasjenige in Jacobis Briefen und Realismus, was den
Spinoza night betrifft, und besonders über seine eigene Philosophie*],[71] all prob-
ably dating from 1793-94.[72] Whereas in his earlier essays Schleiermacher
sought the proper balance between the philosophies of Eberhard and Kant,
here he weighs the relative merits of the philosophies of Kant and Spinoza.
On the idea of what in *On Freedom* Schleiermacher calls "the undetermined
Cause of all determined things,"[73] for example, he writes:

> Here too Spinoza seems to me victorious, or rather, Kantian-
> ism seems to me, if Kant understood himself, to be on
> Spinoza's side. (570)

On the other hand, concerning our metaphysical knowledge of the attributes
of God, Schleiermacher gives Kant's critical philosophy the upper hand over
the pre-critical metaphysics of Spinoza:

> The proposition concerning the essence and attributes of the
> Self-Existing: Now here indeed Spinoza has more information
> than he should have. He would not have had it, however, if the
> idea of critical idealism had come to him, and he seems to be
> quite close to it. (574)

---

70. I discuss Schleiermacher's concept of the goal of moral life more completely in
Schleiermacher's Early Philosophy of Life (Chico, Calif.: Scholars Press, 1982), 79-92.

71. KGA I/1, 511-58. 559-82, 583-97.

72. Meckenstock gives a careful account of the chronology of these writings, KGA I/1,
LXXVI-IX.

73. See above, p. xxxi.

Finally, among Schleiermacher's subsequent writings closely related to the themes of *On Freedom* we must mention his own sermons and his first independent publication – a translation of sermons preached by someone else. In Schleiermacher's sermons his determinism is frequently undisguised. His first published collection of sermons opens with a sermon delivered on New Year's Day 1797, taking as its text the passage from Ecclesiastes:

> What has been is what will be,
> and what has been done is what will be done;
> and there is nothing new under the sun.

The sermon's determinism is unapologetic:

> Of what importance is the position that the heavenly bodies occupy just now? Every position has evolved from those that have preceded, according to the same laws God has prescribed for their movement from the beginning. Of what importance is it whether this or some other small portion of inanimate matter belongs to my body? My body is the workshop of those same forces, the conjunction of which constitutes its distinctive nature . . . .[74]

So also, Schleiermacher continues, in the world of the human spirit, where the person of religious sensibility will recognize unified divine governance beneath the surface of human history:

> That too follows the same laws by which human activity is continually, contrastingly supported or demolished. What is it, then, that we have done? The same that others will do thereafter. Look upon the great secret as to how both worlds to which you belong are bound together, how nature equips humans beings with powers ever new, how through these powers human beings win ever greater dominion over nature, how through this dominion the human community increases, how through this increase human culture is advanced and all human affairs improved! Even here be surprised by nothing, as if it were something new and unheard of. All these things are simply developments of the same divine thoughts, approaches to the same goal of divine grace, according to the same design of divine wisdom. In short, there is nothing new under the sun. (19-20)

At the same time, Schleiermacher makes plain his conviction that the sacred determinism he embraces is not equivalent to fatalism, does not lead to

---

74. *Predigten. Erste Sammlung, Sämmtliche Werke* II.1 (Berlin: Georg Reimer, 1834), 18-19.

moral quietism. Christian people are called to cooperate in the daily work of human betterment:

> Certainly it would be the newest thing under the sun if people
> ever stood still and their life did not improve! (23)

We see here the same conjunction of determinism and moral obligation that Schleiermacher had established in *On Freedom*.

Also in 1797, at the age of twenty-eight, Schleiermacher completed his first independent publication on which he had worked since 1794[75]: a translation into German of two volumes of addresses originally delivered in London in 1795 by the English clergyman Joseph Fawcett. Like Schleiermacher, Fawcett was an independent-minded advocate of determinism. These sermons express the sense of human solidarity that Schleiermacher derives from his own determinism in *On Freedom*[76]. To quote from Fawcett's original: "We are none of us complete in ourselves. We are parts of a whole; we are members of a body."[77]

> The perfectly uninterrupted, and the infinitely extended activ-
> ity of divine power, in the preservation of universal nature,
> presents to reason a contemplation, of all others the most sub-
> lime; while religious sensibility is soothed by the idea of being
> completely in the hand of a Power, to whom it feels the most
> animated love, and in whom it reposes the most tranquil trust.
> (32)

Again like Schleiermacher in his treatise,[78] Fawcett draws from his determinism an ethical sense of modesty, mutual forbearance, and justice tempered with mercy:

> With as much propriety might we ascribe eloquence to the
> . quill, rather than to the writer; or ingenuity to the machine,
> rather than to the inventor; as take to ourselves the praise of
> any personal superiority, with which our Maker may have dis-
> tinguished us . . . . As the consideration that God is our creator
> renders it impossible for us to be proud of any personal excel-
> lence which we have inherited from nature, so the reflection
> that God is the maker of *others*, should lead us to pay a proper
> respect to all mankind, and prevent us from despising any be-
> cause they are poor. The respect arising from this reflection is
> intimately connected with the practice of justice, in our inter-

---

75. See KGA I/1, XXXII.

76. See above, p. xxiv.

77. *Sermons Delivered at the Sunday-Evening Lecture, for the Winter Season, at the Old Jewry*, 2d ed., I (London: J. Johnson, 1801), 51.

78. See above, p. xxvi.

course with those, who are our inferiors in situation. Contempt is the parent of injury and of oppression, both in public and in private life. ... The cure of this conduct is the consideration, that "the Lord is the maker of us all." (44-5, Fawcett's emphasis)

Secondary Literature
Relating to "On Freedom"

The availability of Schleiermacher's early writings on freedom, thanks to the 1984 publication of the Volume I/1 of the *Kritische Gesamtausgabe*, is recent and little secondary response has appeared. I wrote my 1982 study of these materials, *Schleiermacher's Early Philosophy of Life: Determinism, Freedom, and Phantasy*, without the benefit of the KGA. I would now correct a few errors resulting from the unavailability of some sources, obscurities in the some of the available sources, and my struggles with the handwriting and the German of Schleiermacher's manuscripts and texts,[79] but I hope that on the whole that work still serves to augment my more limited treatment in this Introduction.

Certainly the most valuable secondary literature in German is that of Günter Meckenstock. In addition to his invaluable editorial materials in KGA I/1, I recommend his book of 1988 from which I have drawn so much: *Deterministische Ethik und kritische Theologie*. That work is a critical guide to all the Schleiermacher materials of KGA I/1 relating to the subject of human freedom.

---

79. On p. 9 of my book I state that Schleiermacher as a student "avoided direct exposure to Halle's theological faculty," whereas KGA I/1 asserts that "Schleiermacher studied theology in Halle (specifically with Samuel Mursinna and August Hermann Niemeyer)" (pp. XVII-XVIII). On the same page I state that Schleiermacher's three Dialogues on Freedom of 1789 "are not extant," whereas KGA I/1 presents the text of what appears to be the third Dialogue (see above, p. xiii). On p. 44 and p. 55 I state that in order to distinguish his viewpoint from Kant's, Schleiermacher employs the term *esteem* (**Achtung**) to designate the incentive of the moral law, in contrast to Kant's use of the term *respect* (**Acht**). In fact, Kant commonly uses the term **Achtung**.

The Translation's Format

In the original German, Schleiermacher divides his treatise of 137 printed pages (103 pages in Schleiermacher's handscript) with only the following four headings and three sub-headings:

Part I

Part II

Part III

Part IV

On the Distinctive Usage Of

Several Technical Terms in This Doctrine

Section 1:

Preliminary Presentation of

A General Definition for

Every Use of the Word Freedom

Section 2:

Concerning Freedom As a

Predicate of Human Actions

Section 3:

Concerning Freedom As a

Predicate of a Situation

What is more, Schleiermacher relieves the text with very few paragraph divisions. In a word, its density is daunting. For this reason I have liberally supplemented Schleiermacher's headings with others of my own composition – not to impose order but to expose the remarkable intrinsic logic of the treatise's plan and development, so characteristic of Schleiermacher's thinking. I have also freely created paragraphs, trying to befit both good English style and Schleiermacher's flow of logic.

Acknowledgments

I want to express unbounded gratitude to Dr. Terrence Tice, in his role as philosopher, translator and editor, and to Dr. Edwina Lawler, in her role as Germanist and translator, for their intelligent and generous partnership with me in this project. They contributed many weeks of helpful effort, working through the text several times, line by line. My thanks also go to Dr. Ruth Drucilla Richardson of The Edwin Mellen Press for the Press' sponsorship and for her encouragement and final preparation of the disk typescript for publication.

GLOSSARY FOR THIS TRANSLATION OF
"ÜBER DIE FREIHEIT"

abwechseln: interchange
Achtung: respect
Allgemeinheit: universality
Angemessenheit: fitness
angenehm: pleasant, pleasurable
Annehmlichkeit: satisfaction
Ansehn: authority, reputation, appearance
Anstoß: impetus
Antrieb: motive
Art: kind, type (see **Gattung**)
aufheben: cancel, resolve, suspend, negate, annul, deny
Ausspruch: dictum
Bedeutung: meaning
Bedingung: condition
Befugniß: warrant, authority
Begehr: desire (see **Begier, Begierde**)
begehren: desire
Begehrungsvermögen: faculty of desire
Begier, Begierde: predilection (see **Begehr**)
Begränzung: limitation (see **Einschränkung**)
Beschaffenheit: characteristic, condition, character (see **Eigenschaft**)
beschließen: decide
Bestimmung: determination, stipulation, vocation
bestimmt: determinate, determined, definite, particular, defined
Betragen: conduct
bloß: merely, purely, solely
Darstellung: presentation, manifestation, demonstration (see **Vorstellung**)
Einbildungskraft: imagination
Eigenschaft: characteristic (see **Beschaffenheit**)
Eigenthümlichkeit: distinctive character, characteristic, defining characteristic
eingreifen: intermesh
einleuchtend: obvious, evident
Einschränkung: restriction (see **Begränzung**)
einsehen: comprehend
einzeln: single, particular, individual

Empfindung: sensation, sentiment
entscheiden: decide
Entschluß: resolution
entstehen: arise, come to be
Erfahrung: experience
Erfolg: result, consequence (see **Folgen**)
erkennen: know, take cognizance of, acknowledge
Erkenntniß: knowledge, cognition
erklären: elucidate
Erklärung: explanation, definition
erzeugen: engender
Fantasie: fantasy (same as **Phantasie**)
fehlen...gegen: violate
Fertigkeiten: capacities, capabilities
Folgen: results, consequences (see **Erfolg**)
Gattung: type (see **Art**)
Gefühl: feeling
gelüsten: crave
Gemäßheit: conformity
Gemüth: heart and mind
genöthigt: necessitated
Genuß: gratification
Gerechtigkeit: justice
geschehen: occur, happen
Gesinnung: disposition
gezwungen: compelled (see **Zwang**)
Glück: good fortune, luck
glücklich: happy, fortunate, lucky
Glückseligkeit: happiness
Grund: ground, basis, foundation
Grundsatz: basic principle, principle
Handlung: action
hervorbringen: produce, bring forth, give rise to, yield
Ich: I, ego
Imputabilität: imputability
Individualität: individuality
Inkonsequenz: inconsistency
Instinkt: instinct
Kraft: power, force
Lehre: doctrine

Lust: pleasure, longing, craving
Maxim: maxim
Meinung: opinion, viewpoint
Merkmal: defining feature
Moralität: morality
Natur: nature (see **Wesen**)
Neigung: inclination
Nöthigung: constraint
Nothwendigkeit: necessity
Ohngefähr: chance (same as **Ungefähr**; see **Zufall**)
Persönlichkeit: personality, personhood
Phantasie: fantasy (same as **Fantasie**)
Prinzip: principle
Regierung: governance (see **Weltregierung**)
Reihe: succession, series, train, sequence
Satz: proposition, tenet
Seligkeit: blessedness
Sinn: sense
sinnlich: sensible
Sinnlichkeit: sensibility
sittlich: ethical, moral
Sittlichkeit: ethical conduct, ethical nature, ethics
Sprachgebrauch: linguistic usage
Stimmung: attunement, resonance
Streit: contention, controversy
Streitfrage: dispute
Subjekt: subject, subjective being
Tauglichkeit: suitability, competency, fitness
Thätigkeit: activity
Theil: part, aspect, classification
treiben: impel
Trieb: impulse
Triebfeder: motivation
Tugend: virtue
Überlegung: deliberation
Uebergewicht: preponderance
Unbestimmtheit: undeterminedness
Ungefähr: chance (same as **Ohngefähr**; see **Zufall**)
Urheber: originator
Verantwortlichkeit: responsibility (see **Verbindlichkeit**)

Verbindlichkeit: obligation (see **Verantwortlichkeit**)
Verbindung: connection, association
Verfahren: conduct, approach, procedure, process
Vergnügen: enjoyment
Verhältniße: relationships, relations
Verhandlung: deliberation
Vermögen: faculty, capacity
Vernunft: reason
Verstand: understanding
vollkommen: complete
Vollkommenheit: perfection, fulfillment
Vorsehung: Providence (see **Vorsicht**)
Vorsicht: Providence (see **Vorsehung**)
Vorstellung: representation, thought, notion (see **Darstellung**)
Wahl: option
Wahrnehmung: perception
Weltregierer: World's Sovereign
Weltregierung: world governance, governance of the world (see **Regierung**)
Werth: worth
Wesen: essence, being, nature (see **Natur**)
Wille: will
Willkühr: choice, choosing faculty, faculty of choice
willkührlich: choosing, arbitrary (see **zufällig**)
Wirksamkeit: effect, effectiveness, efficacy
Wollen: willing, volition
wünschen: wish
Zufall: chance (see **Ongefähr** and **Ungefähr**)
zufällig: accidentally, arbitrarily (see **willkürlich**)
Zufriedenheit: contentment
Zurechnung: accountability
Zusammenhang: connection, interconnection, interconnectedness
Zustand: state, circumstances, situation
Zwang: coercion (see **gezwungen**)
Zweck: purpose

ON FREEDOM

Friedrich Schleiermacher

Part I

A NEW ACCOUNT OF MORAL CHOICE AND OBLIGATION

Introduction

Current Opposition to Undertaking Such an Inquiry

[219]¹ Given the current situation of the philosophical world in Germany, nothing seems less advantageous for an author than to begin a collection of philosophical rhapsodies point-blank with a treatise on this controversial subject. That is, if there was once a time when this question was the chief object of investigation for our nation's sages and when every new attempt to decide the question of freedom, even if it promised little that was new, was nevertheless picked up with expectation and interest, that time is long past. Instead of counting on forbearance in taking on so complex an issue, one must rather think of justifying such an undertaking. Wherever I look, all parties oppose such an endeavor. Some believe that the question's complete solution has long since been found. Others are of the opinion that a solution could never be found this way. Still others, surfeited with so many conflicting concepts and judgments concerning this issue, fear that all related concepts have become too greatly intertwined and all the words too indeterminate for any new investigation to find its way happily out of this labyrinth, even supposing that a happy outcome is conceivable.

The first of these groups betray the illegitimacy of their presumption by the fact that different factions adduce the same entitlement for their positions. If different parties claim universally valid solutions, then in fact none of the solutions is so, neither the deterministic solution of the Leibniz-Wolff school nor the newer solution contained in the *Critique of Pure Reason*. Even supposing that one of the two opinions is true, still something must at least be lacking either in the grounds from which the result is derived or in the manner of its presentation.

It is remarkable that, despite all the opposition critical philosophy has encountered for some time now from so many sides, this point has received relatively little attention. Most other subjects complained of as incomprehensible by a large segment of the philosophical public [220] have profited from these controversies and little by little have been set in clearer light. Yet

---

1. Ed. note: Numbers in square brackets give the pagination of the *Kritische Gesamtausgabe* (KGA) edition of Schleiermacher's treatise.

this subject still lies in its original darkness where, in my opinion, it cannot possibly receive general approval. Thus we believe that in this respect our investigation, quite apart from the measure of its worth and the correctness of its results, can promise some usefulness in leading us subsequently into a closer elucidation of the Kantian theory of freedom.

Implications of Abandoning Such Inquiry

Those who are of the opinion that no solution to this question on reasonable grounds is possible usually reassure themselves that no solution is necessary: that there is not the slightest difference between the way persons act who accept freedom in one of the innumerable meanings of the word and the way persons act who deny freedom in the same sense, and also that this controversy cannot possibly have so general an interest as is commonly alleged, since even if the controversy could someday be resolved, very few would be capable of comprehending the resolution anyway.

Such a dismissal would, of course, end the usefulness of practical philosophy[2] entirely, since the same argument would apply to all questions touching upon the most important human interests. Yet the situation is not so bad as this. Even non-speculative people have opinions concerning all these things. Even if they do not know how to express a judgment apart from the objects of its application, still the judgment occurs to them when they need it as a ground for their actions. Why should it not also be possible for them to comprehend the grounds through which this judgment interrelates with the system of their other judgments and propositions? Moreover, should it appear that even those who believe they have comprehended these grounds philosophically still act in the same way despite a variety of opinions, this merely gives rise to the strong conjecture that with many people opinion and action, or speculative and practical judgment, are not altogether consonant. This suspicion of inconsistency, in turn, reflects most strongly on those who believe it unnecessary to answer the question of freedom, since they constantly act as if they had long known the answer.

---

2. **Der ganzen praktischen Philosophie.** Ed. Note: Following Kant, Schleiermacher means by "practical" philosophy the philosophy of ethical life, as contrasted with "pure" or "theoretical" philosophy, having to do with questions of knowledge.

This Inquiry to Be Established Upon Clearly Defined Terms

Permit us to make this clear with a few examples. Everyone needs time during which the faculty of desire[3] appears to be at rest, as it were, in order to compare its individual and general activities[4] among themselves, or to judge according to some [221] principle, and this deliberation seldom ends without a resolution[5]. We give some of these activities precedence over others; we decide to postpone this and to actualize that. Obviously we would not bother to make such resolutions if we did not consider it quite possible that in some future case the faculty of desire could determine itself in some completely opposite resolution. Thus not only do we decide something with respect to the faculty of desire, but we decide it with the pure under-standing[6]. We will to make something actual in the faculty of desire, yet without that faculty and indeed contrary to the presumable effects of its objects. This would be an inadmissible undertaking if we did not presuppose that we knew, or at least could very easily know, how the activities of the faculty of desire arise, and how they interrelate, in part inwardly among themselves and in part outwardly with the soul's other faculties. We, therefore, are not warranted to propose maxims for our observance if we do not consider a reliable solution of this problem to be possible.

If we continue to compare the maxims we have formulated, we shall soon become clearly aware that some manifest themselves as a *rule of reason*[7]. The sum of all particular activities that would be in general accord with those rules of reason compellingly presents itself as an *ideal of reason*[8], and there arises in us a demand of a wholly singular nature, namely that we should make this ideal actual. However variously people think of this law of reason and ideal of reason, all still acknowledge something of the kind. The sense that we attach to the expression *moral obligation*[9] is found in accordance with its most general stipulations in each and every system, even in a system in which the expression is vigorously elaborated. This responsibility, so gener-ally acknowledged, would be a complete chimera, however, if we could not do what we should do, and if we did not know that we could, and these

---

3. Das Begehrungsvermögen.
4. Thätigkeiten.
5. Entschluß.
6. Mit dem bloßen Verstand.
7. Vernunftregel.
8. Vernunftideal.
9. Moralischer Verbindlichkeit.

conditions once again point to our having acquired a solution of our question in advance.

Under these circumstances we shall therefore have to venture upon a solution, undertaking it with all the difficulties set in our way by still a third group of opponents. Unfortunately it is very true that the long stretch of time and the abundance of controversies have not served to clarify and fix all the concepts that come into play here, with all their signifiers, but have rather confused and rendered them unstable. Should we wish to begin our play with cards whose value and significance the players do not agree upon, then if our fellow players were aware of this fundamental fact our hopes would indeed soon be at an end. Even if our fellow players should let the trick pass, as is [222] often the case given human frailty, we would only entangle ourselves and our readers in labyrinths of misunderstandings from which it would be impossible to lead them out again.

In order to reassure at the outset those who are so fearful in this sense, we shall completely exclude certain questionable words from our own inquiry. As a further protection against the bad consequences of words susceptible to ambiguous meanings, we shall seek adequate initial clarification of the meaning we shall be using consistently thereafter.

Preparatory Analysis of the Concept "Faculty of Desire"

On the Generic Character of the Concept

Now in order to investigate the conditions and grounds of particular activities of the faculty of desire we must first agree on the generic character and the specific modifications of this faculty, clearly presenting what we understand these to be. According to Kant's definition (KpV 16)[10] the faculty of desire is the faculty of becoming through its representations[11] a cause actualizing the objects of those representations. Excellent as this definition may seem, it contains a difficulty that necessitates my departing from it to a certain degree. That is, this desire amounts to becoming through a representation a cause of the object of a representation,[12] but in that case I have not

---

10. Meckenstock note (KGA), quoting Kant: "'The faculty of desire is the faculty a being has of causing through its representations the actualization of the objects of these representations.' (KpV 16; Ak 5,9,20-22)"

11. **Vorstellungen.**

12. Schleiermacher's note: "Here I have already altered one term of Kant's explanation – to Kant's advantage, I believe. Instead of 'this' representation I have written 'a' representation, since I thought that the concept of the faculty of desire should not determine whether

only desired but also already acted.[13] In order to prevent all misinterpretation let me explain at once that I have not let myself be led astray by a doubly inadmissible usage of language [223] in which one employs "desire"[14] instead of the word "wish"[15]. A wish is a desire wherewith I am explicitly aware of the insufficiency of my physical faculty of causality, and wherein this faculty is not co-determined at all. I would want a definition of desire in which this activity of the soul alone is purely manifested, without necessarily including what we properly call action. This requires me to mount to a still higher concept, and that is the concept of impulse.[16]

Specific Modifications of the Faculty of Desire: "Impulse," "Instinct," and "Choice"

Reinhold is quite correct that a subject's faculty of representation must not be confused with a subject's *power*[17]. However, the way Reinhold derives

through a representation I should become a cause of the actuality of the object of this same representation or of some other."

13. Schleiermacher's note: "It is true that in connection with his definition of the will Kant distinguishes between determination of the will and the relation of physical strength to the realization of this determination (KpV 15), but he never does so in connection with the faculty of desire." – Meckenstock note (KGA), quoting Kant: "'It is different with the practical use of reason. Here reason concerns itself with grounds determining the will, which is the faculty either of bringing forth objects corresponding to representations, or of determining itself, that is, its causality, to effect such objects (whether the physical faculty is sufficient or not).' (KpV 29f; Ak 5,15,8-14)"

14. **Begehren.**

15. **Wünschen.**

16. **Trieb.**

17. **Kraft.** Meckenstock note (KGA): "Cf. Reinhold, *Versuch einer neuen Theorie des menschlichen Vorstellungsvermögens*, Prague/Jena 1789: 'That in the *representing subject*, through which that subject must be thought of as ground of the pure possibility of representation, namely the *faculty of representation*, must be precisely distinguished from that through which the subject is ground of the *actual representation*, which is called representational *power*. This power cannot by any means be thought of as including pure *spontaneity*, through which no representation would become actual without *receptivity*, and through whose effect alone merely the pure form of representations, and only the being affected that is *a priori* necessary to intuition, is brought forth according to the given forms of sensibility. By representing power, therefore, we mean here neither pure spontaneity alone, nor the forms of receptivity and spontaneity determined *a priori* purely according to their possibility, but rather the proper *ground of the actuality of representation*, insofar as it must be present in the representing subject.' (560) Cf. also: 'The relation of the representing power to the possibility of representation determined *a priori* in the faculty of representation – the relation of that power to its faculty, or of the ground of actuality to the ground of possibility of representation, or to representability – I call the *impulse* of the representing subject. This impulse consists of the connection of the power with the faculty, and it must be present in every finite representing subject, in whom

the concept of impulse from power and faculty seems to me not sufficiently clear. In general terms, by impulse I understand the representing subject's activity, grounded in the subject's nature[18], of bringing forth representations. Accordingly, particular impulses arise to the extent that this impulse is considered from some point of view as divided into various kinds. The faculty of determining impulse in general for an object of a particular impulse in some moment of existence is called the faculty of desire.[19] It seems to me evident in this definition that acting[20] proper is not yet co-posited. Acting would be only the application of the [224] physical faculty of my causality to objects in conformity with this determination of impulse. In accordance with desire's being joined in various ways with action, the generic concept of desiring is more closely attached to the subsidiary concepts of wishing or deciding. When deciding[21] is thought of not as a single activity but as a persisting condition, this is commonly called *willing*[22], but this designation is wholly incorrect since willing should relate solely to the will.

There are still other, more important modifications of the faculty of desire besides this classification of desiring, however. That is, insofar as impulse to some particular activity can be determined by a single object alone, the faculty of desire is called *instinct*[23], but insofar as it arrives at some particular activity solely by comparing several objects it is called *choice*[24]. I am happy to admit that we know no representing subject whose faculty of desire would be pure instinct. I could even admit that we can never assert with certainty that any particular action of some being has become actual through instinct alone. Yet it would still seem exceedingly useful, and indeed in accord with common usage, to retain the idea of instinct (since it is there) to designate a modification of the faculty of desire that contrasts with another modification which we call choice. In this respect, the stated modification appears to me to characterize instinct: with any action ascribed to instinct we think of the faculty of desire as being determined by a single object of an impulse alone, and thus absolutely.

---

power is distinct from faculty. To be determined by the impulse to engender a representation is called *desire*, and the faculty of being determined by that impulse is called the *faculty of desire* in the broader sense.' (561)."

18. **Natur.**

19. Meckenstock note (KGA): "Cf. further: 'The faculty of being determined by impulse to have actual sentiments I call the *faculty of desire* in the narrower sense.' (Reinhold, *Versuch* 562)"

20. **Handeln.**

21. **Beschließen.**

22. **Wollen.**

23. **Instinkt.**

24. **Willkühr.**

This characterization will become even more evident if we consider the characteristics of instinct that can be derived from this idea. Namely, it follows (1) that the action persists only until the determining object itself ceases, and (2) that where instinct is present, desire follows immediately upon the appearance of the object, and the tendency toward action follows immediately upon desire. If whatever we suppose to be the determining object of the impulse had already been in the heart and mind[25] for a while before the tendency to action followed, then the impulse appears not to have been absolutely determined by this object, and we no longer ascribe the action to instinct. This is why in the instinctive actions of animals, which on account of the result of those actions we attribute to a mechanical impulse, [225] the action sometimes exceeds the task, or the task is too great for the action. That is to say, so long as the (unrecognized) determining object persists, animals go on acting even if the task is already completed, and as soon as the object ceases, the action also ceases even if their work be still needed.

We still think of an action as instinctive even if the exercise of the physical faculty requisite to an impulse's determination is inhibited. As soon as we have to think of the impulse's determination as incomplete, wavering or relative, however, we no longer represent instinct as its source.[26] When, for example, a mole digs a tunnel, undoubtedly the determination of its impulse is directed not to what occurs but only to what the mole does. It does not desire the tunnel as something to have but only desires to build it, and as it employs its physical faculty to do this, something results that was not its proper natural goal. However, this cannot be the essence of instinct, or else those human actions would also be instinct that in fact we should least wish to confuse with it, namely, actions done only for the sake of their form. This desire, then, is the immediate object of impulse. As it is brought forth, however, another object arises mediately, namely the outer action with its consequences, to which my impulse was not directed but which was the wise goal of the world's Sovereign[27]. This circumstance would involve no modification of the faculty of desire but merely another being's relation to the faculty of desire.

Furthermore, with most instinctive actions we cannot presuppose in the acting subject any clear consciousness of the way the action to which this tendency leads corresponds to the object toward which the impulse is directed. The case is similar regarding all our actions that are stimulated by sensa-

---

25. **Gemüth.**
26. Schleiermacher's note: "Those actions for which we are inclined to presuppose an instinct have still other distinguishing conditions, but they do not belong to the essentials of the concept insofar as it relates to the faculty of desire."
27. **Der Weisheitszweck des Weltregierers.**

tions[28] of the vital senses without our being clearly aware of how they corre-
late with the stimulating sensations. Again this process would imply no particular modification of the faculty of desire, and we must not confuse the action whereby we proceed to work out of an indistinct consciousness of a perceived analogy with the actions of instinct.

A Further Modification of the Faculty of Desire: "Will"

What we call choice, then, involves contrasting determinations. It is the
faculty of desire that [226] can be determined for one object of impulse only
by comparing several.[29] Here, therefore, this determination is not absolute
but is relatively effected through the interrelation of several things. Here the
determination of impulse can be altered through alteration of these different
concomitants, without the stimulating object's ceasing to exist. Here, finally,
is an intermediate space between the appearance of the object in the heart
and mind and the action of desire. The object appears and the faculty of
desire *craves*[30]. In contrast, the complete determination of impulse still
remains suspended by consciousness of the necessity to take into account
several determining grounds, and only when this has occurred does it *desire*.

This latter noteworthy quality has occasioned one German sage to
remark that the human soul's freedom consists in its capacity to postpone its
actions.[31] If we further analyze this thought, if we consider that the faculty of
desire can at a given moment be affected by only one object, and if we render
this statement's indistinct expressions more precisely and according to rule,
then we see that it expresses well the essence of choice and the distinction
between the relation of choice to morality and the relation of instinct.

If a choosing faculty of desire is joined with understanding in a subject,
the understanding composes general concepts out of the common constituents of particular determinations of choice. By comparing results of
these choices, moreover, it composes judgments concerning their subordination which are considered as rules for future cases, that is, as *maxims*[32]. A

---

28. **Empfindungen.**

29. Schleiermacher's note: "Hereupon the Kantian terminology, not altogether correct,
also grounds its opposition between the heteronomy of choice and the autonomy of reason." –
Meckenstock note (KGA): "Cf. Kant: KpV 58f; Ak 5,33,8-33."

30. **Gelüstet.**

31. Meckenstock note (KGA): "Cf. Joch, *Über Belohnung und Strafe nach Türkischen
Gesezen*, 2d ed., Bayreuth/Leipzig 1772, 278f: 'He [Herr Rautenberg, preacher in Braun-
schweig] sets the entire basis of freedom in the fact that people have the faculty of postponing
the execution of their actions until they have considered everything.'"

32. **Maximen.**

faculty of desire for which the idea of manifesting its maxims in particular cases can become an object of impulse is called a *will*[33]. Such a faculty of desire must absolutely be a choosing faculty[34]. The understanding can always think general practical propositions; but since they can consequently stimulate compliance only if some particular object works upon the faculty of desire, several objects must be able to work upon the faculty of desire if the general practical propositions [227] are to be effective as maxims.

This idea of will takes us back once again to the difference between human choice and that of animals. Not essential here is the difference we might mention relating to the various kinds of representations operating in the faculty of desire and to the manifold modifications of their operations. Although, for example, in the composing and recollecting imagination[35] of human beings both sensible and non-sensible representations affect the faculty of desire, this difference does not relate to choice itself. What is essential is that human beings can compare more than merely particular objects. As a result we can say that the human faculty of desire *is* choice, while the animal merely *has* choice; that is, the human faculty of desire is always determined through choice, while the animal merely has the faculty to be so determined. Specifically, since the animal's faculty of desire has only outward objects (by outward I understand whatever is external to the representing subject), it is only accidental that several of them work concurrently, and none can be thought necessarily bound to another. Hence if several objects are not actually manifested simultaneously, desire follows immediately upon being affected, and choice does not always express itself, even if unhindered by instinct.

In contrast, we human beings consider every possible determination of impulse as included under a general practical proposition. Thus for each particular effect of an object we presuppose a practical proposition under which the determination of the faculty of desire occasioned by the object must be included. Therefore a maxim is thought to be bound necessarily to every particular case, and its clear manifestation is expected. It follows that persons who give attention to their actions are at all times aware of their choice. Whenever our faculty of desire is affected from without, we are conscious that this is not yet sufficient to determine it, and every determination of impulse appears to us within the realm between craving and desiring as an option.

---

33. Wille.
34. Muß schlechterdings willkührlich sein.
35. Einbildungskraft.

"Practical Reason" and Its Ever-Present Task

If a subject's will is joined with reason and reason regards itself as the will's principle, practical reason[36] results, which by its nature strives to bring the totality of maxims into unity. If reason could simply enclose the aggregate of all possible maxims within an exclusive system, then to that extent its practical task would be merely transitory and completed in one undertaking. But since on account of the infinite multitude of possible maxims [228] there is no hope of this result and all attempts at such a system are incomplete, reason can compose only the definitive idea of such a system and in each particular case must compare the maxim in question with this idea. The task of practical reason is thus everlasting. It must be active without respite in every action of an ethical person.

The Method of Approach

Two Inadequate Bases for This Inquiry:
Common Understanding and Feelings of Freedom

With these preparatory concepts of the nature of our faculty of desire we can now approach the question of its particular activities. As was already shown above,[37] we must consider a resolution of this question to be possible if we do not want to abandon our entire practical proceeding. What is more, since this question is properly propounded through practical interest and must be resolved if we wish to appreciate even further the obligation of performing certain actions, it must be possible to find a solution capable of gaining general currency. It follows first that nothing can be decided here by an appeal to obscure judgments of common human understanding, still less to expressions of an exceedingly indeterminate and confused feeling of freedom, expressions that by their very nature always require new interpretation. These are all grounds that people can always evade through the manifestation of their individual, quite distinctive consciousness. Since we cannot even say how these grounds relate to the fundamental issue, moreover, they are in every respect much too uncertain for us to entrust to them a question on which all warrant of subjective morality depends. If the question is decided

---

36. **Praktische Vernunft.**
37. See p. 4. Ed. note: All such cross references have been provided by Günter Meckenstock in the KGA edition and are adapted here to the present pagination.

on better grounds, however, then a suitable critique of these common judgments and sentiments[38] would be a very useful pursuit, for despite their testimony, which often seems contradictory, they are nonetheless grounded in the nature of the human soul. At the very least, such a pursuit would serve to remove these judgments' intrusive opposition to eventual principled decision.

A Third Inadequate Basis for This Inquiry: Theoretical Analysis

It has always been equally damaging to this undertaking to change a question that is occasioned purely by practical interest, and that can thus have only a practical sense, into a theoretical question. Whenever we have departed from the practical in order to see how the kind of effectiveness psychological powers have is related [229] to the kind of effectiveness that other, physical natural powers have, we have lost the proper point of view. Then, out of our fear of certain words, we have entangled ourselves in a great deal of useless hair-splitting. Thus if we wished to ask how the faculty of desire's functioning must be constituted in order to harmonize with judgments belonging to common human understanding and decisions belonging to general inner feeling, then a right answer can never follow. If we asked how it must be constituted in order to distinguish itself from the effect of physical powers, then we would not even finish determining the principles of our undertaking. Finally, if we were to set out to harmonize our answer with the theoretical interest of reason, asking how the faculty of desire's mode of action must be constituted in order to be able to be subsumed under the understanding's general laws concerning nature, the matter would indeed be soon decided. All that would remain would be for us to see how well or how poorly the practical claims of reason would agree with the decision. This way of proceeding, however, would actually presuppose the very point at issue. This would be so because among all who have wanted to resolve this question out of theoretical interest, it has always remained a contested point as to whether the laws of our thinking about human beings must be entirely different from the laws of our thinking about nature.

The Proper Approach: Practical, Not Theoretical

Nothing remains for us, therefore, but to engage our question by way of the practical interest out of which it has arisen. Thus we pose the question as

---

38. **Gemeinen Urtheile und Empfindungen.**

follows: How must the faculty of desire's mode of action be constituted if it is to be compatible with an acknowledgment of moral obligation? If we wish to avoid getting tangled up again in incalculable misunderstandings, however, we must first agree upon what we properly understand by obligation to moral law. Moreover, if our answer is to be generally satisfying, we must seek an idea that does justice to all sectors. The very nature of the matter seems to us to lighten uncommonly this otherwise very difficult task. That is, since obligation presupposes only a certain relation of the subject, thought of as active, to the law, what matters is not that all agree on the content of the law but only that all agree on the idea of the law.[39] Under this stipulation all might seem clear enough. However, since all controversies over this point have been occasioned by the fact that we have not sufficiently developed first concepts and have believed ourselves to agree when in fact we did not, we may be permitted to set down particularly the following points as generally accepted constituents of the idea of moral obligation.

Moral Obligation and Moral Choice

The Three Constituents of the Concept of Moral Obligation

[230] *First*, the subject's relation to law that we think of as obligation absolutely proscribes that this law be a natural law of the faculty of desire. Indeed we continually make judgments as if nothing in this matter would occur according to law if we should take away reason and its results, leaving only the faculty of desire. In complementary fashion, we also judge that everything would occur according to law if reason always determined the faculty of desire. Therefore this relation of the subject to law attests, *second*, that this relation is the hypothetical natural law of reason for the will. It immediately follows, *third*, that this relation is the only measure of the inner worth or perfection of the subject[40], and reason makes use of this measure in its judgments.

Reason is aware that it exercises no generally physical and necessary dominion over the faculty of desire. Yet it is at the same time convinced of the possibility that its influence over the faculty of desire, though by its nature indeterminate and accidental, can nevertheless be great enough in any conceivable particular case to actualize whatever is in accord with its law,

---

39. Meckenstock note (KGA): "Cf. Eberhard: *Sittenlehre der Vernunft*, 2d ed., Berlin 1786, 35f, 82."

40. **Für den innern Werth oder die Vollkommenheit des Subjekts.**

regardless of all impulses from elsewhere. The idea of this possible subordination of all the soul's faculties in particular cases, joined with the ideal necessity of morality insofar as actions are regarded as things of reason, then constitutes the idea of obligation in the narrower sense of the word.

I am in fact quite convinced that we can conduct no practical undertaking without encountering the true law of reason and acknowledging its priority over all others. Here, however, I have expressly avoided the law of reason in order to give my exposition of the idea of obligation the greatest possible generality. However, since it might appear that among the adduced constituents of the idea of obligation there are some that could apply only to those who have acknowledge the true law of reason, I may be permitted to justify my stipulations in the following remarks.

First, every regulative practical idea that is thought of as thoroughly determinative for a subject can claim the name of a law of reason, even if it has not originated from reason's essence but is rather calculated for some sensible interest[41], for such an idea can be thought only through reason, and it always documents consciousness of either a mediate or an immediate influence of reason on the faculty of desire. This is the case even with an idea that seems least similar to reason – for example, with an idea mandating that some inner contention between maxims and the faculty of desire be decided simply by way of the sensible [231] interest of the moment. That is, this idea speaks of a conjunction point of the maxims, and by its form this conjunction point is an idea of reason, even if the idea's content is worked out in a completely false manner. Reason presupposes that there are motives other than momentary sensible interest and that its law is therefore not natural law. Finally, reason presupposes that through consciousness of its law the one motive can be strengthened and the others overcome. The natural contention of the faculty of desire with the law is thus presupposed in every law, even the most empirical.

It appears that we may say at least this about such a law: if we were to take away reason and its results, then nothing would occur even according to such an empirical law. This is true because with such law, according to common opinion, there would be no evident difference between consequential conformity (legality) and formal conformity (morality). Yet this difference certainly exists. Philosophers of happiness[42] certainly establish a difference between happiness acquired and happiness produced. They will never judge as follows: these persons have acted philosophically (not to use the word "good") since they have acquired happiness through their actions, whereas

---

41. **Ein sinnliches Interesse.**
42. **Glükseligkeit.**

these other persons have not acted philosophically since by their actions they have missed getting happiness. Rather they will judge in this way: the first class of persons were very lucky[43], for even though they have engaged in no reflections according to the law they have nevertheless attained what the reflections would have granted; but by this mode of acting, in future cases they will fail to produce happiness in the same measure as they have acquired it in the present case, propitious but accidental. Thus we cannot say that they are competent to produce happiness according to rules. The other class of persons, in contrast, have certainly engaged in prior reflections according to the law. Since they have not attained happiness, they must therefore have deceived themselves in applying the rules. Thus, while it cannot be denied that an error of understanding has misled them in this instance, yet their mode of acting is good. To be sure, the difference between legality and morality is not stipulated here exactly as it is by a genuine moral philosopher. Nonetheless, the difference is anything but zero and is just as essential to the system.

Second, even such an obstensible law of ethics, through and through empirical, will be regarded, by those who accept it, as a hypothetical law of reason for the will. Moreover, they will judge the worth of other persons according to their own principle. Consider, for example, those who regard themselves as ends and use all others as means. Even they grant rights to all others over against themselves, and [232] only if they speak of the dignity of others, as contrasted with their usefulness, are they valuing others according to this law's standard. Likewise those whose law of reason always commands action favoring the inclination that has won the upper hand put themselves in the place of others.

Third, it is self-evident that adherents of empirical systems, at least as much as adherents of the pure system, must be convinced of the possibility of always acting in accordance with their system. This is true because they are really seeking success, and their law would amount to nothing if it did not assure them success. On the other hand, one might want to object that this is a matter more of probability than of necessity. The adherents of this system will reply that it is necessary for us always to determine ourselves inwardly according to the law, but that under particular circumstances it is only probable that we shall lay hold of the correct outward measure to attain success.

---

43. **Hat viel Glück gehabt.**

Moral Obligation Presupposes a Will With Its Impulse, "Moral Sense" Or "Respect for the Moral Law"

If one agrees with us about this general idea of obligation, then the question is how the faculty of desire must be constituted if this idea is to be confirmed as reality. If reason has given us the idea of law and obligation, then if this idea is to be realized in the faculty of desire, that faculty can be no instinct. If it were an instinct of the senses, then the faculty of desire would be absolutely determined prior to the law. If it were an instinct of reason, then the law of reason would be a law of nature, which contradicts our first point above.[44] The idea of moral reason, therefore, exerts influence only in choice. (That is, as the understanding can give us maxims purely without our having a will on that account, similarly reason can give us laws without its being practical on that account, if these laws are considered to have no influence on the faculty of desire. Reason becomes practical only through the idea of obligation to its laws. We wish, however, that reason should be practical, and so the question is how the faculty of desire must be constituted if the idea of obligation is to subsist in it.)

Now since laws do not decide particular cases as such, except as they are included under general propositions, maxims are the faculty of desire's only object. Thus the faculty of desire in which law-giving reason is to be truly practical must necessarily be a will. It remains an indispensable characteristic of this will, however, that all possible actions of the faculty of desire (regardless of how they comport themselves against the moral law) must in every possible way also be conceivable as maxims in the will. In itself, the will must be regarded as neither good nor evil. [233] The reason is that if the will were to exclude certain maxims that are in accord with the moral law, then it is self-evident that in those cases where these maxims should determine the will it would be impossible for a person to realize the law; on the other hand, if certain maxims that contradict the moral law were excluded from the faculty of the will, then in all cases where precisely these maxims might come into collision with moral maxims, the law would be regarded as natural law.

Thus this natural undeterminedness[45] of the will is necessary if that relation of the law to the faculty of desire entailed by the idea of obligation is to be possible. However, just as the understanding becomes practical only insofar as maxims we think of do not simply remain in the understanding but also

---

44. See p. 14.
45. **Unbestimmtheit.**

become objects of an impulse, so it is also necessary, if law-giving reason is to become practical and something is to occur according to its law, that reason's dictums must be able to become objects of an impulse. This must be true not simply to the extent that what reason commands happens to be in accord with some inclination, that is, insofar as reason's dictums relate mediately to a sensible object, but rather precisely insofar as the dictums belong to reason and relate immediately to the law. That is, even if in some particular case the law's will should become actual through an accidental relation, the law has no influence on the faculty of desire, and so this relation cannot establish the idea that it is possible in every case to realize the command of reason. This involves a feeling[46], and thereby an impulse, which relates immediately and exclusively to practical reason and at the same time represents practical reason in the faculty of desire. Moreover, this impulse must have exactly the same relation to the faculty of desire as every other.

The entire possibility of the idea of obligation rests upon the existence of this impulse, for this impulse alone relates reason to the faculty of desire. In earlier systems of morality this impulse was called the moral sense[47]. In present systems it is called respect for the moral law[48]. If, however, the newer practical philosophy wishes to argue that the moral sense of earlier systems is not an impulse properly belonging to reason, this argument seems to rest on a slight mistake. Namely, since all empirical systems presuppose an object of the faculty of desire, it appears as if longing for that object would be a feeling possible even without the law – the only feeling required, and completely sufficient to establish the idea that [234] what reason requires can occur in every case. But then we realize that this object is usually not a pure idea of reason but rather an empirical one, to which nothing corresponds *in concreto*, indeed is often an idea contradicting what at first glance seems to correspond to it, as is obviously the case with perfection and happiness[49], for example. We may thus see that if this feeling were not derived from the law, it would never be adequate to the law. On the other hand, it remains ever certain that respect for the moral law belongs to reason in a much more immediate and complete way, since this law has arisen exclusively from the idea of pure reason.

---

46. **Gefühl.**

47. **Moralischen Sinn.** Meckenstock note (KGA): "Cf. Eberhard, for example: *Sittenlehre der Vernunft*, 50-53."

48. **Achtung fürs moralische Gesez.** Meckenstock note (KGA): "Cf. Kant, for example: KpV 130-156; Ak 5, 73-87."

49. **Vollkommenheit und Glükseligkeit.**

The Search for the Fundamental Determining Ground of Choice

The complete undeterminedness of the will that has been indicated and the existence of a representing impulse are a pair of principal characteristics of the faculty of desire, given through the idea of obligation. With them we are now considerably nearer to answering the question concerning individual activities of the faculty of desire. This is true because partly from these derived characteristics, and partly from their immediate relation to practical reason, we will easily be able to see what conditions they must have with respect to their individuality. That is, as we have seen above,[50] each particular activity of the faculty of desire consists in a determination of impulse so complete in a given moment that an activity of some physical faculty in accord with that determination of impulse can follow. Thus the impulse is determined for a single object to the exclusion of all others. Our question then takes the following general form: "Wherein must the origination of the preponderance of one portion of the determining ground of choice over other portions be grounded in each case?"

In order to achieve a more secure elucidation of this question we must strive to bring all conceivable cases under a few rubrics and then to compare these in turn with our known conditions. The first questions, then, are these: Is there, in general, a basis for this preponderance or is there none? And if there is one, is it knowable or not? Since in the interest of greater surety we have decided to rule theoretical interest completely out of the game, we are not allowed to argue from the generality of the proposition offering that basis, which especially in this respect is so greatly disputed. However, from the viewpoint of practical interest the two cases – wherein there is no basis for this preponderance, and wherein the basis [235] lies outside the sphere of our knowledge – are completely equivalent. These two conditions do not, it is true, confute the idea that what is in accord with the law can in every case occur, but they do not allow us to show that this possibility is grounded in the faculty of desire. We would not be warranted to regard practical laws as anything other than merely theoretical ideas of reason. We could not say to what extent an action could correspond to them in any particular case *in concreto*. Still less could we think of their realization as possible in general.

Just as little could we formulate a scheme to subordinate other impulses to the moral impulse. Yet this scheme is the necessary and first consequence that must express itself in our heart and mind as a result of our consciousness of moral impulse and the idea of obligation. Otherwise we could specify no means by which this scheme could be accomplished in accordance with our

---

50. See pp. 6-8.

idea. Neither practical reason nor a striving after conformity with the law –
a striving in accordance with an idea and thus more than fortuitous – would
be possible. We would be forced to give up our practical conduct as unwarranted.

Moral Choice Cannot Be Instinct

If, then, the basis of predominance from which the activities of the
faculty of desire arise must absolutely be knowable, at least insofar as is
requisite to verify that possibility, there are two kinds of objects in which it
can be included, namely, such as can be represented outside our subjective
being[51] and such as can be represented within it. Suppose that external
objects were to include not only the basis for our being affected (for they certainly contribute to that) but also the basis for the preponderance necessary
to every act of choice. Then with every external object there would have to
be given not only a general influence on the faculty of desire but also a
determinate quality and quantity of this influence, not alterable by any inner
characteristic[52] of the subject. (Otherwise the decisive preponderance would
be grounded in the inner characteristics of the subject, which would alter the
influence.) In this case the faculty of desire would still be in essence a
choosing faculty, but with respect to its effects it would be regarded as only
an instinct. The reason is that if several simultaneously affecting objects
partially annul their influence reciprocally, we could regard what remains as
itself an object (since with respect to its influence it would be determined in
only one way). This object's impression would be unalterable, and the faculty
of desire would be [236] absolutely determined to it. Now since neither the
practical judgments of the understanding contained in maxims nor the
practical conclusions of reason in applying laws appeal to single external
objects, and thus the related impulse could not be determined by external
objects either, such an impulse would not even have a part in the complete
determination of the faculty of desire. All this would not be changed in the
slightest if we wished to posit the basis for preponderance in certain objects
represented within our subjective being so far as they are thought of as
individual objects of some impulse, and similarly in external and internal
objects of the faculty of desire taken together.

---

51. **Unseres Subjektes.**
52. **Innere Beschaffenheit.**

Thus we can establish the following proposition without hesitation: no single object of our faculty of desire, whether internal or external, and thus no combination of several such objects, has a determinative influence, invariable in all cases, either upon the faculty of desire in general or upon its particulars, so that the preponderance of impression requisite for any complete action of the faculty of desire cannot be grounded in such objects. Therefore, nothing remains wherein we could seek this ground except what is thought in our subjective being, insofar as it is not a single object of an impulse.

Moral Choice Is Necessarily Grounded In the Complex Variabilities of Our Representing and Desiring

Here again we encounter two wholly different cases. In our subjective being we think in part of what is the unknown and invariable, which includes the final general grounds of all that we notice in ourselves immediately; and we think in part of this notable phenomenon itself, namely the variabilities of the soul[53] and the determinations[54] that are thereby brought forth in the soul's variability. Now it is certain that just as all characteristics[55] of the soul are grounded in its essence, so must be the faculty to desire and to act. Yet what matters here is not the ground of the inherent existence of this faculty in general, but rather the ground determining the individuality[56] of the particular activities in which that faculty is exercised. If these activities are to lie immediately in what is essential in the soul, then that essence would have to include all the results of choice's comparing activity.

For every subject, then, every impulse would have to be determined once and for all, at least as to degree, since in what is essential in the soul no increase or decrease can occur. The impulse that represents practical reason would also have to be determined in like fashion, and in this determination would lie certain characteristic boundaries for each subject as to how far ethical subordination of the whole set of impulses could extend. [237] This latter point, however, contradicts our consciousness of the pervasive possibility of subordination that is given in the idea of obligation. On the other hand, a limiting point for this subordination would be given in each subject,

---

53. Veränderungen der Seele.
54. Bestimmungen.
55. Eigenschaften.
56. Individualität.

in itself and necessarily, and up to this limit the law of reason would again be a natural law for each subject.

We must therefore remain committed to the variabilities and the determinations of the variable in the subject, yet these in turn relate partly to the faculty of representation[57] and partly to the faculty of desire itself. In the faculty of representation everything coheres, and what we separate therein by way of abstraction will not be found sundered *in concreto*. The faculty of desire coheres with the faculty of representation in like fashion. Even if in some particular case the preponderance of one impulse over others is based in such accidental determinations of the faculty of desire as have been produced through its preceding activities, these in turn have their first ground in the state of the faculty of representation (unless one wishes to include quantitative variations of impulses that are innate, that is, actually present prior to all action).

Thus nothing remains here to be separated, and this grounding of the activities of the faculty of desire in the state of the faculty of representation cannot be alien to us if we consider the following points: that it always depends upon the state of our faculty of representation what variety of internal objects of impulse will arise through the association of ideas occasioned by an external object and, together with that object, simultaneously affect the faculty of desire; that it depends upon the state of our faculty of representation how in any particular case the influence of an appearing object may be modified by knowledge of that object; that it depends upon the state of our faculty of representation whether and how we formulate the maxims under which we believe the particular case to be comprehended; that it rests upon the state of our faculty of representation whether or not we take cognizance of certain external objects of impulse as such; and that it rests solely upon this same state to what extent the syllogism basing the application of law on the appropriate maxim will be formally and materially correct.

Thus this proposition appears to be established: the preponderance in which every comparison of choice must end in order to pass over into a complete action of the faculty of desire must in every case be grounded in the totality of present representations and in the state and [238] interrelations of all the soul's faculties that have been produced in the progression of representations in our soul.

---

57. **Vorstellungsvermögen.**

Recapitulation and Reconstruction

Since this thesis was the final option remaining to us, it has to be in accord with the previously established conditions by which we excluded all the other options we have considered. This must be the case if our question is to be answered at all and if we have maintained a direct and correct course for our inquiry. So let us now investigate this issue briefly.

On the Multifarious Activity Of the Faculty of Desire

If a faculty of representation is thought of in connection with the faculty of associating ideas[58] (and this human faculty cannot be conceived of otherwise), and if it must always be active whenever an object of the faculty of desire comes into consciousness from without; if at the same time it cannot be active without bringing forth its own objects for the faculty of desire: then such a subject's faculty of desire cannot appear as instinct in any single moment of its existence. The absolute influence of some one external object does not make it such, nor can the absence of several co-affecting objects ever give choice the appearance of instinct. The activities of the faculty of desire change as richly and rapidly as the flux of external things can ever do. In every moment it is filled not simply with life but with superabundant life, multifariously active. The senses, fantasy, understanding, and reason[59] allow it no rest. It craves, selects, desires, decides, and acts[60] in every moment of its existence.

Will as Neutral in Relation to Sensibility and Practical Reason

Furthermore, since the faculty of representation not only contributes toward determining the influence of objects but also unceasingly presents its own objects to the faculty of desire, various impulses will correspond to these essentially distinct activities of the faculty of representation. One of these impulses will relate to the general rules of the understanding, that is, to maxims, and this impulse makes the faculty of desire a will. Now in relation

---

58. Mit dem Vermögen der Ideenverbindung.
59. Sinne, Fantasie, Verstand und Vernunft.
60. Gelüstet, wählt, begehrt, beschließt und handelt.

to this influence of the faculty of representation upon the faculty of desire it is also conceivable that the impulse relates purely to the form of maxims as rules of understanding, without regard to content. Also, from any action *in concreto* a great many maxims can be evolved, as we consider the action from various viewpoints and according to whether we abstract the action more or less from its attending circumstances. In such a will, therefore, all conceivable maxims are equally possible and are capable of similar influence upon the will's impulse. Thus the will in itself is always undetermined and completely neutral with respect to morality, so that it does not in the least [239] prejudge the decisions of practical reason.

The impulse representing practical reason is possible in exactly the same way as the impulse of the will is possible. Neither impulse will ever become effective as instinct, whether in general or in relation to any one of the objects belonging to it. The reason is that although general judgments of the understanding that manifest rules and conclusions of reason – that is, laws – are the highest product of the faculty of representation, still their influence upon impulse will not be absolute. Impulse is based upon the relation of such judgments to the faculty of representation, and their worth[61] there is not always the same. Specifically, the maxim under which an action is conceived will not always come to consciousness with the same clarity, nor will it always be thought through with the same completeness. Indeed, the very consciousness that we have made this maxim or its opposite our own will not always be of the same degree. Any one of these circumstances will alter the modification of the will's impulse. To cite examples would not be useful at this point.

The same argument applies to the impulse relating to practical reason. This impulse will be stimulated even less frequently than impulses relating to maxims, for it cannot be stimulated unless we think of a maxim, and we often think of a maxim without taking any notice of its relation to practical reason. Often a contradiction between reason and a maxim is not considered clearly enough because the maxim's stipulations occasioning the contradiction are not prominent enough. Even more often, the agreement of a maxim with reason is not considered thoroughly enough. In both instances the ethical impulse is affected too weakly. Here again, therefore, there is no question of an instinct of reason.

---

61. **Werth.**

These Are the Necessary and Sufficient Conditions of Moral Obligation

Accordingly, we see that in this proposition concerning the basis for the faculty of desire's particular activities we have all the conditions required for authorizing our practical conduct. Likewise we can convince ourselves that this proposition includes all the relations of the subject to the law of reason that are necessary in order to secure objective validity for the idea of obligation. That is, since impulses are limited by no determined boundary in the essence of the soul[62], no degree of impulse, however great, can be conceived to which an impulse of even higher degree cannot be juxtaposed. Through this boundlessness of impulses, if I may so express myself, a complete subordination of impulses under moral impulses is easily conceivable. If the activities of my faculty of desire are grounded in the state of my faculty of representation, then they can also be altered by the state of my moral representations. Moreover, since moral representations are likewise not limited by any determined boundaries with respect to their influence and completeness, we can conceive of no situation in which their [240] influence could not be stronger than that of any influence over against it. In a certain situation some sensible feeling[63] might be unduly elevated by my representations, but since the influence of sensible external objects is not absolute, a series of representations is possible through which the feeling representing practical reason might be affected more strongly.

It appears not only that no other possible answer could be in accord with the conditions we have previously established, but also that this would be the natural opinion of every person who is not misled either by misunderstood feelings or by metaphysical sophistries but follows the judgments of common human understanding – judgments that are generally grounded, not in purely moral interest, it is true, but in a certain practical interest. Such a person agrees with our opinion because of an awareness that otherwise the entire interest we take in our own soul would in large part have to be foregone. If we must seek the basis for particular activities of the faculty of desire elsewhere than in the state and other activities of the soul[64], then the inquiries concerning our soul so natural to each of us are cut off at the root – inquiries concerning laws of the soul's various faculties, the way the soul

---

62. **Wesen der Seele.**
63. **Irgend ein sinnliches Gefühl.**
64. **In dem Zustand und den andern Thätigkeiten der Seele.**

apprehends these laws, unusual appearances in particular cases, premises that would have been requisite to some certain result, and the result that certain premises would have produced. This is the case in that we are clearly aware that all the soul's capacities, even those for knowing[65], interrelate most intimately with the faculty of desire and that the substance of all the soul's particular activities, insofar as they involve choice, are by necessity determined through an activity of the faculty of desire.

The Indissoluble Interrelation of Fantasy, Imagination, and Cognition In Our Faculty of Desire

This interrelation is even the case with the faculty whose effects pose for psychologists a perennial problem, elucidations of which accumulate ever more difficulties. I refer to fantasy. The general law that fantasy reproduces in us no other representations and in its productions composes none other than have in some previous moment been part of a total representation – this law can be completely correct, but it is by no means sufficient to explain all of fantasy's particular manifestations. The question always remains as to why, out of the present total representation, fantasy [241] proceeds from just this part, and why out of the representational totality of which this representation is a part fantasy has chosen precisely this one, and again, this particular aspect of it.

Here, at the end of all our efforts at explanation, we must come back to the faculty of desire. The reason is that the expressions of fantasy, which always have reference to the whole of present representations, will produce nothing except what by virtue of those representations can readily become an object of the dominating and momentarily most attractive impulse. Through fantasy, upon which every association of ideas depends, even the particular actions of our cognitive powers[66] are enhanced. Whenever the same fact is applied by one person to interpret some very important proposition, but is used by another to confirm a prejudice; whenever persons develop utterly different trains of clear representations from the same beginning point; whenever persons derive almost entirely different conclusions from the same premises; whenever persons deduce quite different consequences from the same fundamental principles, or induce quite different fundamental prin-

---

65. **Auch die erkennenden.**
66. **Der erkennenden Kräfte.**

ciples from the same results: the ground of these differences can be sought nowhere else than in the faculty of desire. Whenever one person ventures into the depths of wisdom while another, with equal powers of understanding, is content with modest research into nature; whenever one person restricts curiosity to the objects of common life while another, with no stronger consciousness of mental powers, nevertheless plunges into the abyss of religious investigations; whenever one person packs memory with events, another with names, or one loves general information exclusively, and another snatches at every little detail: the intentional course followed by a person's cognitive powers, either overall or temporarily, is determined by nothing other than the fact that at the time the option is taken, this course could be more an object of impulse than all alternatives. Indeed, the first existential ground of all particular actions of understanding, namely the direction of imagination, is nothing other than an activity of the faculty of desire, for attention itself can be conceived as nothing other than desire for the completion of a train of representations, to the exclusion of all others at that particular time. By means of attention, the proportion of spontaneity[67] – now greater, now less – expressing itself in our outward and inward sensibilities also depends upon the faculty of desire.

In short, it is pointless to divide human beings. All is joined in us; all is one. Abolish the regularity of the faculty of desire and nothing in the entire soul is any longer regular. If we deny inner accidental grounds for activities of the faculty of desire, then such grounds exist for no specific action: all is either lodged in the essence of the soul or [242] absolutely determined by external things or not grounded at all. Furthermore, it is easy to see that if we distance ourselves from this opinion, not only must our investigations into ourselves cease, but also we may no longer flatter ourselves with influence over our own wills or over the wills of others. That is, we cannot affect others except through representations, and what would that benefit us if actions be not grounded in representations?

These Moral Conditions Hold Though the Soul's State Remains Empirically Inscrutable

Now it is certainly true that experience can never teach us that from this representational totality such and such an action must necessarily follow. Experience cannot even assure us that a certain action has ever been

---

67. **Spontaneität.**

grounded in such a congeries of representations, for we can never observe the soul's state exactly enough to know about a representational totality in all its aspects, still less to recognize it again. It would therefore appear as if we were dealing here only with probability, but even that approach would be invalid without the basic idea that representations are sufficient grounds for actions. Without this idea we could in no way justify our efforts to affect wills; producing representations could not be regarded as a means to this end, and there would in fact be no means at all.[68]

It is true that if we maintain the idea of necessary causal connection between representations and actions, then we can judge only in terms of probability our assumption that some determinate means will lead to a certain goal. Yet our goal is in fact possible and our method is appropriate to it. Even if some effort involving our own soul or someone else's soul proves unsuccessful, still we know that the fault is not with the essentials of our approach, and observation of the failure can itself serve us as a means for eventually [243] discovering the track to a true, secure effort. In contrast, if we remove that idea, then the failure lies in the nature of the case (if indeed failure is not much too good a word for the only possible outcome of a wholly chimerical undertaking). Even if in that route something succeeds for us, we cannot regard it as the effect of what we have done. Rather it is a mere stroke of luck, an accidental coincidence, from which no learning experience can ever be gleaned and no rule ever induced, even if it should be repeated in the same manner a thousand times over.

This, approximately, is the argument concerning practical grounds upon which we may rest the judgment of common human understanding which validates our opinion. If, on the other hand, it appears that this argument is completely contradicted by common human feeling – which may weigh just as heavily as common human understanding, especially given today's low estimation of the latter – then we shall likewise inquire into its claims. We must let that wait awhile, though, until we have answered more essential and important objections still to be put to us. [244]

---

68. Meckenstock note (KGA): "Cf. Wolff: *Vernünfftige Gedancken von Gott, der Welt und der Seele des Menschen*, 4th ed., Frankfurt/Leipzig 1729: '§512. It would also follow from this [*viz.* from the equilibristic concept of freedom] that all representations restraining us from evil or encouraging us to good would be in vain if they made no impression in the soul, or if they could not lead us to will or not will. Indeed, we could specify no sufficient ground for any matter concerning human actions. In this way the whole of ethical doctrine would collapse, which is built entirely upon motivating grounds, that is, upon rational representations of good and evil.... Overturn this truth, and all certainty in ethical doctrine also collapses, since we have access to the human soul through no other means than representations of good and evil....' (313)"

Part II

MORAL ACCOUNTABILITY AND THE DOCTRINE OF NECESSITY

On the Objection That Determinism Undermines Moral Accountability

A numerous class make it their first concern to find for anyone expressing an opinion concerning some philosophical subject a general label, by which everything the person might say is prejudged. Long before this point in our inquiry this class will have relegated us to determinism[69]. Whether or not any name among philosophical sects admits of more indeterminate significance or greater variation among those to whom it is given, the present author makes no claim that he should be exempted from the general fate of being classified. On the contrary, he is satisfied with the name of determinist, provided only that he is promised that no proposition of any other determinist will be attributed to him that is not clearly contained in what he himself has said or will say.

I am now prepared to illumine somewhat more clearly the question of which objections directed against the doctrine of determinism relate to what has been said in the preceding pages. None of them could be more important than the objection relating to accountability[70]. It is said that such an opinion concerning the originating grounds of human actions leaves those actions no accountability at all. If the grounds of each action are sufficiently and unalterably determined antecedently, which as soon as this opinion is adopted certainly cannot be denied; if each action thus depends upon preceding actions and the first actions always have their grounds completely outside ourselves; if persons must therefore act as they have in fact acted and could not possibly act otherwise: if this is what we are taken to have written, then the thought of such an association of notions must stifle at birth the attempt to assign accountability to an action. That is, if every action is the completely determined effect of preceding actions and circumstances, and every circumstance is in turn grounded in a preceding one, then we come finally to a state in childhood where no morality, indeed scarcely even any choice, pertains to a person's actions. If persons are thus not the cause of

---

69. **Determinismus.**
70. **Zurechnung.**

who they are, how should it be possible for me to [245] praise one and blame another? At most, with a sigh, I shall deem the one as fortunate, though not without deep envy and not without murmuring against the world order, and pity the other, not without secret joy.

The Response to This Objection Is in Practical, Not Theoretical Terms Or in Terms of Sentiment

These are only the beginning of the objections directed at determinism, but I refrain from adding others and content myself with having indicated the thread out of which the others may be spun. Had I undertaken to prove the deterministic system from purely theoretical concepts of reason, I would play a much better game with these objections. I would say to my readers: "I cannot deny that the multitude of your objections weighs me down a bit. This is an encumbrance that I shall be able to cast off only little by little. Before I begin that task, however, answer me just one question, so that I may know how things stand between us. If you were really correct, if it were not possible to unite the doctrine of the necessity of actions with the imputability[71] of those actions and the consequences that follow, what would you conclude from that? Would you bid good night to all inquiry into truth because that doctrine, as you yourselves have admitted, is a necessary consequence of the only conditions making that inquiry possible? Are these concepts too deeply intertwined in your ways of thinking and acting to be extricated in any way? And would you think yourselves foolish if you would thus exchange your accustomed happiness and tranquility, which are demonstrable enough, for a bit of truth, even though its possibility has been so often doubted? If this is your plan, very well, I shall not attempt to seek the resolution of this problem with you. I then have nothing more to say to you, for you are not disposed to capitulate by unconditionally submitting to truth. If, in contrast, you want to make truth a touchstone even for all the concepts belonging to the system of your happiness, and if you want to submit these concepts together with all feelings and opinions to truth, then very well, let us impartially investigate how things stand with the contradictions you present, and let us be content with whatever remains of this concept after our investigation, for there can be only as much truth therein as can agree with a doctrine recognized to be true."

---

71. **Imputabilität.**

We have relinquished this advantageous position, in which the concept occasioning doubt is regarded as itself problematic, so that its reality or nullity alters nothing in the principal issue and investigating it is only an ancillary matter. Instead, we have proceeded purely from practical concern, whereby the issue bears rather more [246] significance for us. If accountability is not to be a necessary practical concept, then the issue does not concern us; but that is certainly difficult to suppose. If, on the other hand, accountability is a necessary practical concept, then either our opinion must exactly agree with it or our entire opinion is false, however exactly it may have appeared to follow from our practical presuppositions, since then it does not accomplish what we have desired from it, namely, complete practical adequacy. We must then abandon either the basic principles from which we have begun or the matter in which we have utilized them.

Accountability Defined: Partial Judgment of Personal Worth Upon the Basis of Action

Granting this understanding of the issue's importance, let us go right to work on it, first reaching agreement concerning the concept of accountability. This we should do because although the concept appears generally consistent, the suspicion is readily cast upon it that it may not be conceived with complete clarity or determined in an unvarying fashion. This is because it so often happens with respect to the concept of accountability that a pure judgment of understanding is confused with something resting upon sentiment, namely with the difference between commending someone and deeming someone to be fortunate, between blaming and feeling sorry for. Sometimes indeed we find the concept of accountability so closely interwoven with this bifurcation of sentiments that it appears that nothing else is to be understood by that concept except authorization to blame rather than feel sorry for someone who in some instance has acted immorally. Though common in other contexts, such an exchange of the concept for the related feeling cannot possibly be allowed here. For the present, therefore, we want to separate the two, dismissing feeling together with its demands so long as we are examining the concepts that provide the only basis such feeling can have for its claims.

The textbooks we ordinarily see tell us that accountability is the judgment that someone is the originator[72] of an action's morality.[73] This

---

72. **Urheber.**

73. Meckenstock note (KGA): "Cf. Eberhard on this: '*Accountability*. When I judge that someone is the originator of an action's consequence, *then I reckon that person accountable for*

definition is quite unserviceable for us, however, for if we ask further what we are to understand by an originator, the answer is a free cause[74], and here we have a term that we should assiduously avoid until we have completed our inquiry. Indeed, this is but the least of our worries, for if by a free cause (insofar as this is supposed to specify the concept of an originator) [247] we wished to understand nothing other than a cause acting by choice – which would be completely adequate to all instances in which this concept appears – we would still be guilty of counterfeiting the concept of cause. If we assume this concept, then our investigation is no longer possible, for the concept of accountability, which is supposed to be wholly practical, is now tainted by a theoretical addition – indeed, worst of all, by an addition by which our opinion concerning its validity, which should be decided by the completeness of its suitability to practical concepts, is to be cast aside at the outset and its opposite posited. This definition therefore goes beyond the concept insofar as the concept is a practical one. We would have to demonstrate that its theoretical component is a necessary consequence of its practical aspect before we could ground our argument in it. In order to conduct this demonstration, we would have to proceed from another definition in which the concept would be set forth as purely practical. Moreover, since we are thus entitled to such a demonstration anyway, it will be just as well for us to restrict ourselves to it and only afterward to see what this concept of accountability stipulates theoretically concerning the grounds of action.

This definition includes yet another error, and even if it is an error only of diction and choice of expression it nonetheless makes the concept of accountability more difficult to understand. That is, by the morality of an action we can understand nothing other than its relation to the moral law, and so we can never say that someone is the originator of the morality of the action. This morality is rather given prior to the action and is grounded in unalterable laws. If, according to the usual ethical treatment of the principle of happiness, we understand morality to be the consequences of action insofar as these consequences are thought of as grounds, this expression of accountability then recedes even further. If, however, we raise morality to something more than a mere calculation of probability, again we must posit this concept differently.

---

those consequences. The originator is the *free* cause of an action, and the action's good or bad consequences constitute its morality. Thus accountability is the judgment that someone is the free cause of the morality of an action.' (*Sittenlehre der Vernunft*, §67, p.69)"
74. **Eine freie Ursach.**

The errors we have just censured lead us now to the following definition: accountability is the judgment by which we assign the morality of an action to the person who performed it in such a way that our judgment of the action constitutes part of our judgment concerning the person's worth. I believe that if we take account of all that sentiment subsequently adds, not even the hardest and strongest judgment of accountability will include more than this. Moreover, it is not possible to draw a more comprehensive conclusion from a single action, for as we establish an aspect of a person's worth, so [248] at the same time we acquire an opinion concerning the way the person will behave in similar circumstances, and, depending on the significance of the action, we determine the extent of the sphere of circumstances that are to be regarded as similar.

This definition is likewise sufficient for those cases in which accountability has an aspect less strong and appears rather to be limiting or completely negative. Specifically, it very often happens that we feel obliged to assign to the agent only a part of the morality we observe in the action. Different people might even define this portion in different ways. And yet the accountability of each one is in accord with our definition. The intention of each is simply to separate that in the action which was merely a consequence[75] from that which was act[76]. This separation might be accomplished according to various ideas, but whatever morality remains in the act we assign to the actor without the least limitation.

Accountability Clarified by Means of an Example

Think for example of a doctor who is just coming from a public performance and is about to savor the enjoyment[77] of reflecting on it in the company of good friends. At that moment he is summoned to someone who is ill. Under the influence of his lighthearted mood, he listens to an account of the sick person's condition, and on the basis of that report he makes a few routine prescriptions and postpones his visit for a while. It happens, however, that the report was not accurate or that other circumstances intervene – in short, the patient becomes a victim of the delay.

Now let us see how variously people will judge this case. One might say that the doctor has the patient's life on his conscience and is accountable for

---

75. **Erfolg.**
76. **That.**
77. **Vergnügen.**

the death. Another considers this merely a consequence that might not have been avoided even if the doctor had performed his duty, but thinks that this much is certain: the thought of the endangered life of another had less effect on the doctor than the thought of his own enjoyment, and he is thus to be regarded as a man who respected a person's life less than a small portion of his own happiness. A third answers that we cannot charge the doctor with a cheap evaluation of life since he was never sensible of this thought; all we can hold him accountable for is that he lacked the skill to weigh properly the actions to which his most sacred duties obliged him. Still a fourth interprets this judgment to mean that the doctor is not in a position to exercise this skill only so long as he is prepossessed by other thoughts. Finally, a fifth says that the ethical nature[78] of the action depends not upon the fact that the doctor did not sufficiently [249] consider the circumstances but rather upon the fact that he was not guided by the idea of pursuing his obligatory duty to the fullest possible completion, before all other considerations and regardless of circumstances.

From this example we see quite clearly that all the variations of accountability are grounded in various estimations of the ethical nature of an action and that once this is established all will take a similar approach. It is also certain that there is no action, however small it may be, to which we have not extended our warrant of accountability, for even if the agent had no ethical motivations, we hold the agent accountable precisely for this lack. For example, if as I am writing this I lay down my pen and stand up, I am not self-consciously aware at this moment of why I am doing so, and yet no one would think it absurd if I were strict enough to hold myself accountable for this action, since I ought not to have performed it without becoming conscious of my grounds for doing so. This applies whenever we observe but a single ethical issue in an action, and we suspend our warrant only when the lack of this first condition renders accountability impossible.

How the Doctrine of Necessity Relates to the Various Components of Accountability

If our definition is correct – and I believe that we can boldly challenge anyone to pose a case for which our definition would not be adequate – then it remains for us to review its various components to see where the reputed contradiction with the doctrine of the necessity of actions might be grounded.

---

78. **Sittlichkeit.**

The warrant to determine the ethical nature of an action requires nothing more than that by its nature this action can endure comparison with the moral law. This comparison, in turn, is possible even if the moral laws exist not as commandments but only as idea. The comparison discloses whether, if all actions are to accord with the moral law, the particular action at hand should occur or not or how far it must be altered in order to occur. This alone is not yet accountability, however.

If we wish to apply this ethical nature of the action to the subject who acts – to the faculty of desire whereby it has become actual – then we would really wish to say only this much: this faculty of desire is suited or unsuited to performing such an action according to the moral law. Now if by this accord we understand nothing more than in the first case, then nothing more is required than that the faculty of desire be a choosing faculty, and from some point of view we [250] can regard the one case as a rule for the others. If, however, we understand this accord to require consciousness of the moral law and reference to it, then we must think of the faculty of desire as being provided with practical reason and an impulse representing it.

Up to this point an opinion concerning the originating grounds of actions has not come into play. Thus the contradiction must lie in the final characteristic mark of accountability, namely, that we make a judgment concerning an action also a judgment concerning a person's worth. Yet this warrant seems neither to promote nor to reject any opinion concerning the grounds of actions. That is, if by the worth of something we understand its suitability to a certain goal, there is no reason at all why we could not base our judgment of suitability upon whatever was effected, without concerning ourselves in the least with how these effects have arisen.

Now we do not want to incur the rebuke that we have tried to elude the whole great controversy by means of a word usage that is inadmissible for this particular case. We wish to grant that the worth of a person is not the worth of a thing, and that we cannot say that the entire goal of a person's existence is exterior. So let us go back to the explanation of personal worth presented above. If we compare that explanation with the earlier proposition that there is no measure of human personal worth except a law of reason, and if we also accept the presupposition that under the idea of obligation the law of reason appears as commandment, then the worth of a person consists in the relation of what the person is to what the person should be. The idea of this worth is almost the same as the idea of morality, and as this relation applies to everyone, the warrant to judge ourselves and others by this relation can by no means be thought away. The intensive and extensive degree of a person's obedience to the law cannot be known from any one circumstance, however, but only from all circumstances together. We have no other means of judging a person's worth, therefore, than by gathering judgments of particular actions that then serve as parts of the general judgment.

The Apparent Contradiction Between Necessity and Accountability Rests upon a Misunderstanding

This concept of accountability, then, follows quite precisely from initial practical ideas, and our opinion concerning the originating grounds of actions was compatible with these ideas. Yet this result is supposed to contradict our opinion. This apparent contradiction leads us to suspect that some [251] underlying misunderstanding must obtain, resting perhaps on an incorrect application of the ideas of reason. In this regard, if judgments of accountability can truly be viewed as parts of the judgment concerning general worth, these judgments must inevitably contain the determination of certain relationships revealed in the actions such that each action is looked upon as a schema of all similar actions (so long as the subject's worth does not change). This in fact appears to presuppose our opinion, since it indicates common conditions and causes of actions.

What will the opponents of our opinion say to this? I suppose they will grant that the more general reflections[79] appear to favor us, but they will claim that our mistake becomes quite clear if we turn more to particular reflections and that outright contradictions will necessarily come to light if we go through the entire series of thoughts required for a judgment of accountability, wishing to reconcile them with our opinion. Someone, for example, has killed his friend in a duel. Can we really hold him accountable? "Certainly, since he should never have become involved in the duel." "But he could not do otherwise, for countless images of all that follows upon the loss of honor overpowered him." "They should not have overpowered him. He must have realized that it is an unreasonable, utterly immoral maxim to risk two human lives in order to avoid uncertain and imagined evils." "But he could not realize that, since this maxim did not occur to him at the moment." "It should have occurred to him, for we must never act without considering the relevant maxim." "But he could not do so, for in the entire course of his life he never had any possibility of acquiring a capacity for considering maxims amidst the storm of other thoughts." So goes an endless give and take, in which every claim of "should" is followed by a proof of "not able,"

---

79. **Reflexionen.**

until finally whoever has the final defense brings an end to this standoff by introducing a "not able" that relates not only to the present moment but also to the whole preceding course of life, thereby leaving room for no more "shoulds."

How then is it possible to resolve this contradiction? How is it possible to make a principle of moral judgments out of the proposition that a person *should* do something which in this moment the person admittedly *cannot do*, that a person should do something, despite the fact that the necessary grounds for its actuality are no longer in the person's power at all?

As evident as the objection [252] seems at first glance, we nonetheless see upon clear analysis that it too does not relate directly to the concept of accountability but again lays claim more to the sentiments relating to that concept. Still, even if we accept the objection as valid, why is it always directed only against the concept of accountability and never against the concept of obligation, especially since this part of the concept of accountability is grounded wholly in the concept of obligation? This practice seems to indicate that the objection applies only to what distinguishes the two concepts, namely, that with obligation we think of actions in general, whereas with accountability we think of the particular, concrete action.

In order to establish this observation beyond doubt, we wish to justify ourselves in relation to the concept of obligation. We maintained that this concept presupposes the possibility of a complete subordination of all impulses under the impulse that represents reason and, by means of this subordination, a complete fitness of all actions to the moral law. Now according to the present objection, even this claim must prove to be false if applied to a particular case. The reason offered is that if a given action has not been in accord with the moral law and yet, according to the doctrine of necessity[80], could not be otherwise, then it follows that it was not possible to conform the action to the moral law. Those who believe that the necessity of actions annuls accountability may not wish to accept this conclusion with respect to obligation as their own. To them we say that we ask nothing more, since our idea of accountability relates quite solely and precisely to this idea of obligation. If, on the other hand, they do acknowledge this conclusion as their own, then we answer that it is a false conclusion, since it replaces the predicates of a concept with the predicates of the concept's representation in space and time.

---

80. **Lehre der Nothwendigkeit.**

The Doctrine of Necessity Shown to Be Both Logically and Really Possible

Just as we said that a conformity of all actions to the moral law is possible, so we wish to state the following. First, it is not possible to think of any problem for which it would be impossible to find a solution in accord with the moral law, not only legally but also morally. That is, in our proposition there is no contradiction between the concept of subject, however it may be determined, and the concept of predicate; or, our proposition is logically possible. Second, it is not possible to think of any case in which this solution might lie beyond the limits of the human soul's capacity. That is, there is no conflict between our claim and the subject to whom it relates; or, our proposition is really possible. This, furthermore, is all that our proposition entails. If those who oppose us demand that in order for this possibility to [253] be proven the grounds of actuality for each particular case would also have to be given, this shows their failure to realize that their demand would destroy the idea of obligation rather than save it. This is because the fitness of actions to the law would then be necessary for every case. From this reasoning it is evident that the grounds of actuality for each particular case must be determined differently from the grounds of possibility for all cases in general. Moreover, our concept of obligation, insofar as it includes the possibility of the complete morality of actions, is saved even if the grounds through which this possibility would have to become actual in particular cases very often *cannot* be available but are rather unavailable.

What now remains for the objection to accountability in reply? Nothing, as we may easily see if, following upon this discussion we once more survey the judgment of accountability as a whole. A given act of choice was supposed to have a distinctly moral character, but it has not received this moral character since the grounds were not there to produce it. Rather this act has turned out otherwise, and had to turn out otherwise, because grounds did exist to determine its actuality in this particular way. In general terms, will this situation hinder reason in its judgment? In no way. The moral characteristic that reason required was not only possible in itself but was also possible in the subject; it was simply not possible at the present time and within this train of perceptions[81]. This temporal determination was not what reason was inquiring about, however. If, in saying that the subject is culpable because the subject did not in this temporal determination produce the reasonably necessitated action, reason is hindered not indeed because of the necessity or impossibility just noted, but rather precisely because the grounds of this actuality that determined the action are included in a continuous train,

---

81. **Wahrnehmungen.**

of which a part arises from distinct, already actualized determinations of the subject: if, I say, reason is hindered in the latter way, then here again no connection is to be seen. Nothing is in fact present that could annul our warrant for accountability. Rather, people have come to be deceived by confused relations between the ideas of reason and the conditions to which reason's manifestation are subjected in particular perceptions. In the end, such always proves to be the reef that causes every wreck we see drifting about in the ocean of philosophy.

Application of the Doctrine of Necessity
To the Concept of Moral Accountability

Yet some charge that determinism treats practical concepts very cunningly, taking great pains to prove that the name and perhaps also the possibility of the matter remain, but that [254] in the laboratory of necessity a person's power goes up in smoke, and so fundamentally we must remain content with a bloodless *caput mortuum*. Is this perhaps to be the case with accountability as well? Are we to have shifted in double measure the difficulties from which we seem to have freed the concept's permissibility over to the concept's application? We shall see!

Personal Worth and Moral Capacity Are Revealed in Actions
By Necessity Grounded in the Soul

What benefits us first of all in judging the accountability of unfamiliar actions is this: that in unfamiliar actions it is much easier to become acquainted with the manifold collisions that can be avoided in particular cases that always occur in conjunction. From this advantage there arises a capacity to discover various moral laws to which the action refers through its various relations. That is, while in our own actions it is usually difficult entirely to escape from our viewpoint concerning them at the moment of the act and its preceding deliberations, in unfamiliar actions it is easy for us to play the role of the impartial observer, passing our eye over all sorts of matters in turn, so as to note even the smallest faults and omissions. Still, this immediate advantage, unquestionably of great importance, arises not so much from the most commonly argued aspect of accountability as from the repetition of the prerequisite determination of an action's ethical nature that belongs to accountability. Moreover, we cannot imagine how we could be hindered in this by the doctrine of the necessity of actions. If, after the ethical nature of the action is determined, we now assign it to the agent's faculty of desire, in doing so we make the following application of this second aspect of accountability: that by taking many such judgments together and comparing them with respect to the subjects who have made them, we seek to ascertain what kinds of moral capacities and weaknesses, or what degrees of these, can be thought of as existing together in the same faculty of desire, either within a unity of character and sensibility[82] or in some conflict among them.

Already this approach appears to bear a closer relation to our doctrine, and far from contradicting it, it rather presupposes it. The reason is that from the way an action is composed of certain constituents we cannot conclude anything concerning certain characteristics of the soul – that is, concerning certain relations between impulses and the efficacy of representations, relations that are apparent in all similar cases – unless actions are [255] regarded as consequences of certain grounds in the soul, which, so long as they are present, must bring forth the same effects. Just as little can characteristics of the faculty of desire be thought of as harmonious or contradictory if we do not regard them as consequences of such grounds or as a conjunction of constituents that either further and undergird or cancel each other in their effectiveness (apart from which nothing can be represented of them). For this result, this effectiveness must be under certain laws in which all its expressions are grounded and similarly regulated. In short, all these applications of the concept of accountability, in which judgments and conclusions are precipitated and interconnected, rest naturally on the axiom upon which all the procedures of theoretical reason depend.

The precise connection between the doctrine of necessity and the practice of accountability will be still more apparent if we consider accountability's final aspect, the aspect most often put forward. That is, if from many judgments of accountability we must render a summary judgment of a person's worth and of the degree to which a person has capacity for ethical subordination[83], if we must thereby estimate the moral difficulties a person might be able to overcome and the degree of sensible power to which a person's ethical power can offer sufficient resistance, then in all of this the idea of necessity is so thoroughly intertwined that separating it from the idea of accountability is unthinkable. Hence we consider all impulses as powers which limit one another in their effects as if by mechanical laws. We consider all actions as one indissolubly coinhering whole, of which we may

---

82. **In einer Einheit des Charakters und der Sinnesart.**

83. **Subordination.** Ed. note: The term refers to our capacity for being governed by moral law.

estimate the aspects not yet known to us from the law of the aspects we already know. Everywhere throughout this sphere, therefore, we are, as it were, pursued by fond necessity. Everywhere, against our will, we recognize the signs of necessity. In the end we are compelled to acknowledge that the very first requirements of moral life, which we have honestly believed ourselves to enjoy in spite of necessity, are blessings secretly bestowed by necessity's hand.

Does the Doctrine of Necessity Undermine Sentiments Concerning The Accountability of Others?

To this point we have restricted ourselves to applications of accountability in which we did not go beyond the concept of accountability itself but merely aimed at considering the train of judgments that accountability places at our disposal, though by analogy viewing it as a given whole, and at making use of that. Now the time has come for us to consider the way judgments of accountability determine our sentiments and our conduct toward others, [256] in order to see whether the warrant of accountability through the necessity of actions is perhaps annulled by anything here. That is, now that we have sufficiently defined the concept of accountability, perhaps we can manage to discuss the sentiments that relate to this concept, comparing them with sentiments that arise from the concept of the necessity of actions. We shall thus be able to see whether the alleged contradiction between the two is actual (or rather, the contradiction between the latter sentiments and the feeling that is general and natural, for it is entirely proper to denote the former sentiments in this way).

Before commencing this investigation, however, we first want to see whether it can have any kind of significance for us. In the course of having established the doctrine of the necessary interconnection of our actions we cast our eye on a concept that is given quite independently of this doctrine and acknowledged to be practical, that is, a concept connected with the first ideas of morality, namely the concept of accountability. It was then incumbent upon us, if we wanted to justify our doctrine, to show that this concept, exactly as given to us, was consonant with our doctrine.

Now we see that this concept, which already involves a process, albeit one of inward action only, is joined with various processes of the person's outward actions by means of certain sentiments arising from the concept itself. Here we do not have an absolute obligation to show that this concept must also be consonant with what our affirmed doctrine claims. Rather, we can first investigate whether any error has crept into these applications from either side and whether these sentiments and ways of proceeding derive purely and without adulteration from the concepts from which they are constructed.

Indeed, even if after all our explanations these applications should still disagree, nothing would be lost for our main point, since these sentiments and procedures are not commanded of us a *priori* and immediately. Rather, it would be incumbent upon us only to offer our good advice toward achieving some tolerable compromise. Still, I think it will not come to this. It is difficult to imagine a truly irresolvable contradiction between sentiments stemming from noncontradictory concepts. It is very easy to believe, however, that an error has been made in the analysis of the sentiments, since, as we have seen, the fundamental concepts are contested and difficult, and this error we want to try to discover.

The issue is as follows: "If," so say the opponents of necessity, "the sentiment that follows upon a judgment of accountability is supposed to apply not only to the act but also to the agent, this can happen only if we [257] think of everything belonging to the action as united in the agent and we thus consider the agent as the power whose effect the action is – as the firm cause of the action. Our language has no words exclusively reserved for these sentiments (for 'praise' and 'blame' apply as often merely to the action as to the action's originator), but everyone is nonetheless in agreement about what they consist in. We gaze with wonder at the magnitude of power required for an action, or with a feeling of tranquility we approve of its harmonious ordering. We despise the weakness of moral impulse revealed by an action, or we abhor the unseemly ordering of the soul's powers that we recognize in it. Thus agents stand before us wishing to be judged and considered only for themselves, clothed in the whole worth of their actions or covered with their entire disgrace.

"Yet, how can we find any room for these sentiments in the conviction of the necessity of actions, a conviction that requires us to feel only the opposite of all this? This conviction indicates to us that the actions cannot be otherwise, since such and such external impressions have struck such and such a resonance[84] in the soul. This resonance of the soul is in turn a product of preceding and occasioning impressions, and so, resist as we may, all is at last dissolved in external impressions. So, of all that belongs to the action, what can we then assign to the agent? Do we see the agent act in some way? We can think of the agent only as suffering[85]! Or where is the power that is

---

84. **Stimmung.**
85. **Leidend.** Ed. note: The term means being passive as opposed to active.

active? It dissolves into infinitely many infinitesimally small external forces that leave us with nothing to think of as firmly active in the subject. True, the action remains lofty, noble, beautiful, small or abhorrent, but to whom do we ascribe this?

"The person stands motionless, as it were. The person changes moral situations like garments, clothed by external powers, now with the purple robe of virtue, now with the rags of vice. The purple is ever lustrous, but do you marvel at the one who wears it? You praise the person as lucky. You envy the person, as is our tendency with respect to everything a person receives from merely external forces. The rags disgust you, but is your passion kindled toward the one dressed in them? You pity the person. You feel sorry for the person, as you do with all external accidents. Thus you see all mortals as transparent as water their whole life through. They flash all the colors, but merely according to the laws of refraction. Of all that you see in the person's actions, nothing belongs to the person.

"Not only does this situation present the ultimate contradiction; it also stultifies from the outset all hope of an amicable outcome. [258] This is true because necessity will hear of no dividing, and if we were to give it even the least bit of room, it would know how to expropriate the rest.

"The sentiments stemming from accountability are apparently the sentiments that arise most readily in all people. In contrast, the sentiments necessity occasions seem to us inwardly contradictory, and all will admit that we can entertain the thought of necessity only with the greatest effort. What can we think, therefore, of an opinion that gives rise to something so utterly contradictory to natural feeling?"

We easily see from the entire construction of this supposed contradiction that it rests upon the reintroduction into the sentiment adhering to accountability the concept of cause and power that does not at all belong in accountability itself, and that the sentiment's derivation is not pure and unadulterated. This adulteration is not at all necessary, however, since these sentiments too can subsist without relating in the least to this opposing opinion concerning the origination of actions.

Clarification of Our Sentiments Concerning Accountability by Means of an Analogy from Art

Allow me to show this by means of an example. Our way of forming judgments and experiencing sentiments in the aesthetic realm has so much similarity to our mode of dealing with the moral realm that I believe I am entirely justified in taking recourse there – not to prove something about the moral realm but rather to present a possibility. Moreover, it seems to me that we handle our sentiments concerning the accountability of artists for their work in a way that would be requisite here.

Once we have determined the artistic worth of a piece of work, we are quick to assign the result of our judgment to the artist. Boldness of composition, strength of execution, refinement of feeling, precise observance of relationships in harmony, chiaroscuro, and perspective: all this we ascribe to the artist. The entire character of the artist is thus presented, enticing us to wonder. However, are we on this account any less convinced that it could not have been any other way, given the situation and capabilities of the artist? In fact we do accept this consideration. We assess the operation of inspiration's moment, when none but grand ideas arise in the soul; we consider how vitally artistic laws and the artist's high ideal play before the eyes of the virtuoso at work, how adept and responsive the artist's tools are to fulfill the commands of genius, so that in fact only exceptional works can result from the artist's hands. We even search the entire range [259] of the artist's talent and education for the grounds underlying distinctive features of the artist's character.

Does all this diminish the strength of our previous sentiments? Not in the least, surely. This is the clearest proof that our sentiments did not at all rest upon our discovering the complete, independent train of conditions associated with the work and that investigating the kind of circumstances that had to come together in order to give rise to such a work has nothing whatsoever to do with our sentiments. We have simply compared the known characteristics of the artist's capacities with the laws and aims of art and have been affected by their suitability.[86] The sentiments of accountability, having

---

86. Schleiermacher's note: "Indeed it seems as if this comparison might appear to favor our opponents' side, since it offers examples in which our opinion concerning a work's origination alters our sentiments of accountability from what would otherwise have been the case. For example, when we praise beginners in art for their work, often this praise would not be deserved at all if we judged strictly according to artistic rules. Is this not because we recognize that given the artist's circumstances the work could not have been better? Here, then, the idea of the originating grounds of an action would appear to mix with sentiments of accountability and alter their color. If this idea were to have such an effect, it would not have to be applied so one-sidedly and falsely. It would have to restrain not only our blame, since the action could not be better, but also our praise, since likewise the action could not be worse, and no sentiment relating to the agent would remain at all. Thus this limitation upon our sentiments of accountability in the aesthetic realm does not proceed from the idea of necessity. Rather it is grounded in a condition in which the aesthetic realm is not similar to the moral sphere but rather quite distinct from it. Specifically, the beginner learns the rules of art little by little and how to utilize them, and because of this learning, not with respect to necessity, we judge the beginner's work not according to the complete content of these rules but only according to the basic principles we may suppose the beginner has already come to know. This condition, how-

so many similarities with aesthetic sentiments, could indeed also exist in this fashion, therefore, without being intertwined with the idea of thoroughgoing causality. Moreover, this must in fact be the case if [260] those sentiments wish to lay claim to the name of a natural feeling that stems entirely from the concept of accountability.

By this we do not mean to have said that all of those whom we have rhetorically introduced experience sentiment falsely. It is simply that they perhaps have analyzed their sentiments falsely and have thereby come to incorrect associations that confuse this apparent contradiction with other sentiments that are quite natural and right. They might therefore allow us to undertake a different analysis, from which in the end they will perhaps not be able to withhold their approval.

Judgment of Personal Worth by Comparison Of the Soul's State to Its Ideal

Accountability immediately presupposes nothing concerning the concept of cause except that an action is really something that has precedence in the soul – something that is, therefore, an effect of the soul, itself regarded as a force or a composite of forces. However, accountability does not at all entail asking how this force came to be active. The action is simply taken to be an expression of the soul, from which the soul is able to disclose its state, and this state is what accountability is intended to explore.

In order simply to evaluate the ethical nature of an action we compare it with the law. That is a quite simple operation, requiring nothing but judgments for which the data are given sensibly. When we translate this action to the person, however, in order to recognize at least one facet of the person's morality, much more is involved. We want to know the actual relations among those representations that have had to arise as motivating grounds within the faculty of desire that has acted in such and such a way. At first we can say only this much with certainty: all of these sensible desires and aversions taken together have been more effective or less effective than the desires and aversions of the moral impulse. But that is not enough for us. We want to know what this faculty of desire will do in other, similar cases, in order to render our judgment that much more secure. So we analyze this situation further. We compose a living image of this soul. Therein we see

---

ever, admits of no application in the moral realm, since we are fully entitled to presuppose in everyone complete knowledge of a right and exact feeling for the moral law, which resides in the soul itself."

contending among themselves the various forces and inclinations[87] that have been vitalized in the action; we see how some become increasingly taut and gain the upper hand, while others grow slack and withdraw from the contest. Thus do we attain knowledge of relationships within this soul. We now know that these are the various expressions of the relationships that have in the end united in this result, and that in similar cases these are the expressions that may be thought of as being harmonious with them.

Now in order to determine worth for the state of soul that contains these expressions, the moral law alone, in its simple form, [261] is not sufficient. With each image we need an equally vital counterimage for comparison. We must know exactly how each of these expressions relates to what a sufficiently strong moral impulse would have produced. Thus we think of an ideal faculty of desire – not, however, a faculty of desire which, like that of the Stoic philosopher, includes nothing except an ethical impulse, but rather one in which the same sensible inclinations arise as in the subject who is to be judged but in which the impulse representing practical reason struggles against them with greater power and better resources. Then step by step we compare the subject's every expression, in the given case and in others that are analogous, with actions that belong to the ideal. This in turn gives us the clearest insight as to which portion of the moral power is too slight and which sensible inclination is too great, so that by this means we can determine the moral worth of the subject in relation to this action.

This continual comparison of the subject with the ideal, which we regard as the subject's natural rule, imparts to our sentiments arising from this accountability that preeminent strength and vitality suitable to all sentiments in which an ideal plays a role. We look upon the person before us as the image of this ideal, and are we not to be preeminently affected by the diversity of actions that we note in comparing the two? Are not all appearances of these sentiments to be susceptive to clarification?

Merely judging the ethical nature of an *action* gives us a very precisely denoted, very prompt feeling, it is true, and yet not a very strong or vital one. It is a momentary product of practical judgment, arising of itself, without preparation and without any exertion on the part of the soul. In contrast, judgment of the *person*, which requires close observation of all that a given action presupposes in the soul, must impart a high degree of vitality to the sentiment it engenders toward the person. This is true in that this sentiment stands in direct proportion to the ease with which we could personify that portion of the moral law at issue and to the ease with which we could represent the self's inner flow. The more difficult it has become for us to think of

---

87. **Neigungen.**

this law as active, the more power we have had to give to the moral impulse of our ideal in order to master all existing difficulties, and the more expenditure of our soul's power of representation it has cost us to produce this faculty of desire, the more worth this ideal has in our eyes and the more we wonder at the person who [262] in this state of soul has acted in accordance with such a law and whom we may therefore regard as this ideal itself. The worth of the ideal itself rests upon this person, and we look up to such a person with reverence. The more lightly we are able to think of the law, the less moral fortitude is required to render it active, and the more difficulty we have recalling the weakness or disproportion that must presuppose in order nevertheless to contravene it, the more resentment we will feel toward the person who does not approximate even these minimal basic characteristics, who remains aloof from even these minimal relations. Accordingly, it can even be repugnant for us to regard such a person as a moral being, since at a given moment this observation brings with it all that is unpleasant about a contradiction of sentiment. So it is, therefore, that with our sentiments regarding accountability we actually view persons as bedecked with the entire dignity or disgrace[88] of their actions.[89]

---

88. Würde oder Schmach.

89. Schleiermacher's note: "The difference presented here between sentiments relating to an action and those relating to the agent bear a great similarity to the sentiments arising from contemplation of works of fine art (insofar, that is, as we posit an informed viewer whose feelings are related to judgments). With the initial comparison of the general impression with the basic rules of the art, relating to composition, chiaroscuro, perspective, and the like, the viewer gives little thought to the artist. The viewer's feeling is strongly determined by the degree of good and bad and their mixture, but it is a calm feeling and does not greatly agitate the soul.

"Only when this stage of contemplation is completed does the viewer's renewed inspection turn attention to the artist. The viewer penetrates the spirit of the composition, sees it active in each individual detail, notes the changing conceptions that presaged the final effort, the artist's approach to the work, the general guiding principles: all this passes before the eye. Stirred with a vivacity totally different from that aroused before by the work's correspondence to artistic principles, the viewer now marvels at the creator's artistic spirit, broad and daring vision, discriminating keenness, animated imagination, freedom of feeling. With this difference only: that here we never personify the ideal of an artist, because the best execution of some particular work is not uniquely definitive; rather, many may be judged equally good and yet differ with respect to character and effect.

"Still other similarities and differences between the moral and aesthetic realms could be presented here – an inquiry that would perhaps not be without usefulness but which we shall leave to another, since at this point it would carry us too far afield. [263]

"In the transfer of sentiments of accountability from the judgment of an action to the judgment of the originator, as is commonly stated in the textbooks, there already exist grounds for different modifications of this process in different persons. It is commonly said that the morally good person is never so greatly in awe of the ethically beautiful as others are; that this applies in particular only to the judgment of the *person*, and with respect to a good action, for

The Familiarity in Ordinary Life of This Process of Ethical Judgment

I believe that everyone will have been convinced that we have nicely clarified (by means of the ideas underlying the comparison) not only the content but also (by means of the complex operation and by means of the sort of images that thereby appear to the soul) the vitality of those sentiments relating to a person as the originator of an action. Yet I expect the following protestations: Is this [264] not an entirely chimerical hypothesis? Does this personification usually occur? And does the promptitude of sentiments connected with accountability permit so complex a procedure? In response: If we seldom notice this action in ourselves, this in my opinion is because it is so very familiar to us from our judging of our own actions, past and future. If we wish to view past actions in the correct light, we always represent our faculty of desire with a stronger moral impulse, but otherwise unchanged. Then we envision ourselves acting better than in fact we had. We thereby trace the entire train of ideas that we would have required for this better condition. Indeed, we even grant this alter ego of ours[90] the meager external resources and the very bodily movements that express a firm will or an inner

---

the good person possesses a certain capacity to think of every moral law in action; that the extent of ethical power required for this ideal seldom appears to the good person as extraordinary, since the person often makes so much use of it; that, on the contrary, the good person cannot imagine the state of heart and mind of an immoral person, especially one in straitened circumstances, and thus breaks out in vehement sentiments towards unethical people. These generalizations should not be taken as characterizations, however, because they will often be imitated by persons seeking the appearance of the good.

"These persons also suffer severe limitations, because the ease with which our thinking can penetrate into the faculty of desire of some subject who is to be judged depends not only on our experience of ourselves but to a greater extent upon the observations we have made of others. Thus persons who, without regard to their own morality, have acquired knowledge of human beings and achieved a facility for putting themselves in the situation of others will be the least inclined either to blame or to marvel at someone else. In contrast, even good persons who, apart from their own experience, are novices in matters of the human soul find it difficult to conceive the circumstances involved in doing some good that lies outside their own sphere or perhaps challenges their weak side. We must be very careful, therefore, not to make the requisite subjective exertion the measure of the ethical strength required for an action, and thus the criterion regarding the sentiments of accountability. Otherwise the good person who at the same time knows human nature would always have but little feeling for other good persons, and only the sentiments of a person possessed of just enough moral sense to follow the ideas necessary for the process of accountability would be able to rise to a certain level of intensity."

90. **Dieser unserer zweiten Person.**

struggle in the faculty of desire. In this way we idealize ourselves for comparison with what we actually have been.

We subject ourselves to this same tension in forming firm resolutions for difficult actions that we anticipate: we transpose ourselves into the moment of the act with all our inclinations, but deliberately with greater moral strength than we know we possess, and then we resolve to accomplish what we have thereby discovered. Often we also transfer this norm to others who are our moral heroes, presuming just enough illusion to lend them the state of our own faculty of desire, and then we formulate our own accountability according to what we find that they would have done.[91]

If we admit this deduction of the sentiments of accountability, then it is quite clear that they are related purely to the concept of accountability, unaffected by an inspection of the entire chain of causes, and that they therefore occur only if we consider the agent's ethical state in relation to the requisite subjection of other impulses to the ethical impulses. If we have allowed the ethical impulses free play, then the stronger the impression they have made on us the sooner another question arises, grounded in our natural thirst for clarifying particular appearances. That is, the more striking the moral state that we have discovered, the more we marvel at the sentiment it stirs, and so it happens that we think of the object of this sentiment as a product of nature and we inquire into the conditions from which it has arisen.

The Doctrine of Necessity Resolves The Supposed Contradictions Among Our Moral Sentiments

Now it is here that the doctrine of the necessary interconnection of actions[92] with the universal [265] chain of causes and effects obtrudes upon us, and from this doctrine those sentiments arise that were introduced above[93] as being in direct contradiction to the sentiments of accountability. This contradiction is resolved, however, by the conviction that the sentiments of accountability presuppose that the subject is the independent originating cause of its state. I do not have to depend on the view that the two different sentiments occur at different points of time. Let them intermingle completely and alter so often that they appear to be fully simultaneous. There will be nothing in the two that cannot coexist even in a unity of feeling.

---

91. Schleiermacher's note: "Consider the ascetic uses of this personification."
92. **Die Lehre von dem nothwendigen Zusammenhang der Handlungen.**
93. See p. 29.

Or is it supposed to be contradictory to think of the state as existing in the subject and then to separate the subject from its state? Is it supposed to be contradictory that persons in their various states, through their various relations to the law and the ideal, make various impressions on me, and yet all appear the same to me if I regard them before and after these states? Is it supposed to be contradictory that I attribute to the subject in its state the sentiments its impression has given rise to in my moral sense and also, regarding it in itself before the whole succession of its states, appraise it as fortunate, or lament that from its determination in time and through the entire preceding succession of states it has come to this?

How could any of this be contradictory, since the first element in each instance relates only to the appropriateness of the state to its rule and the second element to the changeability of the state through its connection with the succession of changeable things! Rather, in the natural course of our ideas both sentiments seem to belong so precisely to each other and to be bound together with such purpose that their precise merging deserves for the first time the name of natural feeling.

Apart from the Doctrine of Necessity, Sentiments of Accountability Lead to Human Alienation, Not Solidarity

Sentiments of accountability toward the person, as long as they are maintained in their purity,[94] distance us from those to whom they apply the more the person's state is different from our own. Either the sentiments place the person at a height our eye scarcely reaches, so that we gape with reverence at the person in the light of a heavenly being whose likes we could never encounter in our own realm, and this cannot help but fill our soul with a despondency extremely damaging to ethical progress; or the sentiments put the person far below us, establishing such an unbridgeable gulf [266] between us that we scarcely recognize our common nature. In neither case do we see in the realm of accountability anything at all that would tend to moderate these sentiments or provide us the means to do so. These feelings would therefore pass into our conduct just as they are. They would humble us under the feet of the ethical hero, as it were, and, in light of their relative strength, rob us of a great deal of our self-reliance and self-confidence. They would fill us with a self-satisfied pride over against others whom we viewed as far beneath us. Disrespect, scorn, and chilly severity would mark every

---

94. **In ihrer Reinheit.** Ed. note: Schleiermacher means: as long as sentiments of accountability are maintained in isolation from the mitigating doctrine of necessity.

aspect of our conduct toward those whose appearance has filled our moral eye with nothing but loathing and aversion.

Yet we realize how necessary and right it would be to alter this attunement of the soul[95] in many respects, and this has led those who are unable to resolve the apparent contradiction between accountability and necessity into a number of byways. They may recommend an arbitrary moderation of these sentiments, completely without basis in their concepts. To be sure, this moderation always aims at taking into account the circumstances and thus is based upon necessity. However, precisely because this is true – because the origin is not acknowledged, because these sentiments are not separated from but are taken to be a modification or an aspect of the sentiments of accountability – the whole of accountability is contaminated, all the associated sentiments are rendered unstable in that no hard and fast rule is recognized, and the greatest confusion is introduced especially into doctrines of legality and the determination of punishments, in both the civil realm and the realm of conscience.

If those of whom we are speaking do not take this way out, they demand a complete separation of our sentiments with respect to the act from those with respect to the agent: only toward the former should we direct the severity and zeal of our moral feeling, while the latter we should regard with eyes of love and forbearance, I know not how. This advice shares a fault with all such well-intended means of covering up the weakness of a defective theory and impeding its practical harm, namely that its hidden harm, both to practice and to theory itself, is greater than the usefulness that can flow from it. This procedure annuls the received doctrine of accountability entirely and cannot be admitted except together with its basis – namely, the truth that the moral law as a rule for human beings must be weakened in our consciousness and [267] eventually must be totally destroyed.

The inadequacy of both these means reveals itself even more clearly in their conspicuous but rarely faulted inconsistency, since they make a great distinction between approaches to the morally better and to the morally worse. They would hold it to be a lax morality, even if they weakened their sentiments against the morally worse or wanted to separate these sentiments from those relating to action. If an observation has the effect of moderating my feeling against an evil that has occurred, why should I not employ the same observation to diminish my feeling for some good, since this follows so naturally from the same basic principles? If I am supposed to set limits to my scorn for a scoundrel, why should I not with just as much justification do the same for my eager reverence for the moral hero? Or is the good so lacking

---

95. **Stimmung der Seele.**

in attraction that we should not dare to cast aside an apparently ascetic means of help, even if this should offend the theoretical system?

In fact, there is no clearer proof that in this viewpoint the system of sentiment does not flow unalloyed from the system of concepts and does not strongly adhere to it. We spare ourselves all of these reproofs, we avoid all of these discomforts and contradictions, by joining accountability and necessity, as accords with the nature of the case. Through this conjunction alone does our feeling attain the attunement required not only by the voice of our heart but also by the solidarity of human society, an attunement not attainable without inconsequence by any other association of ideas. The perceived worth of a morally great person, a model for a moral faculty of desire, has filled me with reverence: should I shake off some of this sentiment? On the contrary, the sentiment is holy to me as an emblem of the knowledge of my vocation and of the proper image of the goal toward which I strive. I wish to make this sentiment as vital in my soul as possible! Will it humble me? Will it rob me of self-consciousness and self-confidence? Will it give rise to small-minded hesitations in my soul? By no means! What I wonder at is the state of a being just like me, a state brought forth by many relations and circumstances and resting upon a gradual consequent strengthening of the ethical impulse. Other relations, other circumstances would not have granted this degree of strength. Happy the person who has been so led. Yet every better circumstance in a given moment would also have allowed a better utilizing of the relations present in the next.

On the Possibility and the Duty of Moral Improvement

Still, a span of time lies before me also, and [268] within it undoubtedly lie the opportunities that so frequently bud forth in human life for strengthening the impulse that speaks for reason. In this way I shall draw near to the morally great person. Undoubtedly I shall use every such opportunity better, the more attachment to and feeling for morality and the more respect for the law I bring with me from my earlier – and thus, conversely, from my present – condition. Thus the consolation of necessity again brings me closer to persons from whom my disheartening sentiments of accountability had often distanced me, yet without robbing me of any of my respect for them. I attach myself to them in the measure that I feel myself striving to be like them.

I feel an aversion to those who live wholly under the power of sensibility[96], who either do not feel or despite their feeling do not avoid sensibility's

---

96. Sinnlichkeit.

most apparent contradictions with the moral law and have dismissed all striving for morality. Should I suppress this sentiment? The intensity with which the ethical contradictions have affected me has the same source as my feeling for the ethical itself and is directly joined with it. At the same time, will I on this account elevate myself above them with self-satisfied pride, feel nothing toward them but scorn, and act toward them only as my moral aversion might have prompted? Another sentiment infuses me with concern and sympathy. This state, which I do not cease to abhor, is also the consequence of a succession of preceding states and of the total interconnection in which they lived. It is the state of beings like me in nature.

Or have they ceased to be like me? Is it altogether impossible that we might draw nearer each other, in that they progress while I regress? The time stretching before them can offer them many occasions for improvement. In time their state can thereby be altered. As for the time stretching before me: will it not include many temptations that could lead me astray from the good, and will I not more likely succumb to them the more proudly I strut around without attention to myself? I am not so greatly elevated above them that circumstances might not produce consequences just as sad for me as theirs have been for them. Far removed from all punitive and damning neglect, therefore, this feeling motivates me to act not simply according to my sentiment regarding their state but much more according to my persuasion of their perfectibility[97] in the future – that is, to regard it as my bounden duty to improve their circumstances so far as I am able, to work through my relationships with them for the restoration of their morality, or at least not to doubt that possibility.

Thus this [269] doctrine, so greatly decried, accords with all our duties. The sentiments resting upon it, which at first glance appear to contradict natural feeling, upon closer observation reveal themselves to be an essential part of such feeling, through which alone our soul is brought into harmony with itself – reveal themselves, in short, as the true ground for the wisdom and practicability of this feeling.

Salutary Effects of the Doctrine of Necessity on Theories of Punishment

I said above[98] that the defective substitutes people often put in the place of the feelings arising from a conviction of necessity in order to imitate some

---

97. **Perfektibilität.**
98. See p. 51.

of its effects would introduce great confusion into the doctrine of punishments – but I should have added, if punishment could be thought of as justified at all without the concept of necessity. I believe I can easily show that
this is not the case, however. Punishment is undoubtedly an evil related to
the senses[99], a chosen action following upon a preceding moral evil. What,
however, is the purpose of this sensible evil? The person punished is
regarded as one in whom the moral grounds of motivation have not had
enough force to produce the obligatory action or to prevent the evil action
the person performed. Thus there were unquestionably stronger sensible
motives impelling the person to evil. Because we can do nothing immediately to increase the ethical force, the effort is made through the prospect of
sensible evils that influence the balance of motives at least to deter the person from the evil action, even if we cannot suspend the immoral disposition[100]. Yet, since in this way the sensible desires and aversions are counter-
poised with respect to a certain object, moral deliberation acquires room for
freer play. This latter procedure is particularly the goal of punishments the
individual inflicts in restraining evil persons[101]; the procedure first mentioned is the goal of punishments sanctioned by society, which always has as
its aim preventing actions contrary to law.

Now how can this entire process occur without a presupposition of
necessity? If an unknown something is the independent ground of actions,
then we do not have the least reason to believe, with even the lowest degree
of probability, that the thought of these sensible evils will have any influence
on people. If it were merely a simple action in which avoiding a threatened
unpleasantness would be at issue, then the process would rest upon the [270]
general experience that people avoid pain and the deprivation of pleasure.
Instead, the action is actually an interconnected action, dependent upon the
influence of sensible abhorrence after the attraction of pleasure in the evil
action has already produced a powerful desire. This being the case, the
influence of this one additional circumstance is unthinkable without the doctrine of necessity, as I believe I have sufficiently shown in the reflections of
Part I. Civil punishments, where the evil is different from mere withdrawal
of good will, involve the presupposed consent of all who make up society, if
such punishments are to have a justifiable basis. How is this consent about

---

99. **Ein sinnliches Übel.**
100. **Die unsittliche Gesinnung.**
101. **Böse Menschen.**

inflicting a positive evil[102] to be presupposed if it is not thought of as a means to the intended end (albeit a means whose degree of effectiveness relative to the opposing attractions is not determined in advance or always the same, but whose influence is generally certain)?

As clear as all this is, some have turned this entire theme of the inadmissibility of punishments back on necessity itself, saying that if from the opposing viewpoint it appears logically impossible to calculate the effectiveness of punishments, from the viewpoint of necessity it is morally much more emphatically impossible to inflict punishments in general. This is said to be the case because since the ethically bad situation is to be viewed as an evil arising from external causes, thus as a misfortune, it is simply irresponsible cruelty to heap misfortune upon misfortune – precisely for the reason that someone has suffered a misfortune to add yet another. Indeed, the evil we do to the evildoer out of our moral disapproval can no longer be justified, for even if necessity does not prohibit our sentiments against the evildoer, yet it must forbid the expression of our sentiments against the unfortunate person. Necessity cannot grant that we should allow persons impoverished by circumstances to feel the consequences of their situation twice over, and weigh them down by unconcealed scorn for their situation.

Nothing is more easily refuted than this whole line of reasoning, however. Why should it not be established by general agreement, which is necessary in any case, to inflict a smaller evil in accordance with specified rules in order to diminish a larger evil – indeed, frequently to prevent it? For everyone who understands the principles of social life, is not an unlawful action a greater evil than the particular sensible evil that [271] ought to be exacted for it? As for punishments within the power of each of us through the expressing of our sentiment and the withholding of part of our good will, these too can certainly be justified if they include only actions sanctioned by our rights and duties toward humankind. Why should I not let the unfortunate feel the disadvantage of their situation if that can become a motivation for their working to better it? Why should I not let wrongdoers know my aversion to their immorality if I thereby reawaken their reflection and ethical feeling?

It is well then for those who punish to be as greatly inspired by the mild feeling imparted by necessity as by accountability's severity. If only punitive laws might be written by lawmakers inspired in this way! Without warping and weakening the state's punitive laws by any false sympathy that would regulate the process other than according to the act's true offensiveness,

---

102. **Die Erleidung eines positiven Uebels.** Ed. note: "Positive" here means the result of willful action.

lawmakers will always be concerned that punishment be as useful as possible. Moreover, without compromising their ethical sentiments, even in the midst of their aversion to the wrongdoer they will be warmed by the feeling of general love and equality, and, so far as possible, every expression of their aversion will benefit those affected.

Interlude: A Dialogue On the Question of God's Justice

Here various incidents caused a lengthy interruption in my sketching of ideas on this subject. I had intended to devote myself to carrying them forward. I wanted to explore how it came to be that we separated the idea of accountability, or rather of morality in general, and the idea of necessity, and how we came to view these ideas, so intimately correlated, as contradictory, when this separation began, and how the many errors in this doctrine arose from this separation. Just then, however, my friend Kleon came in and caused me new disturbance. I had sent him these pages, and he seemed so greatly fired up over their contents, especially over the last portion, that he must have read them through just recently in haste. He could scarcely get through the initial friendly questions of a visit before fervently challenging me to discuss my latest ideas.

Kleon's Initial Questions Concerning God's Allotment of Human Virtue

"You have been very careful," he said, "to harmonize necessity with the arrangement of civil society, the behavior of each person toward others, and the punishments the whole inflicts upon the individual, but have you also considered the existence of a still larger society, namely, the [272] reasonable spiritual realm as a whole? How would I have to conduct myself toward others if in this respect I view them according to your system, and what will you do with the punishments God has inflicted upon members of this society — and also, so that you will not accuse me of an inconsistency, with the rewards? Oh! If I believe you, I shall have a hard time juxtaposing my admiration for an ethically great person with the heterogenous feeling that I count the person lucky. I shall not be able to avoid envying the person, with a sigh and a justified murmur against the governance of the world! Moreover, as regards evildoers, I will pity them — yes indeed, but with a secret gloating. Why secret? To you I can of course admit it. You are its originator and will undoubtedly find its causes very convincing!

"Until now, we still had in virtue[103] one good that we could enjoy without diminishing some other good to the same degree, but you have taken this advantage away from virtue as well. In addition, what kind of moral kingdom of God do you give us instead? As the entire content of the course of time was predetermined in the understanding and will of God, so also the earthly course of each person, down to its smallest details, and thus the person's entire ethical career: all its good and bad actions, all its progress and its backsliding. On the chart of the world let us assign a number to the position of every human soul – or of every reasoning spirit, if all are subject to this law. Then let a blind youth draw the unmarked slips, which so suitably represent human souls prior to all circumstances, and there you have the way the supreme Wisdom deals with its reasonable creatures. All now take their own numbers, and, at the moment they enter into possession through birth, they pledge not to overstep the prescribed bounds of ethical perfection assigned to each, and also not to fall short of them in this world. Indeed, so they must! All the places must be filled. By whom matters not to the Creator, but does it not matter to me?

"In the greater perfection of one person lies the cause of my imperfection, and the greater imperfection of another determines the degree of my perfection. Since all the better people occupy a better place, I must [273] make do with my worse. Since others are there to fill the still worse places, I am exempt from that sad fate. And I am not supposed to envy the former and be glad for the bad luck of the latter? How am I to understand the relation between God and me? Is God the truest originator of my progress in virtue as well as of my falling behind?"

"Now, dear Kleon," I said with a smile, "calm down! You see, you go little enough astray in all of this, and you can make a lot of this delight you speak of if you find it a pleasant sentiment. I heartily wish you luck with the good portion you have drawn in this general lottery. Indeed, to feel this envy is better than to take pity, and you would certainly not want to allow any pity here." Then noticing his incipient annoyance at my joking, I continued: "Still, one thing you seem not to have considered aright. If souls are not supposed to be as much alike as your slips of paper, who then tells you that a blind youth draws the lots, rather than that Wisdom itself gives each soul the place best suited to its particular characteristics? If souls are originally all the same, like your unmarked slips of paper, then is personhood[104] supposed

---

103. **Tugend.**
104. **Die Persönlichkeit.**

to relate to the unmarked soul apart from context or to the soul in context? If the latter, then your personhood depends not upon the individuality of your substance[105] but upon your place in the world. In another allotment of this personhood you now have – and this constitutes your ego[106] – you would have obtained not another place but only another substance, and this I should think would be for you the most indifferent matter in the world. I see that you favor this second case, since indeed original equality must always be the final measure of the justice of whatever happens to human beings.

"But let us abandon this entire petty investigation of personhood; it is not necessary for my peace of mind. Let our moral characteristics always depend upon our place in the world and let God thus be their originator; then certain limits are given beyond which none of us can pass in this life. This thought should be more new and unaccustomed for you than it is incorrect or evil in its consequences. It will little concern the wicked and frivolous that God does not allow them to become better, and all true friends of virtue can find much comfort in these ideas, I think, if they ponder all their implications and [274] look hopefully to the future. I, at least, can view all of these things that you find so terrible with the greatest tranquility."

The Question of Eternal Reward For Virtue As Unanswerable

"Tranquility?" Kleon inquired with astonishment, "and that with thoughts of the future? For me the future grows ever darker with these thoughts, as I told you at the beginning. Its former gleam disappears, and I see before me nothing but black shadows, darkening the present as well. Formerly it gave me the securest comfort to think that true good fortune and true enjoyment[107] in this age and the next were associated solely and essentially with virtue. This solved all the world's riddles for me, leaving no injustice in the world order. What is given and taken by accident[108], as we call it, was only external, changeable appearance, lending now this spot, now another, a false and deceptive gleam. Of their true good fortune and misfortune people were lord and master. Now this connection between virtue and

---

105. **Von dem Individuum Ihrer Substanz.**
106. **Ich.** Ed. note: Schleiermacher's word is simply "I."
107. **Wahres Glük und wahres Vergnügen.**
108. **Zufall.**

good fortune is precisely what troubles me most. If our virtue depends upon our situation, if the virtuous person is therefore to be viewed only as a favorite of heavenly Fortune[109], how unjust, I have to think, that Fortune eternally benefits those on whom it has smiled from the beginning, that Fortune forever separates from itself those whom it has once repulsed, that this whimsical preference explains why some enjoy a true and constant good fortune that resides self-sufficiently within them for a millennium while the vain enjoyment of others depends solely upon the whim of accident."

I must admit that I was a bit concerned about the turn our conversation was now bound to take. It is remarkable and yet quite undeniable that we can contradict the basic principles of thought and action of most people without losing their good opinion of us, but as soon as we lay hands on certain ideas and images they have of eternity and its connection with this world's order, they see us in a very dim light. I did not know this weakness in my friend, but the zeal with which he took up such a matter at this moment augured no good for me. I knew, however, that the expedient of giving the conversation another direction would profit me nothing with him, for I might have tossed out a dozen of the most interesting paradoxes at this point without moving him from his spot. So, in a tone clearly revealing my wish to pass over this investigation, I told him that I would be able to offer him no satisfactory elucidation of this issue. "The future," I then added in such a way as to moderate this tone a little, "is so completely closed to us that we apply all our instruments in vain to force open its lock. We [275] cannot grasp it because we do not survey the whole, and we torment ourselves wantonly when we endeavor to look into it through any kind of imagined chink. We shall see nothing except images forged by our fantasy, and even if we could actually see something of the future, we would not be in a position to distinguish between these two. Be consoled: you find the same difficulties in all systems."

"The same?" he quickly interrupted me. "Exactly the opposite. If others want to know why God does not reward virtue here and now, why the virtuous do not enjoy accidental enjoyments in this life to a greater extent, it must matter to you, on the contrary, to justify providence in such a way that virtue will always be rewarded and that a higher degree of happiness is essentially joined with virtue."

---

109. **Fortuna.**

Theodicy to Focus on a Common Goal Grounded in
God's Wisdom, Goodness, Omnipotence, and Providence

"As you wish," I answered, still in the same tone. "I am as little concerned to resolve the one question as the other. My theodicy consists in a single syllogism, in which the wisdom and goodness of God furnish the major premise and God's omnipotence and providence furnish the minor premise. I do not see anything inadequate about it and I am content with it."

My friend was not to be scared off, however. He looked at me very intently and said very earnestly: "Who could join you in believing that! Is it not a universal human need to seek a more specific solution to this problem, and to muse or to dream, as our thoughts about the present dictate, about the future that stands before us, from which we expect not only compensation for all the privations we suffer here but also resolution of all the riddles and imponderables?"

"And why may I not be an exception to this general rule?" I asked. "You well know that while I am in the first act of a play I do not like to leaf through the last act to see what has developed." I added, however: "If we who know so precious little about the spiritual world on this earth want despite this to conjecture about spiritual arrangements in another world, you must still grant me that we are not modeling our ethical concepts upon established views of eternity; rather we are having to adjust our views of eternity to these concepts. What are you missing in eternity, then? Do you, upon the basis of some kind of presupposition, perhaps think it becoming that God makes eternally unhappy those who have not given heed to virtue's voice here on earth? Or does it seem to you less shocking to think that [276] those who have been less good and upright here will in eternity also have to lag behind the better in perfection?"

Kleon: "But we have grounded both propositions in philosophical concepts, indeed to a certain extent in the concepts of necessity. We say that everything must eternally have its consequences and that a consequence cannot be either better or worse than its ground. Thus a moral state must eternally bear its consequences, and the consequences of a worse state can never in eternity be as good as those of a better."[110]

---

110. Meckenstock note (KGA): "Cf. Eberhard, for example: 'If eternal hell should be nothing other than this everlasting shame that adheres to us from every sin, no one will be more willing than I am to offer this opinion my hand. For the sake of the matter itself I shall gladly overlook all the misinterpretations to which this expression can be subjected. With all the zeal and all the power of persuasion God has granted me, I shall endeavor to impress upon hearts and minds that every immorality has evil consequences to eternity, that every backward

I: "You cannot be serious, dear Kleon, in burdening me with vain attempts to adapt metaphysics to certain concepts – concepts perhaps falsely assumed to be Christian – as a consequence of necessity, or even in expecting any great refutation from me, for the issue is all too clear. In such a reckoning people have forgotten that neither the future state of our sentiments nor that of our morality is grounded solely and sufficiently in our present moral constitution but rather always in external circumstances as well. If these circumstances are arranged in a predominantly advantageous way, why should it not be possible for persons who are presently wicked, despite imperfections that remain as a result of their present character, someday to catch up with their virtuous fellows? Moreover, if this is possible, why should we deny ourselves the comfort of assuming that it is so – for indeed impossibility alone could prevent us from assuming it to be proper for God. In addition, if I believe this, if I am convinced that in the end we all meet at a common goal, and that we all approach it, though by different ways, even if we appear to deviate from it, then the justice[111] of God is vindicated in my eyes, and I need to know nothing further."

Kleon: "I must confess that I am not so easily satisfied. The evil person may be made perfect, I will grant – as fully perfect as the good person, in fact. However, this can occur only very gradually, [277] and these very different paths on which the two are supposed to travel for so long a time do not cease to disquiet me. The one is more nearly perfect for a longer time and has won for the determination of one's self a certain large portion of existence which the other has lost, and upon the basis of our presupposition that is what I still cannot tolerate."

I: "Listen, dear friend. Your two persons seem to me like your two children when they learned to read. The one learned the letters very easily; the other learned them with difficulty, but thereby quickly grasped their associations, at which the first had needed to work for a very long time. Consider that people have more to do toward their perfection than even the best of them attain in this life. If one person has not come so far, if that person must devote a significant portion of another segment of life to catching up with some other person, perhaps the one will traverse more rapidly some succeeding way which the other is required to travel more slowly. Thus if we proceed to a certain point of time, the two will soon have come equally far."

---

step we make in the path to perfection will remain a deficiency for the entire sum of perfection and for the entire length of the path covered throughout our eternal existence.' (*Neue Apologie des Sokrates*, Vol.1, 3d ed., Berlin/Stettin 1788, 429f)"

111. **Gerechtigkeit.**

Kleon: "This is like all of your analogies. Though we be short of our ethical goal, still we have before us no greater step than that made by good people in this life, namely that they arrive at knowledge of the law and that at least generally their ethical impulse speaks to their actions, even if it does not always go so far as to direct all of them. Further, from that moment onward they must necessarily be happier[112] than others. They journey in truth and in unity with themselves, enjoying indwelling blessedness[113], while others are subjugated to their passions and are a mere play of external accident. Why do they deserve this long and great privilege of happiness[114]?"

Though Consciousness of Virtue Affords A Certain Enjoyment, Virtue Is Not The Natural Measure of Happiness

"Happiness," I replied with laughter: "so this is where all your objections are leading? Do you not know that happiness is banned from philosophy?"

"Oh!" he said. "I do not want to make happiness a principle; I do not want to do anything for its sake. Yet, when it comes to vindicating God's guidance of humankind, it is worth our trouble to ask why a person's better or worse sentiment is so essentially connected with a higher or lower degree of morality, since morality itself is in turn dependent on an arbitrary heavenly apportionment." [278]

I: "What if I completely denied the matter whose foundation you demand of me? What if I say that people are not happier because they are able to be more virtuous and, conversely, that people are not more unhappy because they had to be more wicked?"

Kleon: "What? Shall we break off now? I see that you have no wish to resolve my doubts, since you toss me a paradox in which you cannot be serious."

I: "And why not? My truest and most complete seriousness . . ."

"Wait," he broke in, "you must not have understood me. I well know that in this world the misfortune which tends to arise from the imperfection of our state and from our associations can far exceed the good fortune arising from virtue alone. Even if experience has shown me no example, I still see this possibility. In the other world, however, we shall no longer have to fear

---

112. Glüklicher.
113. Seligkeit.
114. Glückseligkeit.

such glaring contrasts, and there, I should think, it would be clear that a happiness awaits the virtuous that is appropriate to them, one which the wicked may have no hope at all of reaching."

I: "So your view is this: insofar as there is no accidental good fortune or accidental misfortune in that state, the virtuous must necessarily be more fully blessed, since virtue itself necessarily brings good fortune with it. Let us calculate the total influence of virtue upon our good fortune, however. It is true that mere consciousness of virtue, apart from all effectiveness from without, affords us a happiness that absolutely cannot be attained by any other means. Still, vindicating providence in relation to this contested issue depends not upon the kind of happiness, nor upon its source, but rather upon its degree, for the latter constitutes its magnitude. Does virtue turn the scale here? I scarcely believe so."

We now did some calculating together and found the following. Consciousness of virtue affords enjoyment; but the joy that consciousness of a hedonistic life system that is wicked, egoistical, or without principles creates could be equally as vital for adherents of all these systems. What is more, even with the fortune that appears to spring from virtue alone – or conversely from wickedness alone – its magnitude does not depend upon the degree of virtue – or upon the degree of adherence to some other system – but upon other characteristics of the soul and other circumstances. A cold, morose heart [279] that knows no golden mean between indifference and admiration, for example, will not derive nearly as much enjoyment and self-satisfaction from consciousness of the same virtue as will a person of joyful disposition who is accustomed to wandering in the warming atmosphere of cheerfulness and love. Virtue makes us happy to observe the actions that virtue occasions, yet we all gain enjoyment from actions that accord with our systems and in which we can see our systems reflected, as it were. In both cases, however, the degree of this enjoyment and the frequency of its gratification[115] are determined not by the extent to which we are possessed by our system but rather through circumstances and occasions. As systems, both virtue and vice exclude certain kinds of enjoyments, but both can elevate those enjoyments remaining to them to a certain degree of permanence through gratification regulated by certain considerations, through order and moderation. Even here no marked superiority of virtue over vice could be asserted.

Finally, as for the presupposition that the immoral must eventually become moral, there is still this difference: the virtuous remain constant in

---

115. Genuß.

relation to their striving, but with others a time comes when they must change their principles, their strivings and their mode of sentiment. This does not necessarily mean less happiness, however; in fact, this whole change of mind and all the new viewpoints it offers the soul are a great source of satisfaction[116]. Granted that persons often come to feel remorse during this period, still not only is this a mixed sentiment but the joy over each action carried out according to new principles is also proportionately greater.

"You see," I said to Kleon, who had been forced to grant all of these particular results, though not without resistance, "that the extent of our virtue is not the natural measure of the degree of our happiness. Do you believe that providence will arbitrarily make it so? Even less so! If, as you yourself seem to believe, before we attain our true perfection we are determined to run a far longer moral course than our small steps can complete in this life, then unquestionably we shall often have to encounter the rough, craggy terrain of misfortune. Let us welcome this in that life also; it will always led us to the broadest, most romantic reaches of our horizon. [280] So if your only fear is seeing the virtuous too happy, do not be concerned."

Divine Apportionment of Good Fortune, As of Moral Perfection, Accords with God's Infinite Wisdom and Love

Kleon: "I see that you always know a way out, but what a heaven you have! It looks so much like our mother earth that we might swear it is only earth's reflection – as on Sicilian coasts at the first rays of the rising sun a deceptive image of the region may be seen hovering in heaven's faint clouds. But my dear friend, if we must give up these concepts of a higher happiness that virtue essentially and necessarily brings with it, how are we supposed to arouse virtue in the great mass of humankind still clinging to sensibility?"

"Do not believe," I said, "that these motivations are as effective as people commonly imagine. Yes, this happiness consists in the exercise of virtue. How, therefore, can we do something for the sake of this happiness if we are not already enamored of virtue, which has ever had no other means of recommending itself to us besides its inner beauty? Whoever is capable of experiencing this beauty needs no other enticement. For those who cannot feel it, all else will be in vain; they will remain for yet a while in their own path and chase after another good. For those who have taken even a single step along the path of virtue, however, should a prospect of rewards, of many

---

116. **Annehmlichkeit.**

enjoyments, enable them to persevere? Nothing else matters to them any longer; for them there is no other good fortune and they would not abandon this good fortune even if it should be less than some other. How gladly they tolerate the claim that all other kinds of good fortune please at least as well. Yet, I have already told you that I would not be able to satisfy you. One must be more familiar with this way of thinking in order to develop a taste for its other grounds of reassurance."

Of all that Kleon had been forced to concede, this he most gladly granted. He still wanted to say nothing concerning his own conviction; that, he said, required quieter hours. However, it appeared as if the whole revolution of ideas had left him a bit bewildered. He had something more to say about bias and injustice. He reverted to old objections and still could not rest content with the idea that one person should for so long a time be more nearly perfected than another.

"Dear friend, do finally stop creating imagined, petty objections to a beautiful whole by pitting some one particular part against another. If without including any thought unworthy of divinity you can think of the unequal apportionment of external goods in this world, and even more of the [281] degrees of development, so endlessly varied, to which a person's powers of soul attains or can attain; more yet, if both of these thoughts serve to convince you more and more that not everything can end with this life but that a state of compensation and of communal approach to a communal goal stands before us: why should not the very diversity of moral perfection serve that goal all the more, the more important and characteristic this diversity is for us? If it is true that all of us in this world, whatever our dispositions may be, can, in our own ways and in the particular circumstances we have to traverse, enjoy the same amount of contentment, tranquility, and good fortune as others; if we either do not perceive at all or perceive with equanimity the differences between our state of perfection in this world and that of someone better; if in another life these differences in part will disappear entirely and in part, through a linking of circumstances worthy of divinity, prove to have been salutary and necessary for our betterment and perfecting: what an impression would a whole so formulated not make upon its alert, noble-minded earthly observer! Or would this impression be unpleasant to you alone? Would perception of this whole miss its great aim for you alone? Impossible! This infinite diversity, this multiplicity appearing to be imperfection, when compared with the highest possible universal perfection to which it leads, must fill everyone with all the wonder of which sentiment is capable.

"If God cannot but guide into the way of perfection even those who in this constricted state have had the misfortune of falling under the sway of vice, leading them to one goal along with the rest, why do we wish to imagine obscurities where there are none? Why do we not rather acknowledge, in devotion and most reverent delight, the infinite wisdom and love of that Being who would wish to grant us – and all reasoning members of the divine kingdom who can rise to this view, without real detriment to a single individual – the incalculably great and instructive view of how our nature extends from the bestial coarseness of cannibals who feed on the flesh of their fellows, and from the horrible depravity of the wickedest villain, to the astonishing perfection of the wisest mortals, and even to the godlike virtue of a Christ or a Socrates." [282]

Issues Concerning Our Feeling of Freedom

On the Deceptive Power of Our Feeling of Complete Freedom

It is quite natural that also in this respect this connection[117], so utterly neglected, and indeed not thoroughly developed even by the determinists, should give rise to great alterations in our suppositions and feelings, and no one will be surprised that Kleon should have found separation from his accustomed ideas so difficult. The point on which he alighted, however, is by no means the only one, nor even the first, at which I expected him to demand explanations. Another consideration, at least, seems to lie even closer to us, as it is found within the bounds of this life and relates to the conduct of our own moral life. That is, besides the feelings that arise in us toward others regarding the accountability of ethical actions, there are other, similar sentiments more intrinsic to our own ego, sentiments that manifest an experience belonging necessarily to the completeness of our ethical consciousness. With these sentiments the feeling of freedom[118], so often cited against necessity, makes its appearance much more clearly as an essential and inseparable constituent. This feeling unfailingly awakens in us as often as we become expressly conscious of ourselves as moral beings. Should it be anything other than the result of a strengthened consciousness of that distinctive character of our faculty of desire that makes us capable of morality? If it is this, how can we continue to join necessity with it, since this most lively feeling inwardly releases us from everything that even appears to resemble necessity's

---

117. Ed. note: The reference is to the connection between sentiments of accountability and the doctrine of necessity.
118. Freiheitsgefühl.

yoke? We sense this in a stark, cool examination of ourselves even apart from all external occasion that might lead us to deception. There we must admit that in our desiring we lie outside the sphere of all sensible necessity, that even an infinite mass of motivating grounds can never be thought sufficient to determine our desiring, and that we can withstand those grounds without any ancillary aid apart from the only other ground that can be mentioned, the existence of our power to will[119].

We so delight in this self-feeling[120] that often in such moments we let a myriad instances of our fantasy dazzle us, simply to relish examples of this sentiment that are fabricated and yet are experienced as true with the full vitality of inner assent. Under the most propitious assumptions, and in such a way as not to hinder our other aspirations, we let all the good come forward that most flatters our most cherished inclinations, and we think it possible and as entirely within the order of spiritual [283] things that, without any opposing, repellent grounds, we may neglect this good and not appropriate it, so that if asked, we would be in a position to answer only that we did not will to[121]. If we wish to experience a still higher degree of the delight this consciousness gives us, we direct its energy to virtue itself. We picture an opportunity for the greatest moral actions, under conditions with no sensible counter-attractions, and although we do not approve straightaway, we think it just as possible that even here we could coldly pass the opportunity by. Thus we feel ourselves equally free from, equally unnecessitated by ethical and by sensible goods.

It is not even thinkable, moreover, that this feeling is merely a product of fantasy, which, in moments of dominion, might through its illusions know how to place us in a world other than the world we really inhabit. Rather, without our choosing to invoke this feeling, we discover it in regard to particular times and actions under all kinds of circumstances. It is the only presupposition under which we resolve to act ethically or can at any time think of ourselves as acting ethically.

Indeed, all the feelings that constitute moral consciousness and that always lead us in our actions can relate to this feeling. Whenever we begin to consider an imminent action, this feeling precedes all more refined elucidations: we incontestably feel that we are compelled to none of the action's possible modifications – neither to the first option that occurs to us, nor to

---

119. **Unserer wollenden Kraft.**
120. **Selbstgefühl.** Ed. note: The reference is to the feeling of freedom just mentioned.
121. **Daß wir nicht gewollt haben.**

the most vitally attractive option, nor to the option we regard as clearly the best.

An Extended Presentation of the Mistaken View That Only a Feeling of Complete Freedom Makes Moral Life Possible

We commence our survey with this feeling of complete independence. How, then, we ask, could we resolve ethically to deliberate concerning the action to be done if we had even the slightest idea that we were compelled in advance, either to action in accord with the law or to any other not in such accord?

Only with this feeling, it is said, can we be glad about our previous actions or in some other case look back with pains of regret.[122] We are glad to glimpse the good we have done at various times of our lives only because we feel that we could just as well do evil, and similarly the evil distresses us because we feel that in any of these [284] moments even the highest degree of contrasting good was equally within our power. Thus this sentiment guides us in our moral considerations of the present and the past, and likewise in our outlook for the future as well. Only in the consciousness that we are not controlled by strings but rather that under all circumstances and in every moment of our life it depends upon us alone to be something, and that we must always be what we want to be – only in this feeling, it is held, can we occupy ourselves with moral plans for the future, to propose what we shall become, what we shall accomplish and how. Only so is it possible to preserve the reflection that we can work for our betterment.

When we realize how necessary this present striving for the more distant future of our own morality is, not simply as a matter of fantasy but for showing us the way ahead with steadfast and sufficiently understood resolutions, how necessary these sentiments concerning the past are, so rich in instruction and so motivating; how necessary this unconfined deliberation over what is to be done at the present moment is, itself tied to the great idea of self-sufficiency; and when we realize how indispensably necessary all of this is for maintaining the moral life of every person, and how all of this can occur only if we completely exclude consciousness of necessity from our train of feelings, what are we to think of the ethical practicality of this doctrine of

---

122. Ed. note: With this sentence Schleiermacher begins a presentation in which he entertains his opponents' objections, one so long and detailed that it is easily mistaken for a statement of Schleiermacher's own point of view. This hypothetical presentation continues until the sentence beginning "This is the speech put into necessity's mouth . . ." (p. 70).

necessity? Will the doctrine be in a position at some point to rebuild what it has torn down, even if only to a certain extent? Can it possibly provide us other subjective motivations for ethical conduct?

Nothing could be less true! All the sentiments deriving from this doctrine land us in dull indifference and complete ethical paralysis, as must obtrude upon anyone who regards the doctrine from the point of view in which we have presented the feeling of freedom. At the first thought of a serious deliberation concerning the role I shall take in a coming action, I languish, for this deliberation is an illusion, a mere toying of my soul with itself. What will happen is already weighed out. I am not in a position to alter anything among all the circumstances of my soul by which the impression of objects and the prevailing of one of my inclinations over the others in the moment of action have long been determined. Assuming that I want to think and act consistently with my theory, why should I not entirely give way to this feeling of being completely determined and directed from without, and thus remain unconcerned about my action? Why, on the contrary, should I delude myself with a procedure involving a deceptive sentiment [285] that is utterly opposed to that one and strives only to annihilate it? No, as natural as this striving may have become – to think of myself as free and to act accordingly – I will try to root out this habit reinforced by prejudices. I will not trouble myself concerning my actions; I will do nothing except what in each moment I must necessarily do.

I look back over my actions in the past; I note good and evil. True, I am glad about the former and I grieve over the latter – but how? Only as in relation to all good and evil that I see around me, for what is supposed to move me to greater involvement? I see no basis for surpassing joy over the good I did or for heart-rending, painful regret over the evil I initiated: I could as little have changed them then as I can now prevent either from having happened. I did what I had to do, and because both good and evil actions belong to me in equally small degrees, I can now look back on both with a certain coldness that allows these sentiments little influence. As for the distant future, it can still less occur to me to make plans for it with respect to myself. I would appear quite laughable to myself if I wished to determine my future moral stature. Oh, it will determine itself; or, more precisely, it is already determined by what will occur during the intervening time and by what is already determined. I simply lack the ability to read the book of fate; otherwise I could see my ethical conduct for every moment of my life entered therein as precisely and infallibly as the state of the heavens in the astronomers' tables. If I shall disturb nothing therein, why should I currently trouble myself over this? In due time I shall discover what has been determined for me during this period.

Thus does necessity convince those who, against their own will, as it were, think about fashioning their morality. What sort of conclusions, then, will necessity not draw from those whose actions already follow other goals and who, when they rationalize principles for their behavior, are concerned only with finding excuses for themselves? These people have found in necessity everything they sought. Formerly, at the moment of action they had their determinate series of passions; now that they regard that series as constraint[123], they will be even less tempted to disturb it with reflection. They believe themselves all the more authorized [286] to rest content with the past the more clearly they imagine themselves aware of the thread by which necessity has led them from one place to another, and with similar resignation they view every possible place to which they might still be lead by this most comforting thread.

A Feeling of Being Externally Unconstrained In Choice Does Not Contradict The Doctrine of Necessity

This is the speech put into necessity's mouth, and together with what was said above[124] concerning sentiments of accountability, this twofold presentation includes all that inner feeling usually alleges in its struggle against necessity, so far as I am aware.

Here we must follow the same course we took in our earlier investigation. On the one hand, too much truth is evident in the natural feeling put forward by our opponents for us to fail to acknowledge its source in our concepts and our consciousness of ourselves. On the other hand, we cannot decide to acknowledge as correct a feeling that is supposed to be grounded in some way contradictory to our accepted doctrine of the necessity of our actions. We are therefore bound to investigate what in the various effects and expressions of this feeling such a contradiction really presupposes, and it

---

123. **Nöthigung.** Ed. note: This term will prove to be basic to Schleiermacher's argument. He does not explicitly define Nöthigung. In general, however, the German word may convey a positive sense, as in the English "coercion" and "compulsion," or a negative sense, as in "impediment" and "restraint." The English word "constraint" seems best suited to bear this dipolar implication, being defined by the *Oxford English Dictionary* as "the exercise of force to *determine or confine* action" (emphasis added). See below, p. 118.

124. See pp. 29-56.

would have to be damaging if we did not at the same time discover that this presupposition cannot coexist with others.

I do not doubt that most readers who have attentively followed our preliminary investigation will have discovered a certain mixture of the true and the false in the language of this feeling. To analyze this more clearly we need to review what was said. It was not incorrect to call this feeling the result of our consciousness of our faculty of desire's distinctive character that makes us capable of morality.[125] In this connection, if we go back to what we established at the very beginning concerning the nature of our faculty of desire,[126] we shall recall that this capability relates particularly to our faculty of desire's characteristic of not being absolutely determinable by any one object, and the so-called feeling of freedom appears to relate chiefly to this characteristic. It is the feeling of our exercising choice, and this relation is confirmed by all that feeling's appearances. [287] It awakens with reflections concerning ourselves[127] and what has changed and continues to change in us, even unrelated to any particular practical occasion.

This, moreover, is quite natural, for as persons who in all our actions must be conscious of our choice, we must be even more aware when many possible determinations occur to us that could have influenced our choice. It is natural that we take pleasure in this feeling, because it indicates such an infinite multiplicity within ourselves. This multiplicity explains all the poeticizing that fantasy does in order to heighten the gratification we have in this feeling. We serve up an attractive object of impulse and gradually combine ever more new attractions with it as some of its charms grow stale in our minds. We continue this process until we are conscious of appetite[128] in the highest degree, and then we cast it all away without having initiated any action of real desire.

Indeed, to show that the ethical impulse can just as little determine our whole faculty of desire by means of a single object, we provide ourselves a context by seeking such an object here also. Yet what is it, we may ask, that we set over against all these attractions? According to the doctrine of necessity, must there not inevitably be a counterpoise among the grounds of motivation? The answer is nothing other than that which impelled us to the

---

125. See p. 66.
126. See pp. 7ff.
127. Bei Überlegungen über uns selbst.
128. Des Gelüstens.

entire fiction: our enjoyment in becoming conscious of a preeminent characteristic of our soul. By this we do not wish to feel a release from all necessity, however, since this release cannot be manifested in any example and our fiction would thus be a vain undertaking, but rather a release only from the constraint of objects. This latter can be manifested, in that we determine our faculty of desire by means of a representation relating to pure self-consciousness[129].

Self-Conscious Deliberation Contains A Secret Admission of Necessity

There is no problem with thinking of this self-consciousness as being desired sufficiently to ensure the inadequacy of all other attractions, considered in themselves, to compel us. When we think of what joyful excitement we feel at being freed from a constraint relating merely to our external circumstances, it will not surprise us that our fantasy should so greatly undertake to become aware of being freed in relation to an essential part of our nature. For the most part, indeed, fantasy undertakes such means of rescue for the sake of this self-consciousness. The reason is that if in reality this rescue depends upon giving rise to some object strongly affecting the faculty of desire, then the person would have to be a great psychological oddity [288] who would refuse it merely to prove choice *to oneself* and thus the nullity of this object's constraint, because such a person must certainly feel that this conviction can be attained much more easily.

This origin of the true feeling of freedom is attested by the instances in which it most readily arises in relation to particular actions, namely, those instances where we want to establish something in our faculty of desire by means of our deliberations[130]. In such instances, then, we must naturally be more clearly conscious of its relevant determination than in instances where, from lack of skill in employing the faculty of will, we yield to first impression and follow our desire without any notable intervening alterations. Even here, however, where this feeling joins with real actions, it is not a matter of becoming conscious of complete freedom from the law of necessity. Rather, as we extinguish the first impressions of objects in our soul and proceed with deliberation, we feel that those impressions lose the magnitude of influence that could give them the appearance of constraint, and that the resolution we

---

129. Das bloße Selbstbewustseyn.
130. Überlegungen.

shall reach will depend upon the total connection of this object with all of our inclinations, indeed with the state of our faculty of knowledge also – will depend upon the way we instruct this process and upon the completeness and conscientiousness with which we will compose our acts[131]. This is what we wish of our deliberation; this is what is warranted through the feeling of freedom. All of this, moreover, seems to contain a secret admission of necessity – as we have conceived it – more than an apparent contradiction to it.

A new consciousness reveals itself here, however. We are aware of a variety of examinations to initiate and carry out which are to determine our faculty of desire, all having their advantageous as well as their disadvantageous aspects; but we have not yet discovered the closely bonded and no less delicate and secret sequence of ideas that has led us, or will lead us, to prefer one alternative over the others. This ignorance of what is supposed to take place in us should give us the idea of a sum of causes = X, apparent from its effects, but unknown as to its conditions. In relation to external things we call this chance[132], and it is fundamentally just as inexcusable to ascribe this to a complete lack of causes internally as externally. Within ourselves we are more in the state of feelings than of concepts, and we are conscious of having acted ourselves, or of wishing to act, without feeling the impetus[133] that [289] determines the degree and direction of our power. Because of this, the deceptive feeling easily arises that the degree and direction of our power have been determined without there anywhere being any ground for this determination. On account of its close connection with respect to time and object, this feeling becomes united in consciousness with the feeling of choice and is falsely regarded as one of its components, and thus arises the strange corollary: a sensation of the complete absence of all necessity in the causal connection.

Determinations of Will, Even More Than Determinations of Choice, Arouse Our Feeling of Freedom

Often this feeling may originally relate not to consciousness of choice alone but particularly to consciousness of the will, the second characteristic

---

131. **Akten.** Ed. note: The term, in distinction to the usual **Thäten**, entails deliberation, self-possession.

132. **Zufall.**

133. **Anstoß.**

of our faculty of desire that makes us capable of morality. This second characteristic can give rise to the same appearances as the first, but with this difference: in this fiction the faculty of being determined by our consciousness
of a maxim is opposed not to the impression of individual powerful objects
but to the entire relational result of all impulses and all representations of
the faculty of knowledge. This is done in order to secure victory for the particular impulse "to realize the maxim" over the result that would have been
sufficient to completely determine a choice that would not at the same time
be a volition[134]. Because we are not so continuously conscious of our faculty
of will as of our faculty of choice, however, the desire to make this volitional
characteristic truly vital in our consciousness can have a prior influence upon
real actions. Not infrequently it happens that we hold back from something
pleasant or undertake something unpleasant simply to demonstrate to ourselves the strength of the will's impulse, inasmuch as we are conscious that
our faculty of desire, considered purely as choice, would in this case have
yielded the opposite result. Yet even in that situation it is just as true of the
feeling of will as it is of the feeling of choice that it exists purely and without
the fictional corollary of contradicting necessity, but this strange component
very easily attaches to the feeling of will when it awakens on the occasion of
particular actions.

This attachment especially occurs when, in a moment wherein we are
already firmly determined with respect to the content of an action we are
committed to, we remember a maxim and begin to ask whether the form of
the action does not run counter to this maxim. All that otherwise determines
the faculty of desire (for as we have said, the will's impulse does not come
into play with every action) has completed its operation and produced a
result, yet we are nevertheless thinking of overturning this result. This
thought is striking to us, and stirs up a false feeling of [290] the absence of all
necessity, all the more so since the only cause that is able to produce this
revocation is revealed clearly enough in our concepts, and yet is often hidden
from the eyes of our feeling. Specifically, every maxim joins a desire or an
aversion with certain actions that are thought of as objects of an impulse.
This desire or aversion is the only one affecting feeling immediately, and
since usually it has already been present as a particular representation in the
process of choice, we overlook the great influence it now obtains by being
thought of as a rule. We take our general desire to be only a reiteration of
that individual desire, and thus we cannot recognize the cause that now ele-

---

134. **Ein Wollen.**

vates one single result, to which formerly the desire only contributed or for which, as only a small part of the minority, the desire was in no way a match.

This deception becomes even easier if in such single actions we strive to become conscious not only of the will in general but particularly of the will's characteristic that moral and antimoral maxims are equally possible in it. After we have set aside the decision of choice and all the particular movements of feeling belonging to it, so as to investigate the maxim alone, then we want also to feel that no maxim, either single or in conjunction, is in a position to constrain the will's impulse. Since we have already stationed ourselves so completely outside the state of our faculty of desire, it is all the easier for us to regard it for a moment as if it existed in itself, without respect to our state. We represent to ourselves a maxim totally opposed to the maxim that has been stimulated in relation to the impending action, one that lies outside our system of maxims in general, and we are pleased to think of this maxim as determining our will. Moreover, since we have abstracted from all opposing decisions arising from our state, there results the most deceptive feeling that without any ground we could determine ourselves for the one maxim equally as well as for the other.

Should the decision actually be made, our state returns to effectiveness. That is, the faculty of knowledge decides upon the maxim that relates to the impending action in accordance with the accustomed system. Then the strength of the desire for unity among maxims, or the strength of the inclination to bring the practical faculty into play, delivers the decisive stroke as to whether this or the opposing maxim should be followed. Further, the relation of the will's impulse to the sum of individual impulses belonging to sensible choice determines overall whether the maxims will be followed or the first decision of choice will obtain the upper hand. [291]

Thus We May Separate True and False Understandings of Our Feeling of Freedom

Thus characterized by their origin, the true and false constituents of this inner feeling separate from each other. On the whole faultless at the beginning, this inner feeling gathers impurities only amidst its passage among the great multitude of objects through which it is led. If these impurities are suitably screened, then the end of this feeling is as pure as its beginning. If we are not aware of the impurities, then this feeling is contaminated in its consequences and associations. After our deduction of this feeling, however, it cannot be difficult for us to accomplish a basic analysis of these consequences and associations and to show what rests upon the true and what upon the false portion of feeling.

This much can be determined in advance: it must be possible, everywhere and in all cases, to conceive and sense the sentiments arising from the true portion of this feeling, together with their related states, in a unity of consciousness. It must be possible because these sentiments rest upon nothing except consciousness of those characteristics of our soul in which the possibility of these states is grounded. Furthermore, it must be possible to unite these sentiments with the feeling of necessity and with the sentiments derived from necessity and those corresponding to them, for only the two kinds of sentiment together have the same ground, namely, consciousness of the characteristics of our practical nature.

In contrast, those sentiments resting on the incorrect portion of feeling will indeed contradict necessity, but they can be recognized as false precisely by the fact that they exist only as momentary sentiments and can never occur as feelings of our interconnected existence. This follows quite naturally, because to attain those falsely derived sentiments we will have passed beyond consciousness of the actual state to consciousness of general characteristics, and yet we will have mistaken the one for the other through a deception that must destroy itself if the deception is to endure through many states – which would of course be necessary if feeling is to become feeling of general existence and its nature. So it is true that once we are accustomed to this deception, such erring feelings can arise with all the actions and states of our life, but in each action and state the feeling necessarily seems discrete and disconnected.

Some Ethical Consequences

The Proper Role of Our Feeling of Freedom

With these assertions we can now proceed to investigate the sentiments that were assumed in the presentation above[135] to be subjective ethical motives, resting on the feeling of freedom and [292] contradicting all necessity. If that was as much as to say that the feeling of freedom alone produced these sentiments, but that necessity with its consequences would not be capable of producing them, then we can gladly grant the second point but must entirely deny the first. It is a rule allowing no exception that every subjective

---

135. See pp. 66-70.

ethical motive, insofar as it may really be held to be such, may have its origin only in an ethical impulse representing practical reason. True, all other impulses can lead to lawful action and lawful conduct, but never based on true ethics. Still, even this would not always happen. The supposed consciousness of freedom as the feeling of a particular modification of power would always impel actions in which it could become most fully aware of free expression; it would therefore always oppose the prevailing motives, including the ethical impulse as soon as it showed power over the faculty of desire. How, therefore, are we to take this feeling for an ethical motive?

We can therefore say only this much: consider those occasions when we either deliberate concerning impending actions or make preceding actions the objects of sentiment or lay plans for coming actions; if at those times the ethical impulse is to express free effectiveness, the requisite presuppositions exist only in relation to the feeling of freedom, never in relation to the consciousness of necessity. The first of these cases – deliberation over what lies before us – does indeed presuppose the consciousness that we are not constrained by objects, and since deliberation commonly consists in searching out one or comparing many maxims, it also presupposes consciousness of the will's impulse. Yet, though this be granted, it is in the inner axiom of the ethical law's binding relation that the ethical impulse has its full warrant to impel the faculty of knowledge to investigate what in this case accords with the ethical law. Will the feeling of necessity refute this warrant?

We are convinced that nothing will occur except what is grounded in our state and thus in the whole succession of all preceding states. However, this activity of the ethical, or at least of the pure impulse of will, also occurs in accordance with our state, and we rejoice over this because it is a sign of perfection in our state [293] that presages a good outcome for the impending action. Moreover, if a misunderstanding ill humor concerning the yoke of necessity – a humor we cannot presuppose in a well-instructed adherent of this doctrine – does not infect the soul's natural course, then, consequent to these deliberations grounded in our state, something will happen that would not have been brought to pass in another state deprived of such deliberations. The necessity of that false feeling of freedom is therefore incomprehensible. Rather, that feeling's contradictions would be obvious in this case, were it not for the fact that the feeling usually depends on the impression of only a single state, without connection to future or past.

On Regret for Past Actions

Matters are quite otherwise with sentiments concerning our past actions. These too can arise only from the ethical impulse if they are to be really ethical, and here again necessity will not oppose them. It is true that what has occurred in accordance with all that has gone before could not have occurred otherwise, but is the state this betokens any less bad for that reason? Should not regret on this account be more vivid than every sentiment concerning external ethical or other evil since regret cannot alter what happened?

In this same respect, regret must be weakened by the feeling of freedom, which certainly makes regret a futile sentiment! The action I deplore is barely connected with my present ego. My power is determinable without causal force[136]. By means of a certain secret sympathy – not all that easy to understand, in fact – this power should always determine itself as if the ethical impulse had determined it. This past action was an isolated aberration of this power. True, it unpleasantly affects my ethical feeling, but since all the expressions of this power together are not a path but only individual steps, this past step has no influence upon the direction of those that follow. Moreover, these reflections must almost destroy the sentiment of regret, or at least give it the chill that above[137] was debited to necessity's account.

In contrast, how differently the following reflections enliven feeling: the poor state of the past is a ground shared with the present state, which clearly bears its traces. Thus the overpowering sensible impulse, whose strength I do not feel so much at this moment, is perhaps only sleeping, only to subdue the ethical impulse at the next opportunity! How well justified my sentiment of regret becomes! This is so in that it links a significant portion of my existence to the moment of action. [294] And how useful that sentiment is! It is the work of enlivened ethical feeling, communicating the more strength to ethical impulse the stronger it is itself. I welcome that blessed sentiment as an excellent means – grounded in the nature of my soul's better part, still coming to light – of impeding the evil I have had to fear in consequence of preceding evil.

---

136. **Causalzwang.**
137. See pp. 68ff.

On Planning for the Future

How is it, then, with the proper goal of all these sentiments: plans for the future, resolutions for future self-betterment? This goal requires consciousness that we feel the soul's ethical impulse to be unbounded in itself, that each stronger stage of that impulse and every higher step of ethical submission is not impossible. With this consciousness, ethical feeling delineates our ethical needs for the future, more vitally manifesting themselves in this moment; and with this same consciousness, ethical impulse strives to foresee those needs as appropriate for us at the moment of their realization.

Now it very easily happens that we think of both this consciousness of a greater possible strength of ethical impulse and, arising from it, the greater ease of regarding as ours what is not yet ours, as effects of the false feeling of freedom. As a result, it will depend only upon the act of a declamation[138] for us to become what we intend to become. But what else follows from the false assessment of those feelings' origin? We are filled with greater conviction that whatever we intend to occur will actually do so, since at the time of realization there will be no ground determining actuality other than the act of declamation. However, from the moment of resolution to the moment of realization, striving toward the wished-for state is completely excluded. One reason is that in this feeling of freedom we are not aware that everything that yet lies between the present moment and the anticipated one, as a means or as preceding links of the chain, really belongs to the attainment of that state. Thus we shall only be lulled into unconcern by this supposed certainty, which always does its utmost to make us miss our goal. Indeed, another reason is that a false feeling of freedom is not content to have us surrender our feeling for a continuing portion of our existence, but also, whenever it relates to some period of time other than its own, must represent the two as isolated, unconnected moments.

Will necessity offer us anything worse, therefore, if we should prefer to associate our sentiments with the feeling of necessity rather than with this other chimerical feeling? Necessity likewise allows [295] the ethical impulse's striving for the future, because it can unite itself in a single consciousness with the feeling of the ethical impulse's unconditioned magnitude, a feeling that underlies those strivings and is quite in accord with it. Nothing is taken away, then, from the strength and vitality of our wishes and resolutions.

---

138. **Aktus eines Ausspruchs.**

Modesty, Discretion, and Fruitful Ethical Activity Arise from
The Doctrine of Necessity

Necessity does bring more modesty to our sentiments, however: we cannot look forward to their fulfillment with the infallibility of a wonder worker! We attribute our present ideas to no false, foreign source but only to a superior activity of ethical feeling. Will our train of ideas entail that at the time we are to realize these ideas this same activity reawakens and presents us with our goal in its original purity and clarity? Even more, will the ethical impulse (which now, at a distance, we feel so powerfully for this objective) – will its longing to validate these ideas be strong enough then to prevail over opposing inclinations? All this the feeling of necessity presents as depending upon the content of the intervening period – upon the strengthening or weakening of ethical feeling contained therein, upon the increasing or diminishing power therein of ethical impulse through action, both generally and in the particular respect under consideration. All this makes us modest, in contrast to that proud but all the more insidious certainty.

Yet, along with this modesty we are infused with discretion and activity. We do not, out of proud presumption, restrict our desire for future moral good to the single moment at which we are supposedly guaranteed its possession. We seek it from this moment on, and our desire for it causes a far more lively desire for the whole of morality, without which we know it is impossible to reach the good. Necessity does not say to us: "You will be so because you now want to be so." It rather says: "You would have become so less than perhaps you will, had you not so vitally desired it in advance."

So it appears that the antipathy against necessity occasioned by the supposed damage that could accrue to these subjective ethical motives is likewise based on self-deception. Necessity seems to contradict these subjective ethical motives only insofar as one insists that these sentiments must arise wholly out of necessity. The reason is that as the entire doctrine is explained, these motives come more and more clearly to light as a non-faculty that cannot injure necessity at all, since necessity is in accord with the nature of the case. This is true in that it would be utterly inconceivable that appearances of ethical feeling in connection with certain kinds of [296] objects should be grounded in knowledge of the relations belonging to our originating power, and, given the various errors to which such knowledge is subject, this would also be a very unwise arrangement of nature. The false feeling of freedom suggests an opposing promotion of these sentiments simply because it presumes to complete them, but this is to confuse ethical feeling with the feeling of a certain modification of our power. The inadequacy of this confusion is proven by the fact that it disrupts the interconnection of life[139], as it were.

The Rule of Necessity Heightens Our Sense of Self-Activity, Personality and Ethical Maturity

As clear as all this is, I believe that a large number of readers, while not denying it, will still maintain that necessity greatly diminishes their feeling of personality[140] and self-activity[141]. We do not want to dispute this observation, but it would be interesting to investigate its actual source. Perhaps the following consideration will suffice. When we make a decision, or arrive at the result of a comparison, in relation to matters that the Stoics[142] reckoned as the *proegmenois* – that is, matters that cannot be decided by their relation to the moral law – we will be conscious of less self-activity when we have to admit that we do not see into the ground of this decision than when we can convince ourselves that we have given this option priority over that because we consider and experience things in such and such a way. Moreover, we will sense less personality when we do not know how this state interconnects with our preceding states than when we can say: "I have arrived at this way of experiencing things little by little, in this way or that." Here, therefore, our feeling of self-activity and personality is greater the more we are able to see into the mutual interconnection of the various individual workings of the soul in relation to an action, and into the interconnection of an entire state with preceding states according to the rule of necessity, which is thus presupposed; and our feeling of self-activity and personality is smaller the less of this we are able to elucidate in this way – thus, in general, the less necessity seems to be present and the more the soul's workings seem to correspond to freedom.

So it is also with actions relating to some greater [297] perfection of our soul (but still lying outside any immediate ethical criterion) – a new

---

139. **Den Zusammenhang des Lebens.**
140. **Personalität.**
141. **Selbstthätigkeit.**
142. Meckenstock note (KGA): "For this Stoic teaching cf. Diogenes Laertius: *De vitis philosophorum* 7, 105-107, ed. Meibom 429-431; ed. Long 341f."

discovery in the realm of knowledge, for example. We attribute more worth to it the more we know how we arrived at it and the less we are able to believe that our soul determined itself with respect to it with no existent ground for this determination. Such things affect us in the same way when we regard them as matters for our future determination. We are convinced that our future judgment and our future activity cannot be measured solely by our present feeling and the strength of our present exertions, and this does not seem strange to us or weaken our feeling of self-activity, whether we presuppose necessity more or less explicitly.

How does it happen that the opposite of all this occurs as soon as we view actions from the ethical side, that this interconnection we have discovered is so repugnant to us? In all of the other cases we regard an action simply as something that occurs, and it is more our own the more we know that and how it has occurred in us. With ethical actions, in contrast, we regard an action as something that should occur in a certain way. We fasten our whole personality to consciousness of this idea, and our self-activity to our actions' conformity with this idea. Yet, this in turn becomes a basis for misunderstanding: neither in our concepts nor in our feelings do we know how to properly unite this consciousness with the fact that what occurs is nevertheless an action. Let it occur as it should or as it should not: either way it is repugnant for us to see that it had to occur as it did, because we always believe that this "must" will harm the authority of "should." Without noticing, we confuse two quite different things: the ground explaining why the action occurred as it did and the idea for the sake of which it should have occurred – that is, this idea's degree of effectiveness as related to us. Thus when we see that the ground changes with our circumstances, we believe that the idea is itself grounded in those circumstances. This really would do harm to the idea's reputation, and this disgusts us. We rejoice, on the other hand, when the ground of action appears to exist without respect to circumstance, because we believe that this is a proof that the idea also exists in this way, since in general circumstance only destroys the idea's effect.

This is an illusion, however, from which we ought to have freed ourselves, even regardless of anything else. Moreover, if we correctly think our way into necessity – if by means of constant application to [298] every conceivable action we have made ourselves familiar with the considerations setting forth the compatibility between necessity and the whole ethical nature of actions, so that this conviction gradually passes over into our feeling – then we shall soon be freed from that illusion. Also, this feeling of necessity will then no longer harm our consciousness of personality, not even in relation to ethical actions insofar as they are regarded as such. Rather, even here we shall no longer hesitate to give the name of self-activity to individual conduct graspable in this way. We shall also call our own the actions that occur through us, the more so the more particularly they interconnect with our previous actions and with the whole modification of our capacity for action.

Only one observation remains to be made here, namely, that with the feeling of necessity, consciousness of personality increases with ethical progress. So long as the ethical impulse struggles with sensible impulses to gain the upper hand, or sensible impulses struggle with one another, not only the individual action in its relations, but also the strength of the impulse in which it is grounded and which reveals itself as now stronger, now weaker than others, will appear to be produced by circumstances, and the soul will appear less secure and self-reliant. Once the ethical impulse has attained a certain strength, however, it grows by means of judgments, by means of free development of ideas, and by means of small actions. Our more conscious actions, on the other hand, begin to occur of themselves according to the ethical impulse's rule, so that the soul seems to act in accordance with circumstances but not to be altered by circumstances.

In contrast, according to the feeling of freedom, if it is consistently developed, consciousness of personality and of self-activity must diminish in just this same measure. The reason is that the more constant the ground is according to which the soul determines itself, and the more active it is in every case, the less that ground can be misconstrued, and the more prevalent the ethical impulse is the more it wins the reputation of necessarily determining in every case, whereas according to the assertion of the feeling of freedom, personality consists only in this: that such a thing is not perceived in the soul at all.

Part III

HISTORICAL SURVEY: CONCEPTS OF FREEDOM, NECESSITY, AND ASSOCIATED FEELINGS

Introduction

Two Possible Approaches: Theoretical and Actual

[299] If by means of these arguments it has become as clear to some readers, at least, as to the author, that all the exceptions taken to the doctrine of necessity from this side rest upon some kind of illusion, they may very naturally pose the question of how it happens that since this doctrine has been well known for so long and has been systematically accepted by a great many thinking people, it has never universally overcome these illusions. Instead, a great many people continually must have advocated the opposing viewpoints that rest in part upon precisely these illusions.

The issue being defended here could be very little damaged even if no answer to this question existed except *non liquet*[143]. Yet the author finds himself driven for his own sake to seek an answer, because this dry *non liquet* could easily give him the appearance of being eager to write entirely upon his own authority, whereas the real basis, as we could easily show from the fortunes of philosophy, is that what is called for has never been properly brought together in systematic philosophy[144]. From the way we arrived at the idea of necessity in the first pages it appears that we were able to avoid all theoretical means and convince ourselves of necessity purely by reflecting on practical ideas. Especially here, however, there is a great difference between the way a concept arises and the way it is deduced. The whole question is about how something happens, and this can never be posed at the instigation of practical ideas alone, for these assert only that something should happen or should have happened. The question can be answered under the guidance of these ideas, however, once it is posed either through an investigation of the relations of these ideas to that which happens, or independently through immediate intellectual curiosity concerning how all that happens in ourselves has arisen.

---

143. Ed. note: "It is not clear."
144. **Systematischen Weltweisheit.**

The first entrance into this labyrinth reveals a multitude of paths, all equal with respect to their value and all leading to a certain point. It allows room for a boundless host of empty conjectures, and even if the idea of necessity should occur among them, yet in this way it is always lacking the determinateness [300] through which alone it can keep itself free from all errors and refute all apparent objections. Moreover, it can maintain this determinateness only if it relates to general theoretical interest from the outset. The second entrance brings us immediately into a place where we have no option except either to take the way of necessity – clearly sketched for us here, and the only way we see to enter upon – or to wander around in the remaining wasteland, for from this point of view no alternative set of ideas can appear to us in any other way.

If we decide upon the first entrance, as is quite natural, thereafter we completely lack the capacity to counter objections, which cannot be dealt with, given the basic proposition from which we have set out, because these objections relate to ideas of what should happen, and these ideas stubbornly maintain their complete lack of dependence upon rules concerning what does happen. If both disadvantages are to be avoided – if we are to find a satisfactory answer here where speculative interest and practical interest conduct their boundary dispute so stubbornly that they reject every compromise, whether through surrender or mutual accommodation – then this will be possible only if we start from the point at which we have come upon a secure and determinate idea. We are also required, accordingly, to investigate the real significance of these ideas and the significance of their relations to what happens in our soul – which, since both are in our soul, we alone can declare – and thereby to inquire whether these relations are in accordance with this idea or in opposition to it. That is, we must more or less follow the way we have actually followed from the beginning.

Historical Obstacles to a Clear Doctrine of Necessity

Has the way of necessity been taught all along? On the contrary, until now it has always been obstructed by great obstacles. Either the principle of causality or the basic practical ideas were lacking. If these practical ideas were pure and unadulterated, then speculative interest was not in a position to have been able to give the first determinate idea of causality. If speculative interest was excessive, then practical ideas were suppressed and misunderstood so that they could not render the proper evaluation of the matter. Not that people ever ceased to make judgments according to the principle of causality and in their actions to be aware of their faculty of will and their practical reason – particularly in the broader sense we have adopted, wherein every system of actions has its practical reason. Otherwise all the soul's operations would have ceased. Still, it makes a great difference whether we are conscious of these operations merely as powerful feelings or whether we also know the full worth of the fundamental concepts to which alone these feelings [301] can relate – whether we assign these feelings to the place they must occupy in the system of concepts and whether, with each expression of those feelings, we inquire which of the basic concept's criteria, and which relation of this basic concept to others, may document its correctness. Only in this case – and apparently it has almost never existed – will our knowledge of these principles be sufficient to perform the requisite assistance in this matter. The alternate case, in contrast, will give rise to all the contradictions and mistakes that have prevailed in this doctrine up to now.

Just as the course of life brings outright misunderstandings and *non sequiturs* when we blindly yield to feelings basic to our behavior without tracing them back to the judgments from which they have grown – since feelings then easily overstep their bounds and extend to objects that cannot be subsumed under the grounding judgment, or in their ardor carry us away to perform actions that judgment would not have prompted, or, tracing back to concepts alien to their origins, occasion a mode of acting[145] that is entirely distorted and wrong – so too with those feelings relating to the fundamental laws of our soul. Without the exact determination they may obtain only from concepts, they partly cannot be understood, partly cannot be united with one another. This is still the fate of all who think about what we call freedom and the feelings that constitute it: with the notion of blazing a middle trail between necessity and its opposite, both feared as if they were cliffs, they are invariably hurled over the one cliff or the other. Or when they believe themselves to have settled upon one of the two opinions, then it happens either that they often unknowingly stray from it, or that they are able to repel attacks directed against them only by resorting to sophisms and peremptory decrees. It has ever been the same with systematic philosophy[146] which, from a lack of these two main supports, philosophizes falsely concerning the whole question. A closer look at history will reveal that this lack alone causes not only the appearance of the many false, confused and inconsistent theories on

---

145. **Handelweise.**
146. **Sistematischen Philosophie.**

this subject but also the poor grounding and the scanty progress of the one true theory that exists.

Greek Antiquity

From Lack of Questioning, Through Philosophical Fantasy, To the Idea of Unified Purpose

If we pursue our considerations of [302] the history of philosophy to the end in order to find the end of the labyrinthine thread, we discover it far sooner than we believed. To our amazement we see that there was a long period in earlier philosophy during which no formulated question concerning this point of controversy is to be encountered. Far from indicating a good state for philosophy, however, this signifies quite a one-sided, wholly incomplete state. People were not even far enough along to pose the question.

With the Greeks (and I shall restrict myself to them, since our philosophy stems from them alone) the colorful play of an alert and ever active fantasy preceded the first attempts at philosophizing. Supported by the dark tenets of a mystical antiquity, Greek fantasy invoked an invisible being for every observed unity among nature's workings, which these beings arbitrarily controlled, as the Greeks felt that their thoughts controlled their own bodies. Under the pretext of explaining this world, Greek fantasy created another world, one admittedly even less explainable, but precisely because of fantasy's indeterminacy, this left unbounded room for imagining otherworldly laws and affairs. If the kind of interconnections fantasy stipulated among its beings was not at all in accord with the rules of understanding – indeed, had the perpetual tendency to deviate ever more widely – yet, insofar as fantasy had to do with the creation of a world or a system, as these two are in fact one and the same, it was in fact under the sovereignty of reason, for here fantasy too must continually give rise to a certain kind of derivative unity. Thus reason was also active here in a certain way: it acquired a certain direction, and thereby this play of fantasy not only gained influence upon the first attempts at reasoning according to higher laws of knowledge but by means of this influence also determined to a certain extent the whole course of Greek metaphysics. That is, as soon as reason had matured enough, thinkers arose who realized that all of this when viewed as poetic composition was indeed very beautiful, but that it contained nothing to justify claiming it as the true explanation of their existence. So philosophically they saw themselves virtually compelled to discard the entire previous apparatus.

They were by no means left completely free in the course of their philosophizing, however. The questions to which earlier poetry supplied an answer were already there, and the more stubbornly this answer was rejected, the more insistent was the need to give a better answer in its place. And what had these questions been? [303] Fantasy coldly neglected the daily *things of nature* which are always in the state of death. Among them, the rare changes that now and then occur, if they have been observed individually, bear clear traces of an alien source, and this could have led to a development of the relevant principles of understanding; but this did not happen. Imagination was then attracted only to those natural occurrences offering it an image of life, a continually changing reality, or a reality exercising the same dominion over a great multitude of similar things.   Imagination, with its usual quick industriousness, transferred to this realm the ideas most familiar in self-consciousness – since in self-consciousness imagination must itself be quite active – namely, that presentiment[147] of results which precedes actions, making known their intention. Thus the first business of fantasy in its observations of nature was to ask: What sentiment lies at the basis of this change, for what purpose does it occur, and what sort of unity is to be brought into this purpose? That is also the first question that confronts philosophy, and its answer is the first that philosophy must attempt.

In contrast, the interest of understanding in establishing and developing how, in general, something exists and happens for us, and is known as existing and happening, must be neglected from the beginning. It could never lie in the path of fantasy, which never cares to investigate how and why it acquires its objects but is always concerned only with how it assimilates them and what it wants to initiate by means of them. True, the interest of understanding soon had to manifest itself in those who noticed fantasy's continual activity, but the effect could no longer be decisive. That interest did not alter the whole course of philosophy; it only gave rise to new modifications in the cultivation of ideas already in motion.

The more that thinkers now saw causality's interconnection among natural events, the more doubt arose as to whether the idea of unified purpose could be generally applied to the whole of the world and to every individual part. This dynamic nexus, where it simply could not be rejected, appeared to them a more adequate basis for clarification than the former ideal. However, they set the two in opposition to a certain degree, because they still had not seen enough of the laws of knowledge to be convinced that, even with the most agreed upon unity of purpose, each individual event requires such a causal connection in order to be known by us. [304] Thus, concerning the

---

147. **Vorempfindung.**

applicability of their first idea, they were divided into the three main viewpoints of ancient philosophy.

Those who were most fully convinced of the reality of causal interconnection completely denied unity of purpose; the extra-worldly beings whom they accepted were true not philosophically but only theologically, and with respect to the *causa finalis* of the world's events they affirmed chance[148] in the strongest sense – that is, affirmed a complete lack of final cause. The rest, who still asserted unity of purpose, were themselves divided over the way in which this could be the case. Some asserted that unity consists not only in the events themselves, with respect to their outcome, but also in the events taken together with their interconnection; they made the law of causality, so far as they knew it, part of the unity of purpose they had urged much earlier, and the being whom they made the subject of this unity was a wise being. Others did not risk this leap but thought that in order to unite both principles it was enough to assume a certain predetermined and eternal harmony between the two – not provable, it is true, but possible; they had experienced the idea of unity of purpose without and before the idea of mechanical *causa efficiens*, and they wanted to retain it unalloyed; thus they said that purpose lies merely in the events, and despite and through the inner interconnection of events nothing ever occurs except what is comprehended in this unity of purpose. Now the being who was the subject of this unity could not be thought of as endowed with wisdom, and that being became a kind of hypostatized necessity: Fate.

Consequences of Antiquity's Lacking A General Principle of Causality

Investigation of these two viewpoints sufficiently proves how far removed ancient philosophy was, not only from knowing the true state of affairs with respect to the proposition of causality, for this has been set forth only recently, but also from conceding to causality the generality that in practice it arrogated for itself, completely unnoticed. For if that generality is granted – presupposing along with events their consequences, and along with the whole sum of consequences their intercooperation – then one would have to assume incomplete knowledge on the part of the being in whom unity of purpose is represented, if that being was not supposed to think of individual parts of purpose within this interconnectedness.

---

148. **Ein Ohngefähr.**

All of these viewpoints, however, were concerned only with explaining change in the world. Only later did the interest of understanding, which was a cause of the division, occasion a sort of questioning about the origin of things concerning whose change people had reasoned for so long. However, the way [305] the whole matter was handled shows that here too the interest of understanding, even though it posed the question, was not predominant in efforts to answer it. The philosophers still did not operate out of the principle of causality. They stopped short with answers that would never have sufficed for that proposition. Rather, in the early poetic times of philosophy they searched only for sentiments and designs that might explain the genesis of so great a manifold from a presupposed smallest possible number of different elements.

In still later times they asked about these elements themselves, and since they attributed separate, individual agents to the particular characteristics manifested in material effects, they arrived at simple fundamental elements of which all matter was supposed to be only combinations. Moreover, they were completely satisfied with this result of transcendental physics, even though they still had found no necessary connection whatsoever between the existence of those simple things and the genesis of their combinations and had still less inquired into the ground of the actuality of those simple things. They merely exulted over the happy discovery of unity in the derivation of composite concepts from a few simple ones.

All of this seems completely foreign to our main question today, and these ideas have therefore been merely touched upon rather than developed. However, it was necessary at least to mention these viewpoints in order to make it clear that all of the main issues of ancient philosophy, which appear at first glance to be able to proceed simply from the principle of causality, in the theory itself were not based upon that proposition at all, and that it therefore did not occupy the place in that philosophy that would have been due it.

As soon as philosophers began to perceive the universality of a few great laws of nature, they had to acquire a concept of the necessity of their effects as well. However, since in fact an event together with all of its circumstances and determinations can never be manifested as the effect of a law of nature, even this knowledge did not suffice to give the principle of causality the representational comprehensiveness it deserved. Further, in their observations of particulars, instead of proceeding from the presupposition that there absolutely must be an interconnection of events upon which this particular event follows, and then according to this rule seeking an aggregate of events that might in itself contain the cause of the perceived event, they did not concern themselves with this at all. For them the formula [306] underlying the relations that appear upon observation of a particular event was always simply that everything happens according to a purpose or, to the contrary, according to chance.

If they thus observed the world and all that happened in it more from the point of view that whatever happens *should* happen than that it *must* happen, more according to the idea of appropriateness to a purpose than to the idea of inner connectedness, and if therefore in their philosophizing about the world they could not manage to draw forth the principle of causality from the confusion in which it lay entombed and put it in its true place, then how could it be possible in observing what happened in their soul, where teleological ideas are much more conspicuous, that this principle could have been fundamental and could have prevailed over this teleological interest?

They saw unity of purpose – which for the world they had to posit in an alien, quite unknown being – set forth in their own faculty of choice and dependent upon their knowledge of themselves. The first, most natural question, therefore, was which of all the possibly relevant ideas was most correct; so, once they had come to an agreement among themselves, all actions would be included in this unity, with respect to both their possibility and their actuality. They could not join their speculative philosophy with the principle of causality viewed as an axiom that had to be applicable also to actions of the soul; accordingly, the determinate idea of necessity, which on one side is basic to the controversial question of freedom, certainly could not exist. Nor, however, did they have enough familiarity with reasoning about the proposition of a ground[149] to be able to attain the other approach to this question presented above[150]; they never had room for the kind of comparison between what should happen in the soul and what does happen that could have enabled them to do so. The ideas of ancient philosophy concerning the meaning of the moral law together with responsibility to it and the accountability arising therefrom were correct enough. However, the very law that was supposed to assume this position was altogether too diversely stated, and from this diversity arose continual warfare of each against all the others.

It is the chief concern of all who wish to lay any degree of claim upon principles to justify their accepted practical system fully, at least to themselves. Each of these systems [307] of ancient philosophy that set up ethical laws was to a certain extent grounded in an alien theoretical supposition (one that had to relate to knowledge of some particular aspect of human nature).

---

149. **Nach dem Saz des Grundes.**
150. See p. 85.

This procedure cannot be otherwise as long as reason derives the basic practical law elsewhere than from itself. Because this was so, all observations concerning particular actions were directed toward establishing sufficient ground for the system, strangely enough by means of characteristics of action that were in accord with that very system.[151] Thus such people always remained inside the circle of practical ideas and merely compared the general with the particular included within it.

Even if this polemical interest was sometimes satisfied enough to make room for the observation that often something did not happen that according to the accepted system was supposed to happen, given the conditions of the time this could take only two directions, neither leading to our question. Either they placed the blame for this lack of agreement upon the practical ideas, and thought that the understanding had let itself be taken unawares, for a moment believing a maxim to be in accord with the accepted system when in fact it was not; they then thought of ascetic precepts by which awareness of the system's main points could at that moment be attained with sufficient clarity. Or, if they ventured beyond the boundaries of practical ideas and regarded this disharmonious action as something that had happened, still they did not inquire after its causes; rather they subsumed it under the teleological ideas dominating speculative philosophy as a part of the wise purpose of the supreme being, or as a determination of necessity.

From this effort many new ideas, questions, and doubts could have indeed arisen, had not the more immediate polemical practical interest always had other needs which interrupted the complete execution of such an undertaking. It never happened this way, however. Even if it had, the path from there to our controversial question, though it was almost the shortest way to come, would still have been continually the broadest. So to me, at least, it seems quite natural to conclude that we find in ancient philosophy almost no traces of this entire article, and that in general, no sooner is there talk about it than people have begun to philosophize about the Christian religion.

---

151. Ed. note: Reading from the Ms. **"die dem System gemäß war"** instead of the KGA's **"die dem System gemäßerer."**

Medieval Christianity

The Augustinian Doctrine of Grace Opened a New Debate, Yet Lacking A Correct Idea of Necessity

The dispute over grace that Augustine opened, and that ever since has never really ceased to divide the church, offered the first occasion for such philosophizing. [308] Philosophically regarded, parties to this dispute could assert one of three things: either what happens in people through the powers of their soul and the natural course of things never deserves the name of the *good*; or people generally do not have the faculty of making the representation of moral actions into an object of their faculty of desire; or, finally, people do possess this faculty, but it is always too slight to carry through its intention against some sensible impulse, and some such impulse indeed confronts it in every case. The first assertion is a mere quibble over the meaning of the word "good," behind which people have sometimes hidden during this controversy but which is able to change nothing beyond linguistic usage. The third explanation differs from the second – if we do not forget that, in both, complete volition or knowledge of the good as such would already be a good action – only in this: that the second denies human good from the side of possibility, the third from the side of actuality.

Although this controversy, choose whichever of its three explanations you will, does not directly include our question, still the assertions made are of such a kind as to invite a search for instances that either confirm or refute them. This need, moreover, leads naturally to a closer examination of the way in which ethical actions are brought forth in the soul. Therein arose a comparison of the practical ideas with that which occurs; this, in turn, opened a free field to vacillating, unlimited surmises and theories, and it occasioned the confused treatment which the scholastics conferred upon our issue. Naturally the correct outcome could not be found in this way, since the correctly determined idea of necessity still could not be taken over from the speculative realm. However, before we come to the time at which this could occur, we must, in order to be able to elucidate the events of that period, see what new hindrances to the conclusion of this matter were in the meantime created by the course philosophy had taken in relation to religion.

It is in fact too great an honor to call the exertions of the dogmaticians in this matter philosophizing. This term properly applies only to a procedure of developing thoughts from a basic concept or principle, and for them this was unfortunately all too impossible. The authority to which they were bound in their reasoning is so disconnected, and its individual constituents are so dissimilar, that often it must have happened that invoking some philosophical [309] doctrine to elucidate some dictum, they bumped up against another dictum undermined by this same doctrine, directly or indirectly. Thus they were always compelled either to proceed arbitrarily, in order to carry through in their chosen direction despite all difficulties, or to pull themselves out of a bad situation by means of a host of sophistical expedients.

Consequences of Conceiving Moral Law as Divine Will

The internal disputes that arose among them cannot be further developed here, even with respect to our question. We shall stick merely to their influence on philosophy and the philosophers. The rather generally accepted doctrine of human inadequacy[152] and of the depravity[153] that had affected even human reason naturally meant that previous moral systems were altogether discarded – all the more so since the sacred Codex offered much more material for practical than for speculative philosophy. Therein were found a multitude of practical maxims, which in many earlier systems were not presented as parts of ethical legislation at all and in other systems were not expressed with the same exactitude and clarity. Thus revelation was made the basis for knowledge of these maxims, and this fact gave rise to a peculiar but important change. That is, this relation was only accidental: it was quite conceivable that one could attain knowledge of these maxims in another way. Indeed, as soon as these maxims were regarded as ethical laws, deduction from a general first principle was required. One could not simply take this for granted, however. What had been only the occasion for perceiving these maxims was made their proper and inner basis of knowledge as moral law: their existence in revelation was made to imply their necessity, and that which makes known the practical necessity of a proposition was also required inevitably to lay down the basis of its obligation. The basis of obligation to those moral laws, therefore, consisted merely in their being declarations or commands of divinity (for if one had wanted to assume some other cause of obligation, there would have had to be another way of knowing this obligation, since no general first principle from which those commandments might be derived is established in revelation).

---

152. **Unfähigkeit**.
153. **Verderbniß**.

This tenet, much older in theology, first went over into philosophy proper in a very natural way when people began to elaborate natural right. These efforts proceeded from the positive legislation of Rome or of Judaism (politically considered), where [310] the obligation of every tenet rests upon the authority of the lawgiver and what really mattered was simply to put those ideas in a light that could justify the way the lawgiver wielded authority, since every individual tenet related to that authority. Thus one had to search out those general tenets that had been chosen above others to serve as a basis for legislation, likewise for something that would procure obligation to them. One could well see by now that this had to be something apart from and prior to the lawgiver, who was to regard it as previously assumed. Still, it was very natural to stick to the well-trodden path of grounding obligation and to look for these first tenets in the authority of a lawgiver – a lawgiver, however, who did not have to look elsewhere for justification, and that lawgiver was the Deity.

This newly-assumed first ethical principle gradually gave rise to a great change in every practical idea. We shall point out only those changes having a marked influence upon our question. In all previous practical systems each particular law was derived from the system's first principle. Whoever had initiated an unethical action – presupposing that it was not merely an error of understanding arising from an incorrect application of the principle – never considered the whole sum of legislation but only considered a particular instance of the principle. This maneuver permitted different accountability for different actions, since it was quite possible that a person who in certain cases knowingly violated one consequence of the basic principle might in other cases act according to other ethical laws for their own sake.

In this later system, where ethical law was considered to be divine legislation, all of this became something entirely different. True, to a certain extent one had a basic principle here also: that one must do the will of God. Yet, the particular propositions comprising the will of God could not be derived from this principle. These all had to be given separately, and I can apply the principle to each individual law only insofar as I think of each law as a part of the collective unity known to me. Here, therefore, if I knowingly violate one commandment, then, apart from what I might have done otherwise or what I might do later, in this one action I have in fact transgressed the entire law, for the obligation of every particular law [311] is derived only from the obligation of the whole, which I should therefore have previously considered.

Reducing Accountability to The Idea of Divine Punishments
Contradicts the Principle of Necessity

Thence one necessarily comes, albeit by an entirely different route, to the Stoic paradox that, particularly with respect to accountability, all transgressions are equal.[154] In reaction to this, sentiment is naturally indignant. In this dilemma, moreover, one is all the more glad to take refuge in a second theological tenet that can serve at the same time to strengthen belief in the first and, indeed, says the same thing, only in a different form. It is the tenet of equal divine punishments, whether temporal or eternal (though the latter is probably more consistent). To be sure, both tenets are always more harshly and coarsely expressed in theology than in natural philosophy, but these two intermingle. In addition, the more one wished to ascertain the way accountability is determined in this system, the more one had to make use of this image of punishment, so as to have something vivid to focus on amidst these incomprehensible notions. So it happened that the idea of accountability was reduced wholly to divine punishments – something that gradually would have been effected also by the idea that the obligation of laws is grounded merely in the will of the Lawgiver and that legislation is therefore positive[155].

In this state of affairs the proposition concerning the grounding of obligation was now established as an axiom, applying generally to all objects of our knowledge and lying at the basis of all our judgments concerning these objects, and this axiom was applied also to human actions. The necessity of human actions, which followed from this application, soon revealed itself to be in obvious contradiction to this theory of divine punishments. If actions are only results which according to all the pertinent data could have occurred in only one way, then the warrant for inflicting a punishment for these actions would be automatically suspended; according to the data really supposed to pertain to the actions, the punishment could not be carried out.

Herein human punishments had something that could not be adduced in relation to divine punishments. They were not justified by the effects their announcement could bring about, because where it happens that the effect of the announcement fails, it would always be unjust to inflict punishment for this failure, which was itself a result and unavoidable. Rather, the rescue of

---

154. Meckenstock note (KGA): "To this Stoic teaching cf. Diogenes Laertius: *De vitis philosophorum* 7, 120, ed. Meibom 440; ed. Long 347f."

155. Ed. note: As before, "positive" here means the result of willful action, in this case God's. See above, note 102.

human punishments consisted in this: that they alter the data for actions that follow [312] the punishment's application.[156] Now this could not be said concerning divine punishments. The reason is that those who thought of punishments as eternal were naturally convinced that once they are carried out, nothing further can follow. In addition, even those who assumed a limited duration instead of this eternity did so more out of a certain natural sympathy than out of more rigorous ideas of punishment in general, for most of them regarded punishments not really as intentional means of betterment but rather as natural consequences of the damaged reputation and justice of the Lawgiver, who moderated these consequences, in light of their magnitude, only out of goodness.

The contradiction in this doctrine of divine punishment was thus apparent in all its modifications. All means of resolution were bound to appear inadequate upon closer examination. Only the doctrine's underlying good intention was able to protect it from the severest exposure of its inadequacy. The worst was this: that in the way just indicated, this doctrine had become the main pillar of all morality. Advocates of necessity could not point out the doctrine's nullity, however, because they had merely borrowed their tenet from speculative philosophy and, given the state of affairs, they lacked opportunity for perceiving necessity in a new vision of practical ideas and even more lacked the means for realizing such a vision. So either they remained silent, since on the one hand their feeling assured them that they were falsely accused, but on the other they saw no sure way to extract themselves from the fundamental issue; or, where various subjective grounds did not permit them this silence, they sought out sophisms and spun circles, praising every new rescue from the issue, though fundamentally they were all nothing other than sophistical and circular. The other party thus stuck stubbornly to the assertion that the doctrine of necessity suspended all morality since it overthrew the legitimacy of divine punishment.

As greatly as theologians and philosophers were divided and redivided over the grounds of this assertion, they were nonetheless in agreement concerning the issue itself, and on this account they denied the validity of every general axiom proposed concerning actions subject to practical ideas. This was not the end of the matter, however. Human actions were now considered under the aspect that they do occur, and the question could not [313] immediately be dismissed as to how they would be produced if they did not

---

156. Schleiermacher's note: "On this account, capital punishment was not included in this rescue; it was first impugned by advocates of necessity, on the grounds that if it is carried out, it can motivate no further action."

occur according to the principle of necessity. This question had to be fully answered if the doctrine of necessity was to be considered completely refuted.

Seeking a Complete Opposite To the Doctrine of Necessity Gives Rise to Indifferentism

Also the age was no longer to be helped by chimerical, highly venturesome hypotheses and turns of phrase. The idea of a sufficient ground with necessity constructed upon it was so definite that no middle way was available. One had either to approve it or to assert its complete opposite, and thus arose *indifferentism*. At this stage of the controversy, however, the talk was not yet about the correctness or the necessity of likewise proving this idea independently of the contrasting idea that preceded it. Rather, since necessity was presupposed in order to defend practical interest, and since indifferentism was the only other hypothesis by which that interest could be rescued, one felt obliged only to demonstrate the possibility of the latter.

In this respect, people imitated the procedure of those who defended necessity. That is, in order to clarify once and for all what they really intended, the defenders of necessity posited a completely indeterminate and universally applicable case, stating: As I deliberated over a certain action, thinking of it at first as no more than problematic, the outcome of this deliberation could not possibly have been otherwise than it was, all things being equal – namely, not only the objective circumstances of the action but also the subjective state of my whole soul, and especially of my mood at and since the moment of my first thought about this action, my accurate or inaccurate knowledge concerning it, and a multitude of other fluid circumstances that are similar. The outcome could not have been otherwise because there must be a sufficient ground to explain why, of all the possible ways to decide this matter, only this way has become preeminent for me, and yet this ground can lie nowhere else than in that part of the general train of events that can be thought of in connection with the decision.

For the defenders of necessity, positing this general example was supposed to serve only the presentation of their own view. The defenders of indifferentism made use of the very same example, saying: In the moment of a certain act or resolution I could decide in any conceivable way, and nowhere in the preceding course of the world is there a necessitating ground sufficient to have determined this way to the exclusion of every other. Nor did they content themselves [314] with allowing this general example to serve their own goal. They also sought surreptitiously to obtain a proof, for they said it is obvious that, in accordance with self-consciousness, in the moment of decision each person really stands in this relation to the impending action. This was the ground on which they built, and their building materials were taken from those illusions of self-feeling that we have discussed in the preceding Part,[157] though not in relation to this particular system. Those feelings and this system are so closely related that it may be almost impossible to determine whether it is more the case that the doctrine is confirmed by these illusions or that the illusions arise from the requirements of the doctrine.

The darkness spread over the entire dispute by this complex interweaving of various errors was nevertheless not so thick that one could not have seen how this way of representing consciousness permanently nullified our way of judging actions. In order to prove the possibility of this complete absence of sufficient ground it was thought necessary to adduce instances where it would be impossible for us to find such a ground for action and where we would be conscious of this absence even after the action and would confirm this consciousness through our judgments. Accordingly a great host of particular cases was presented just to prove the tenet. In some cases the action is so slight that it never occurs to us how it happens but only that it does. Closer attention reveals that far from accomplishing this proof, however, these cases make us aware of just the opposite. Either we fear that we have thereby let go of the ground of motivation that was nearest to us and have laid hold of its opposite, or we do not want to appear indebted to this proof of freedom and thus stick to the more familiar ground of motivation. Other such cases include actions that we do not perform expressly for the sake of the idea of freedom but that happen in us of themselves, as it were, without any clearly enunciated will. They consist either in suddenly rejecting a train of thoughts or in a bodily motion, one that cannot occur without choice yet occurs without our being conscious of any choice we might have had.

However, basic psychology shows us – partly in the workings of fantasy, [315] partly in the impressions of vital senses and in the relation of the soul to the control of the body, long not recognized in all its grounds – how such actions can arise without their lacking a sufficient ground. Moreover, even if we cannot always exactly specify the more immediate determination of these general grounds as they apply to a certain moment, indeed even if we could not do this in a single instance, equally little would be proved by this. When

---

157. See pp. 66-83, esp. 66-70.

the particular moments that must come together in order to constitute the *causa efficiens* of an event are so slight that they escape our eye, then the ideal whole constituted by these moments naturally suffers the same fate. In the material world, however, this happens many thousands of times daily without our believing ourselves justified in jumping from "do not see" to the conclusion "does not exist." Why should we do so when what is in question is an action of our soul?

The proof that something has a cause lies qualitatively outside the sphere of experience. When we presuppose that proposition, however, it can probably guide us to where in a particular case we should seek the appearance corresponding to the concept. For this purpose it need only lift out by analogy several appearances from among the infinite multitude. On the other hand, not only is a direct proof that everything has no cause likewise outside the sphere of experience, but this would also be quantitatively impossible to prove apagogically[158], for it would be an infinite task to show that among all perceived appearances none could be the causative ground of some given appearance. And yet such are the grounds upon which indifferentism seeks to win acceptance. We have to wonder how it has found so much acceptance, despite weaknesses of these grounds. This acceptance seems almost inconceivable, in fact, when we consider that even granting its grounds as valid, indifferentism establishes almost nothing that would bring the doctrine of necessity to be rejected on account of its failures. Far worse failures afflict indifferentism itself.

Apparent Advantages of Indifferentism Are in Fact Illusory

Necessity was a hindrance to ethical conduct only insofar as ethical conduct was taken to depend upon the theory of divine punishments. Indifferentism, though appearing on the surface to preserve the connection between these two, in fact does not even support either separately. That is, how can I be punished for something when I could do nothing ahead of time to advance or thwart it? Not my principles in themselves, it is true, but their every appearance [316] in my soul, their influence and the ideas they stimulate, all belong to the general train of experiences and events, which is supposed not to contain anything whatsoever of the ground of actions. Or how can I be accountable for an action when we cannot determine the extent to which it

---

158. Ed. note: A term from Aristotle referring to a demonstration that does not prove a proposition directly but rather shows the impossibility or absurdity of denying it.

belongs to my soul? And yet this is obviously the case within the system of indifferentism.

It is poor help here to seek words that do not exclude but rather only conceal the idea of grounding and being grounded, or to content oneself with such ideas as appear valid only so long as they are not sufficiently definite. The indifferentists say that actions spring immediately from our will, but they are far from connecting these words with the idea of them we have presented above.[159] Nor have they done so with the idea of the faculty of desire, nor with any other clear idea. Only this much is clear despite all this indefiniteness: since actions are here regarded with respect to their ethical nature, it is unthinkable that ethical and unethical actions could spring from this will in the same way, for otherwise the difference between good and evil persons would thereby be suspended and accountability annulled. We must therefore divide this will once again and assume varied conditions, or whatever else, within it.

Now if these conditions are inborn or bestowed upon a person from the beginning, again no accountability is possible, for we do not know whether or not these conditions relate to general ethical characteristics of actions in such a way that someone who has once brought forth actions in relation to certain ethical laws must, by virtue of the will's conditions, always, or at least in all similar cases, bring them forth in the same way. If these conditions have only developed, then either they are the fruit of such changes as operate according to the law of causality, and then even actions based in conditions of the will have their sufficient ground in these changes; or they have no ground at all, not even immediately, and are based on chance; or we must again seek a general subject in which they exist, and then our investigations begin all over again. Thus we can by no means settle for the proposition that actions arise from an indeterminate something resembling nothing. Instead, we are always driven from there either to [317] knowledge of a sufficient ground, or to complete chance, which certainly annuls morality more than anything else.

If all this was actually to be of no benefit to indifferentism, help still came from another side, offering a new prospect. The party that carried the doctrine of supernatural grace to its highest peak had negated a necessary requirement for the validity of practical ideas, namely what we have earlier[160] called the neutrality of the will: the conviction that ethical as well as unethical maxims can with equal likelihood become objects of the faculty of desire

---

159. See p. 11.
160. See pp. 23-24.

– that is, become determinative of the will. Necessity did indeed grant this neutrality, but it did not demonstrate neutrality, since in every action it placed the will in a state of having been determined, attaching the will momentarily to one object exclusive of all others. Thus necessity certainly made this two-sidedness thinkable but could not prove it. Indifferentism, in contrast, appeared to re-establish this two-sidedness completely, applying it to every case, and maintaining that in every moment when action was impending it was equally possible for the will to manifest any one of the maxims that could stimulate us, not only as an object of impulse but also as *actual*.

For some people, this rescue of one of our faculty of desire's most preeminent characteristics might initially have developed the idea of indifferentism out of the natural illusion of self-consciousness discussed above;[161] for others, it might at least have served as a powerful confirmation of belief. Nevertheless, this advantage that indifferentism would assert over necessity is also a chimera, and it is easy to see that necessity has taken the measure of this issue far more accurately than indifferentism. This two-sidedness must certainly pertain to our will when we think of it prior to any state or regard it without respect to its state. However, as soon as we think of it in a state, then certain of the determinations – all of them equally possible – will have become actual rather than others, and as long as they exist at the same level of strength, they naturally exclude the effectiveness of the others.

Almost nothing except the history of indifferentism's origins, therefore, is necessary not only to convince us of its groundlessness but also [318] to explain the proceedings that from the first seem so little to confirm its value. I also believe that nothing needs to be added to establish our final judgment, which is the following: that indifferentism is one of the errors in philosophy arising from the need to preserve the authority of two covertly contradictory presuppositions. It could not possibly prevail, therefore, because it could not achieve this impossible goal. On the other hand, it could not be completely struck down either, because determinism, which at that time derived purely from theoretical principles, could not deny the independent authority of practical ideas and could not ward off the challenge to establish them sufficiently. Nor did it find, either in its capacities or in anything else at its disposal, the means to expose the covert contradiction. For us this is easy, however, because we are long accustomed to the truth that morality is to be thought of as sufficiently established independently of divine commands and punishments.

---

161. See p. 98.

This incapacity of determinism, unavoidable at that time, bestowed upon the error opposed to it the proud reputation of being unvanquished. To this incapacity were joined illusions that error made use of for proofs. Such error flatters people's vanity – which very often does not know exactly why it is puffed up – with consciousness of independence from general law, though without being able to provide any intelligible concept of the positive characteristics of its state in the absence of such a law. Thus indifferentism retained its advocates, as happens with all philosophical opinions, so long as philosophy has nothing except opinions. These two opinions therefore could only coexist side by side, without legitimate general grounds for deciding which side really represented the truth.

The Rise of Fatalism

Indifferentism, and even more the grounds upon which it was defended, gave rise to yet a third opinion – or rather, arising as it did in the period of unbounded hypotheses concerning this point of controversy, this third opinion managed to be sought out anew and brought to light with new titles to assert its rights. Indifferentism had based its first attack against necessity upon the dependency of all moral ideas upon theological ideas and particularly upon concepts of divinity's moral predicates. It had thus acknowledged these primary theological ideas as incontrovertible principles, and the metaphysical predicates of divinity [319] could not be separated from the moral. Therefore the decision it made, which was supposed to serve to rescue the moral predicates of divinity, was also necessarily so contrived as not to give offense to divinity's metaphysical predicates. Unfortunately, however, that was not the case – at least not according to the principles from which one had to proceed at that time.

Indifferentism and the Concept of Divine Foreknowledge Combine to Imply Fatalism

According to indifferentism, if the faculty of foreknowing actions from their grounds were taken away from us, the loss would not be great. We would still have the perception of those actions that actually occurred. Moreover, even for actions that are still to happen, according to this opinion, we still retain probabilistic conjecture, regulated by most of our earlier perceptions. So the lack is filled for us. But what about the Supreme Being?

Even if the intuiting knowledge that appears to be possible only under conditions of finite existence were not denied and there were some other kind of the same knowledge for the Supreme Being, how is that Being supposed to attain exact and incontrovertible knowledge of the determinations of things, which are intrinsic to their reality even before they have become actual?

It is true that some have thought there could be probabilistic knowledge that always proves correct.[162] Even if we grant this, it still does not suffice for the eternal prescience of God. This prescience requires not merely the outcome of knowledge attained bit by bit but rather knowledge in the highest degree certain, in itself and by its nature. Now for knowledge that is supposed to precede experience and to manifest in all of its determinations what is still indeterminate, no other source is thinkable except the source through which it is supposed to be determined. For everything that occurs in a necessary way, however, this source must exist in the interconnection between causality and that which is to be determined; no other condition of knowledge is thinkable. Indifferentism has taken away this condition from the Supreme Being, not only for human actions but also for all changes in the material world brought about by those actions and hence, by and by, for the greater part of the course of the world. Accordingly, divine prescience is as good as negated.

Now let our most recent philosophy argue over this as it may, in that earlier period one could not do so, and [320] no other way out was really open for this grim issue except *fatalism*. This word has been given so many meanings, as a sect name designating a point of view concerning the interconnection of human actions, that I must first explain what I wish to be understood by it. Several philosophical parties have not only considered the subject of self-consciousness as it is revealed to us in the faculties of representation and desire but have also speculated about the nature and kind of power at the basis of these faculties, and from this general error they have arrived at completely different ideas. When they then spoke subsequently about the interconnection of actions in terms of these self-established ideas concerning the substance at the basis of our faculties, the general grounds they gave for this substance assumed particular content in accord with these points of view; but the relation of these grounds to the subject itself was none other than simply that of causative necessity – which determinism in general, without respect to any particular opinion about the substance of the soul, had granted.

---

162. Meckenstock note (KGA): "Cf. [Moses] Mendelssohn, *Ueber die Wahrscheinlichkeit,* in *Philosophische Schriften* 2,275-280; *Gesammelte Schriften* 1,512-514."

The materialists, for example, had established that the substance of the human soul is matter, so when they wanted to account for the grounds of actions, they could not possibly say anything except that actions followed according to the laws of motion; but this was simply to grant that actions spring from each other according to the law of causality. The pantheists had established that no particular substance lies at the basis of our faculties but that our whole ego belongs to the one necessary Substance. They therefore had to maintain that the grounds determining changes in our egos were to be encountered not in the substance they denied but in the Substance they granted. When they added that our consciousness deceives us here, they did not thus deny that there is a natural interconnection of these changes or that there is a general law of consciousness – all the less so, since they ascribed a general and (since all was a single unity and therefore nothing therein could be posited as determined otherwise) unalterable necessity to their one Substance and everything belonging to it. There is thus no other law here, no other necessity, than that which determinism also advocates – except that, by virtue of the admittedly rash concept of the subject's substance, necessity is determined closer at hand. If someone has labeled these parties fatalist, the aim could only have been to make them hated – an idea that should never be a determining ground in philosophical terminology.

We are concerned here not at all with this kind of fatalism but with [321] another. This other kind applies to changes in the human soul the idea of fate that we have seen earlier[163] at the basis of a theory of the world's governance, and it seems to be the only idea of fate rightly deserving the name. In that context fate was a third idea alongside chance and the governance of a wise being. Unlike the idea of chance, fate did not exclude all fitness of events to the idea of a purpose; but neither did it allow so complete a determination of events in and through their interconnection as did the idea of governance by a wise being. Instead, this idea of fate asserted that every particular fact, regarded purely in itself, unalterably occurs in accordance with a certain purpose – without respect to what has gone before and what will come after, and without its already being given of itself through the former or in turn containing in itself the latter.

---

163. See p. 89.

Fatalism Denies the Immanence of Divine Wisdom in the World Order

Now this way of thinking had long been abandoned in favor of the better idea of wisdom, and this could continue to be the case in relation to changes in the world depending purely on the rule of nature. For changes connected with acts of human choice, however, equilibrism made such a mediating idea once again necessary. The reason was that no true interconnection of actions with respect to their efficacy was any longer thinkable. Thus, on the one hand, one had to give up the idea of wisdom, which not only actualizes every particular part of its purpose but also has eternally ordered the connection of parts both in such a way that every part has been effected in accord with the laws of the world by the parts that have been actualized before and in such a way that through its natural effects every part will in turn contribute a subsequent succession of parts in accord with the plan of the whole. On the other hand, however, one could not allow the idea of chance to creep in, as if these actions were by nature wholly unsuited to be conceived in a plan; otherwise, on account of the influence of actions upon changes in the material world, no plan would be possible for these changes either and the idea of wisdom's governance would be totally useless.

With respect to these actions, therefore, God's foreknowledge was necessary, but a foreknowledge not somehow requiring knowledge of a cause from which the action must necessarily follow. In addition (if one does not want to think of God's creative ideas as limited by particular characteristics of certain things, which is an obvious imperfection, and [322] if one does not want to exclude the entire spiritual world from the sphere of one's thematic ideas[164], which would likewise be a great limitation) God's foreknowledge also requires regulation of actions in such a way that, of themselves and without difficulty, they mesh in the determinate order of the material world and its accidental changes, and in such a way that, among themselves, they constitute a whole foreknown by the Supreme Being.

Although equilibrism was greatly frightened by these claims of theology, fatalism applied all of this to human actions, maintaining absolute predetermination of every event, without respect to the means thereto and the consequences thereof. Precede what may, every action nevertheless occurs through a mystical act of the divine will, as in the idea of a Supreme Being. Accordingly, as in determinism, every action is equally necessary – and for that action to be otherwise at the moment of the general plan to which it

---

164. **Thelematischen Ideen**. Ed. note: The phrase designates ideas of or pertaining to volition.

belongs, that is, at the moment it occurs, is equally as unthinkable. Yet, this necessity originates not from the action's being grounded in a preceding interconnected sequence, but rather from its dependency upon the Supreme Being's will, which here rests merely upon that Being's knowledge of its plan.

If we wanted to present this doctrine in a single example as we have the other two, we should have to say this: At the moment I performed this action I was in no way constrained to do so by my preceding actions or by my state, for I was conscious that this bond did not exist, that so far as these grounds were concerned I was free, and that I could always have acted otherwise (so far, equilibrism). Indeed, it could just as well have been the case that something else could have preceded, different from what actually did so, and I would nevertheless have acted – or rather, would have had to act – in exactly the same way, because this action was precisely so and not otherwise in the plan of the world-governing Being, and in every moment of my activity I am completely dependent upon that Being's will, without any intermediate grounds. So if, according to pure equilibrism, the subject *happens upon* the action, and if, according to determinism, the subject *is brought to* the action, then according to fatalism, the subject is unalterably determined to the action.

Equilibrism's Kind of Fatalism Contradicts Moral Accountability

I believe this discussion makes it quite clear that if the equilibrists have sometimes charged determinism with being fundamentally one and the same with fatalism, they could be referring only to that fatalism, improperly so called, which they attribute to the materialist. (The doctrine of the pantheists comes somewhat closer to the doctrine we are now considering, but because of differences [323] in its grounds and points of view, it does not belong here; the two doctrines are similar in content but wholly different in form.) That is, the contradiction between fatalism and the determinism we have considered here is too clear to require serious review. The most essential difference we can conceive here is whether I say "I could not at this moment act otherwise, because I have previously acted and thought and sensed in such and such a way," or whether I say "I cannot at this moment act otherwise than I have actually acted, even if I had previously acted and thought and sensed in a wholly different way."

It is also clear that fatalism in itself includes no complete opinion concerning our controversial question, in that it declares only the relation between actions and the world's Sovereign, but not between actions and the characteristics of the subject. With respect to the latter, fatalism always pre-supposes the answer equilibrism has given and is thus its complement. Yet, although this is true, it is clear from the history of philosophy that equilibrism has never accepted this complementarity but has rather disputed fatalists with the greatest fervor, so that to justify its zeal in opposing other parties, it has customarily reproached them for serving under fatalism's banner. The cause of this conduct is easy to explain. In relation to other parties, fatalism is one of those all-too-obliging friends who in order to spare us some small embarrassment uncover our most hidden secrets, thus becoming a far greater danger to us than that from which they would have rescued us. Thus in the course of showing how indifferentism could be united with the ideas of spec-ulative theology, fatalism proves that indifferentism was incompatible not only with the ideas of practical theology, which it really wished to maintain intact, but also with the moral ideas upon which practical theology was based.

Indifferentism, in matters pertaining to its distinct ideas, contented itself with denying all relations between a subject's actions and the subject itself so far as it is thought of in some state. Whenever someone asked about this, indifferentism thus avoided the categorical answer to which, as we have seen above, it always had to return, namely that there is no such relation and that action does not belong to the subject at all. Fatalism opened a new way of understanding this matter. Equilibrism left me ignorant of the extent to which action belongs to me. Fatalism added that action was necessary on account of the commanding will of a Being of infinite efficacy. That in myself which might oppose an action, without my even knowing it, [324] can thus be overthrown in a moment by the power of this will. This Being's will is thus at every moment the natural law of my actions, and it is not possible to comply with the moral law except by accidental agreement.

It is important to note that this impossibility lies not in my individual sit-uation but in my character as a human being – indeed, in my character as a spiritual being[165]. This is so in that this fatality of my actions follows imme-diately from the freedom that equilibrism assures me precisely because I am a spiritual being. Even assuming that all my actions were most virtuous and in complete accord with ethical law, I am not on this account moral. I cannot make the judgment of actions into a judgment of myself, for despite all my subjective incapability, the actions would be coerced from without.

Furthermore, if every individual action had remained the same, even if all preceding actions and sensations (assuming that they had seemed able to contribute something) had been otherwise, still this contradiction means that

---

165. **Ein geistiges Wesen.**

whenever we wish to precipitate a judgment concerning our worth out of an observation of some particular action, we shall do better to precipitate it out of what taken all together we call disposition, since we do not tie our view of that so strictly to our system, than out of the action, which can be posited as contradicting dispositions. If we observe this procedure with every action considered individually, then little by little every action is excluded from the right to help determine a judgment of my worth, and no such judgment takes place at all.

This presupposition that we are not brought to actions by dispositions causing them but are determined to actions independent of disposition's outcome, utterly negates convictions concerning obligation to moral law and the possibility of accountability for our acts of choice. It also validates the experience of all who wish to excuse themselves from important moral transgressions. Far from acknowledging the necessity of determinism – for they probably feel that their conscience would only accuse them even more vigorously – they will always turn to fatalism for their sophistry. Indeed, as to the superstition among uncultivated peoples, and also among our own lower classes, about possession by evil spirits: what does it contain but fatalism – actions brought about from outside, cut off from the interconnectedness of the subject's states – except that here freedom from obligation to the law and from accountability is not the result but the origin of the theory, and that here people shrink from attributing to the Supreme Being the unconquerable coercion by which they shield themselves.

When our [325] greatest romantic and dramatic poets portray full-blown villains reflecting on the grounds and occasions of their actions, fatalism always manifests itself. That is quite natural, for the villains view themselves as instruments of heaven determined to work out these events: their dispositions are something quite independent and thus not the cause of what now disturbs them, of what they must have done in any case. And so, luckily, the moral law finally disappears entirely from their view.

More Recent Systems of Ethics

I hope that this discussion will have reached at least the one part of its goal, namely to show how these erroneous opinions could arise and could have been so widely propagated after the correctly defined concept of necessity was found. With regard to the other point that was intended, however, it is not yet clear enough why the proponents of determinism, convinced of its theoretical rightness, were not able to discover why they could not derive from their theory complete victory in the practical realm. Along this path, moreover, we must discover the contradictions responsible for this failure and must undertake a survey of the practical ideas we have received only recently from a completely different source.[166]

Theoretical Reason Gives Rise to the Ethical Systems of Happiness and Perfection

Yet, perhaps this can be done somewhat more clearly. Those for whom an interest in religion at least outweighed an interest in speculation were incapable of making this discovery; those for whom the interest in speculation outweighed that in religion saw that the practical law had to acquire its obligation from somewhere other than revelation or the idea of the divine will in general. They therefore undertook to bring about a real reformation of practical ideas. For this purpose they commissioned reason to draw up a law, or to seek one already in existence, and to sanction it in such a way that it did not need to borrow obligation from a being outside themselves. The way this commission is put (and indeed this content was that to which the newly-discovered contradiction first had to bring reason) shows already that reason was not thereby declared the absolute sovereign of everything else, that the basis of obligation was supposed to lie not in reason alone but in the whole subject *human being*. Since none of the other human faculties was named as particularly [326] favored, reason settled upon the only universal, namely consciousness.

Reason could not act freely of itself in consciousness but had to accommodate itself as practical reason to some particular result theoretical reason had achieved in accord with that disputed principle, the causality of actions. Thus, instead of proving itself as a faculty of laws and giving a law with obligation grounded purely in the existence of this kind of reason, here too reason in its practical activity, at least, was only a faculty for comprehending the interconnection of things according to principles. Moreover, it gave only a law the obligation of which rested upon the interest of consciousness, and the systematic correctness of that law was supposed to be proved from that acknowledged interconnection of things and from the determinate *consequences* of each action of the heart and mind.

---

166. Meckenstock note (KGA): "An allusion to Kant, *Kritik der praktischen Vernunft*, Riga 1788."

Reason could not stop here, however. A double consciousness presented itself to reason, representing a differentiated interest, with each side claiming activity of its own in the form of lawgiving, even if the two should agree about the content of the laws: namely, consciousness of the characteristics of particular successive impressions upon receptivity and consciousness arising from consideration of relations among the powers and faculties of the soul, given rise to by every kind of subordination of inclinations and sentiments. So this double consciousness was divided into the systems of happiness and of perfection[167], and the quite natural subordination of practical, law-giving reason to theoretical reason that was occasioned by this state of affairs impeded the proper course of the moral reform that was in progress.

Divided consciousness could have been happy in this state had it been able to ascribe true worth to feeling, which declared consciousness right or wrong in itself, without first investigating the consequences of actions as would have had to occur according to the system of divided consciousness. If consciousness had known that another law lay at the basis of feeling, regarded as a law of reason different from its own law, it would still have been able to find a narrow path that in the end would have brought it to the true practical philosophy. However, the arguments over moral sense had already taken another direction. The question was not whether a law lay at the basis of feeling. Rather everyone was [327] occupied with clarifying whether this feeling ought not to be placed at the basis of the entire ethical law.

Theoretical Misunderstandings Damage The Case for Practical Determinism

This unfruitful result dealt something of a blow to determinism itself. True, most of the equilibrists' objections to determinism, concerning its union with the moral systems of happiness and perfection, were merely misunderstandings. For example, when the determinists say that we have the faculty of acting according to such laws as reason has acknowledged and name this faculty freedom, they are not saying that we are compelled to act according to these laws; when they explain reason as the faculty of comprehending the necessary interconnection of things, it does follow that reason cannot choose to alter anything in the laws it has acknowledged to be in accord with this interconnection; but it does not by any means follow that

---

167. **Die Systeme der Glückseligkeit und der Vollkommenheit.**

the will is wholly altered by this interconnection – on the contrary, the will's neutrality between claims of sensibility and claims of reason is affirmed. Still, the bad consequences that followed from these misunderstandings are important.

First, the obligation of this law, since it related to a theoretical and indeed wholly subjective idea, had no general necessity, and yet one was clearly conscious that necessity unavoidably belongs here. This always gave equilibrism opportunity for new attacks. Second, there had been a mistake of which we have already spoken once,[168] and which was actually difficult to avoid so long as practical reason was not purer and the law was not derived merely from it but was adapted to other ideas. That is, it was supposed that one had no impulse that related purely to the realization of the law (since moral sense was not a motivating but was rather a judging feeling); rather, in every case one confused predilection for realizing the law with predilection for the object in itself toward which the law commanded one to strive in each particular instance.

Of course, such a consummate force could in any case repel impulses opposed to the command. However, the force itself, if it encountered no external opposition, could also either exceed the law in strength or fall short of it. Moreover, one could not say that the force should have been exactly conformed to the law. The reason is that in general the law cannot determine in advance the strength with which every object of impulse may be desired in every possible case. That cannot happen until the particular object [328] shall have been given, not only conceptually but also individually, so that all its consequences could be considered.

For these reasons, the human soul has never had a means, even in itself, for producing the restriction necessary for every particular case. Yet, according to all of our previous propositions, this is required if we are to be able to think that in every case the law would be fulfilled for its own sake. Here, then, one would always have had to make modifications of accountability and seek loopholes. Moreover, determinism could not reject the reproof that it falsified the concept of accountability, and this evil could not be removed until one attributed to the law a feeling that related to the law alone.

Now one could reply that I myself have already established[169] that this feeling is conceivable with every law, and thus that this way out could easily have been found. This is true insofar as we think of the law purely in itself.

---

168. See pp. 17-18.
169. See p. 18.

If it is conceived falsely, however – if it still needs verification outside itself, so that to a certain extent its content contradicts the form it should have – then it can well be that the existence of this feeling, which follows from the form of practical law, likewise contradicts the verification upon which that law's content rests. This is clearly the case with happiness. The law at the basis of this system usually reads as follows: act in such a way that you keep in mind not only the impressions of the moment but also the perceived satisfaction of anticipated impressions in general. This law, furthermore, receives its verification from the supposedly inevitable pursuit of the most pleasurable state.

Now if one assumes a feeling that is not merely judging but also motivating – the only kind of feeling that relates to this law – and if one supposes that we always act in accordance with this feeling, then only two ways exist (for the law's form and content here are too different not to be separated in reflection). Either one has considered feeling to be dependent upon the law purely through content, and then there occurred the confusion between impulse for the law and impulse for the current, accidental object of the law, or one has regarded feeling to be dependent upon the law through form, and then a person seemed to act not for the sake of the satisfaction of impressions in general, according to the system, but rather always for the sake of a particular impression, namely the impression of the feeling for the law – and what is more, for the sake of an impression that [329] was not even included in the sum of the other impressions.

The case is the same with regard to perfection, where one has appeared to act not for the sake of harmonious relations among all the soul's powers, but rather from a despotic predominance of one power over all others, namely the power of the lawful will. Hence one preferred to regard the feeling for form, the existence of which one could not deny as a feeling, either natural or acquired, as a feeling in the presence of the law. One also sought to show that according to the system it was erroneous to include the feeling among those inclinations that could through regulation be brought into harmony and satisfaction. [330]

Part IV

ON THE DISTINCTIVE USAGE
OF SEVERAL TECHNICAL TERMS IN THIS DOCTRINE

Introduction: The Importance and Difficulties
Of Clear Definition

When the author looks over the path he has traveled with his readers thus far, he sees that he has done all within his power to develop and, from his perspective, to evaluate the systems opposed to his opinion and the objections derived from these systems and their wider implications. That is by no means all that is incumbent on him to do, however, if he wishes to reach his goal: to clear the way of everything that might hinder the reader and to render his opinion so familiar that the reader will be able to view from every side whatever is commendable in it. Specifically, a great multitude of particular ideas remain that appear to belong to the realm of this question. Even though they are for the most part to be derived from one or the other of those opposing systems, or even if they are to be thought of as general ideas apart from them, they are represented in completely different ways in each case, and most readers will here and there reflect on and search out how they are supposed to connect these concepts with the opinion they are being asked to accept. They may encounter no small difficulties merely in finding the point of view from which the majority of these ideas join with this opinion or can even be properly compared with it.

All of these concepts will hinge upon various applications of the word freedom and other associated words. The author acknowledges his duty to offer readers help, not only by presenting these concepts in a definite order but also by indicating the point of view from which their relation to his opinion can best be viewed and evaluated. Indeed, he thinks himself all the more obliged since he admits that in his own investigation he has very assiduously avoided these words, or at least their variant, irregular, and singular meanings, and has thus prevented the combining of these ideas with his opinion, so far as this depended on him.

The title of Part IV will sufficiently inform the reader of the sort of course the author plans to follow. He expects no general approbation, however. On the one hand, only a narrow view of the general history of philosophical concepts is required to know the kind of influence linguistic usage universally exercises over [331] the cultivation and association of ideas, to know how frequently modification of meaning in a word's usage produces gradual and even unnoticed alterations in ideas based upon completely different usages of that word, and how necessary therefore clear definitions of words[170] are, indicating the various relations of concepts in order to understand oneself and deliver oneself fortunately out of an issue.

On the other hand, it is unfortunately a very well known objection against philosophers who assert something distinctive, that definitions of words are precisely the means they use – partly in an insidious way, partly deceived in their development of ideas – in order to elude difficulties they ought to admit.[171] Therein they attribute different meanings to words that signify the ideas of others and then know how to prove that the contradiction between the defined idea and their proposed system is only apparent, or that not only a contradiction between the idea and their system but also a contradiction of the idea with itself or with others of the same kind are equally likely propositions.

This common objection has never been urged more strongly than in our day, and in our day never more forcibly than against this doctrine, and among all the parties contending over this doctrine, never more pretentiously than against the determinists. With respect to the greatest number of his readers, therefore, what expectations can the author have except unfavorable ones concerning the way he wishes to conduct this part of the inquiry? That is, he does not trust himself enough to be convinced that the good opinion that his readers might thus far have formed of his sincere will and calm understanding can be great and stable enough to remove all suspicion in this regard, and he therefore wishes that the explanation he now offers them may at least contribute something toward this end.

Given the great difference among nuances, themselves often wavering, which the sense associated with these words evokes in the individual mode of representation of each person; given the infrequency with which people clearly develop these ideas of such familiar usage in terms of their content; and given the difference between what people really think in that process and what they presuppose as having been thought on the basis of the conclusion they draw from what they think – a difference that often arises from this lack of development, a difference we usually call by the sanguine word inconsistency[172]: in light of all this, it is of course impossible that the author's

---

170. **Andeutende Worterklärungen.**
171. Ed. note: Reading from the Ms. "**einräumen**" instead of the KGA's "**[Unsichere Lesart].**"
172. **Inkonsequenz.**

definitions should contain in precise detail what [332] each individual person thinks in that process, or would like to have thought. This is not his intention, however, and he does not wish to persuade anyone that this will happen. He will by no means counterfeit a proof that this one concept among all those commonly accepted is the only correct one that corresponds to the composition or history of the word. He never wishes to utilize anything from his declared concept to stipulate whatever concepts his readers may have. Rather, he begins with these words simply because in this way he will most easily arrive at a concept concerning at least the features and compass of which his readers will be in agreement with him. He will then show how this concept relates to his ideas developed above, leaving it to his readers to assay whether this concept is their own. Once they are *clearly* aware of the difference, they can then make for themselves the relative application concerning what has been said regarding his ideas.

Section 1. Preliminary Presentation Of a General Definition For Every Use of the Word Freedom

If we wish our inquiry to investigate the word and to trace all of its various states, as it were, then we must necessarily begin with a state we can consider as original to all subsequent states, with a meaning[173] that is basic to all others and can be found reflected in them. Yet, given the great abundance of various applications to totally different objects that this word must satisfy, such an undertaking might seem almost impossible. Readers will little wonder, therefore, if we ask them to make a few restrictions in the claims they think to make on us in light of this chapter's title.

On the Relation Between Technical and Common Meanings Of the Word Freedom

If our word had remained a purely technical term[174] in speculative philosophy, our task would have been far easier and we could justifiably be held to the strict standard of sufficiency. If the word then had to be related to several objects, we would accept the relation as correct only insofar as it was

---

173. **Bedeutung.**
174. **Kunstwort.**

allowed by the rule under which the relation had been made. Moreover, if the word took on various determinations[175] in various systems, the character of the system would very easily reveal what sort of determinations it necessarily [333] had to exclude from the original concept, and what sort of new determinations it could have given in their place.

Yet, it is far from the case that our word has remained within these limits. On the contrary: it is in everyone's mouth. It has had its meaning chiseled and daubed by almost every author of popular philosophy. Also, in that it has passed over into the most ordinary usage of common life[176], it suffers under the arbitrary train of thoughts in everyone's fantasy and must daily allow itself to be joined with wholly alien matters and to be translated into widely distant spheres. Such being the case, it may be supposed in advance, even apart from all knowledge of the matter, that in so many hands, almost always damaging, the word may have taken on various meanings permitted neither by its relation to the analogy of language nor by its connection with its originating first concept. One would therefore want to demand that the concept we believe to lie at the basis, let its compass be as small as it may, should nevertheless be so deftly and from all sides so accurately tailored that we may affirm both that all other concepts would have to have arisen from a logically correct application of this basic concept to some definite object and that we would be in a position to demonstrate the method of this derivation.

Yet, this much is certain: as many various modifications as philosophers have made of this word, still every concept that they impute to it, along with others so designated previously, must have in common some principal feature[177] that justifies attaching the same word to this concept. As arbitrary as the train of thoughts of a mere reasoning human being may be, still no absolute leap can be thought of here; and as often as people have made a new application of this word to some object, still they must have perceived some relation between this object and the idea – perhaps indeterminate – that they usually connect with this word; and often, at least,[178] they must be aware that the idea has arisen out of many ordinary applications of the word.

---

175. **Verschiedene Bestimmungen.** Ed. note: The reference is to various aspects of definition.
176. **In den gewöhnlichsten Gebrauch des gemeinen Lebens.**
177. **Hauptmerkmal.**
178. Ed. note: Reading from the Ms. "wenigstens oft" instead of the KGA's "wenigstens deßen."

Search for a Generic Definition of Freedom, Guided by the Concept "Absence of Constraint"

Thus there must be a first concept that is at least the general guide to all the rest, and it must be possible to find it, even if this should be possible only by gathering all of these common features and comparing them with one another. Yet, this first concept remains only a guide, and it can very well happen that several of these concepts may be viewed as derivative from the illusion we have mentioned, rather than from this guiding concept, or that the influence of another concept must be presupposed, through which certain determinations have been imparted to it. In both cases we must be careful not to take the correctness [334] or incorrectness of the derivation as the measure of the truth or falsity of the derived concept itself. At most the derivation would show only that one has falsely judged some of the concept's relations with other concepts, or that one should not have designated the concept with this word – all of which can occur without detriment to the concept's inner truth and correctness, which must be tested by quite different measures. By itself the correctness of this first concept could not even be ground for a judgment concerning the correctness of all the consequent concepts, in such a way that they would stand or fall with it. It is quite possible that the first idea might be indistinctly or incorrectly formulated but then gain in distinctness and truth through its connection with various others.

Our intention is to descend from this first concept, once we have found it, to the others, grounding our discussion of them in that concept. It would thus redouble our distance along a very difficult journey if we had to make our way analytically, step by step, through all of these derived concepts in order to collect the features that we could gather into the first concept. It would therefore be desirable if we could shorten this task in some way. For this reason we prefer to content ourselves with a single, albeit indeterminate feature which occurs to us as something common enough to all and which will be conceded by everyone. Perhaps it will give us opportunity to attain an adequate concept.

At the basis of every concept of freedom always lies the absence of constraint[179] – either by what has preceded in time, if the object is thought of as given in time, or by what has been previously conceptualized, insofar as the object is represented outside all temporal relations. Now of these two kinds of objects to which this defining feature of the concept can be applied, there is no doubt which is to be regarded as original and which as derivative with

---

179. Die Abwesenheit einer Nöthigung.

respect to the concept of freedom. Kantian philosophy,[180] which specifies that the idea of necessity is grounded in pure understanding, posits that idea in relation to the conditions of sensibility in such a way that no other application is wholly justified except to objects of this knowledge (and a wholly justified application of the idea must have preceded before another idea is allowed the same name on the basis of similarity). Not only that; Kantian philosophy also teaches that sensible perception [335] of the objects commensurate with this idea of necessity must precede in order to bring the idea to consciousness. Even the opponents of this philosophy maintain that all ideas of necessity – whether true or merely apparent – always arise only from appearances joined to perception.

We must therefore seek our concept at the point where freedom is applied to things that occur and, indisputably, among these things, at the point where the defining feature from which we have begun is most universally asserted, without any special application to particular kinds of objects, insofar as possible; for such an application must necessarily lead, if not to limitations that completely alter the principal concept, then at least to more constricted determinations that may enlarge the concept's content but will thereby narrow its range and, through alien additions in any event, render it unfit to be used as a universal generic concept[181].

Kant's "Transcendental Freedom" Provides A Starting Point for Definition

Nothing is conceivably more general than the case where freedom is predicated of something purely insofar as it happens, without any regard for its distinctive character or for its relationships[182]. Now this is exactly what Kant calls transcendental freedom,[183] and if we accordingly wish to advance from the indeterminate defining feature that has brought us thus far – mere absence of constraint – to a proper definition, then we are completely relieved of the burden of composing one, as we need only to adopt the elucidation of this transcendental freedom that Kant has given us. As is well

---

180. Meckenstock note (KGA): "Cf. Kant: KrV B 266f; Ak 3,186,4-24 and B 279f; Ak 3,193,25-194,20."
181. Als allgemeiner Gattungsbegriff.
182. Auf seine eigenthümliche Beschaffenheit und auf seine Verhältnisse.
183. Meckenstock note (KGA): "Cf. Kant: KrV B 561f; Ak 3,363,8-364,16."

known, it reads as follows: "transcendental freedom is the faculty of initiating a series of events."

Yet, by the nature of the case we must first make a few restrictions, for transcendental freedom is itself only a special kind of freedom. Now the concept regarding some particular kind must always include certain features not found in the generic concept, and in a definition of that particular kind these features must be presented in such a way as to exclude the characteristic features of all other kinds. If, therefore, we have acted correctly in turning particularly to this kind because here the concept is purest and is present in its greatest range, then we cannot take the explanation chosen by the philosopher as a definition of this kind of freedom to be an explanation of the generic concept without first trimming away the features that determine the concept in such a way that what designates [336] this particular kind is coposited and all other kinds are excluded.

In this relation, the first question would be this: whether the generic concept of freedom always entails initiation of a series of events. For the kind of freedom thus defined, this is obvious: if I consider something purely as effective and effected in time, then I regard it in its relationship to the universal causal interconnection in which, together with its causes *a parte ante* and its effects *a parte post*, it constitutes a series. But will that be the case with all other kinds of freedom as well? In general, whenever a question arises concerning whether some object should be denied a certain predicate, then the object should at least be observed in such a circumstance or in such relationships as have given rise to the idea of this predicate as applicable. Thus if freedom always entails negation of constraint and if the different kinds of freedom differ only as to the kinds of constraint involved, if therefore the question should arise whether an object is free with respect to one of these kinds of constraint, then something in that object must have given me occasion to investigate its relationship to this particular kind of constraint.

Now this can have happened in a twofold way. First, I saw that the object itself brought forth something through this kind of constraint, though even this will not have occasioned my asking whether the object was also brought about by this constraint if I regard the constraint here as only accidental. Indeed, an accidental constraint could well seem to be a contradiction. It is not, however, and I believe that an example will suffice to clarify what I mean. In the course of solving a complex calculation consisting of many different terms, it can happen that some number is multiplied by another to yield a product. There is constraint here: the product had to arise necessarily from the connection between the two factors. Yet with respect to these two numbers – the product and the first factor – the constraint is only accidental; it pertains not at all to the relation in which these two numbers stand according to their synthesis[184] but only to the relation in which both stand to a third relation, quite foreign to them, namely the idea of the calculation. Thus the constraint is for them only accidental, as they are also accidental for the idea of calculation in which the constraint was grounded. This is also why I proceed in my calculating in terms of this operation, and it never occurs to me to ask whether the first factor of this product has likewise arisen through the same constraint, through the multiplication of some [337] other number with the second factor. This question arises only if I regard this second factor as an exponent and thus regard the constraint it entails as law, and forthwith I think of both numbers – the first factor and the product – as members of a series.

So also when the question of an object's freedom arises from observation of its effectiveness. This will not happen if I think of this effectiveness as functioning according to its relation to some wholly foreign idea and as accidental for such objects. It will happen only if I define that function in such a way that I must think of it as a law for the objects' individuality. As soon as I think of constraint as a law, however, I must think of the things determined by it in a series. Now the law knows no limits in its progressive application, and thus the series is infinite – unless the series is very short, the law being limited by the idea that defines its completion.

This brings us to the second way the question concerning an object's freedom can arise, namely, when something contained in the pure concept itself makes us think of a determinate constraint. This happens because that too can be the case only when we think of the object's effectiveness according to a certain idea. This effectiveness then requires its own law, and that law requires a corresponding series of necessary effects until it has achieved satisfaction for its idea.

Excluding Kant's Phrase "From Itself" Yields the Desired Definition

Thus the generic concept of freedom must always include relation to a series. It is almost self-evident that the issue cannot be mere existence within the series but is rather that of a beginning in the series. If the member of the series of which freedom is to be predicated can likewise be thought of as produced from a preceding member through the law of the series, then for that member no one can assert the absence of precisely this constraint. So

---

184. **Synthesis.**

nothing that remains in our definition could contain the determination establishing the character of this kind of freedom to the exclusion of all others, thus making the explanation unfit for the generic concept, except the expression that the object of freedom must initiate the series *from itself*.[185]

This expression is not sufficiently clear and requires closer analysis of its meaning. The meaning is not difficult to find insofar as it relates to transcendental freedom, since here objects are regarded purely without respect to their special characteristics. To the extent that they happen and in turn are effective in time, they can be thought of in no other series than the universal series of causes and effects, and no other idea of constraint can be applied to them [338] except that of the universal causal interconnection. If some of these objects are therefore denied the constraint of this *a parte ante*, they cannot be thought of as subject to any other and thus initiate the series of effects following upon them entirely from themselves – that is, without real interconnection with other appearances *a parte ante*. Now this exclusion of all other kinds of constraint – which are all either grounded in the causal interconnection or are purely idealistic – is transcendental freedom's distinctive characteristic, and this is what must be altered if its explanation is to be used as a generic concept.

Nor is it any longer difficult to determine what aspect of this defining feature can be applied to all kinds of freedom. Freedom's subject was denied that constraint *a parte ante* which grounds the law of the series in which the subject was thought to exist. Naturally, in every other series having a different meaning, being free cannot indicate a complete negation of all interconnection, as is not the point here, but can indicate only a negation of the interconnection of that series. Understood in this more general meaning, this same expression can be retained in an explanation of the generic concept.

We may join the concept of freedom with some object, therefore, in a twofold way. Either we begin to search for the origin of a series and go back until we encounter a member that belongs to the series surely enough, in that the next member follows from it according to the law of the series, but a member that cannot itself be thought of as determined through the law of the series; or we have begun by observing the efficacy of this free member itself, in that the law according to which the member produced the series is evident

---

185. Ed. note: Schleiermacher has not earlier quoted this phrase "from itself," which he here identifies as the distinctively characteristic element of Kant's definition of transcendental freedom, but it is to be found in Kant (KrV B 476; Ak 3,310,16-20). Excluding this phrase leaves Schleiermacher with his desired generic definition of freedom: the faculty of initiating a series of events.

to us, yet we see at the same time that the member itself has not arisen according to this law. In both cases we see that our concept really relates only to the action through which the series is produced, for only this action is the first member of the series, in that the entire series never arises from subjects but only from alterations of subjects. We transfer the concept of freedom from the action to the subject of the free action only indirectly, namely, when we think of the subject's faculty for performing several such free actions. And so Kant has expressed it in his definition.

Threefold Plan for the Remainder of the Treatise

Before we go on to show how this definition can actually be applied to the various kinds of freedom, it will be necessary to classify these kinds somewhat so that we can [339] proceed with a certain degree of order. Since we have to do only with human beings here, we exclude from our discussion all those meanings of freedom not relating to humans. However, in the course of our several justifications, we shall touch upon all the meanings that do pertain to human beings, even if they would not directly relate to our principal question, so as to verify the correctness and fruitfulness of our definition even with those meanings.

Now either this freedom is known in human actions as grounded in their individuality – that is, is seen in those determinations or kinds not relating[186] to anything in the concept of the acting subject – and then this freedom is immediately related to the actions only and is transferred to the subject only insofar as the actions with all their characteristics belong to the subject. Or freedom of action relates, according to its kind, in part to the *situation* of the subject – that is, to the outer conditions[187] of the possibility of certain actions, to the subject's relations to other things that restrict or advance certain of the subject's powers as to the degree and direction of their expression according to a rule – and in part to a *faculty* of the subject – to the inner conditions of the possibility of certain actions with respect to the subject's functions. In these two cases freedom relates immediately to this situation and to this faculty, and it is only indirectly transferred to the actions, insofar as they belong to the situation and faculty. We must therefore deal with a threefold relationship of our concept: namely, with freedom as a predicate of

---

186. Ed. note: Reading from the Ms. "**welche sich**" instead of the KGA's "**welche sie.**"
187. **Bedingungen**

human actions[188], with freedom as a predicate of human situations[189], and with freedom as a predicate of human faculties[190].

Section 2. Concerning Freedom As a Predicate of Human Actions

Three Kinds of Freedom As a Predicate of Actions

Since the concept of freedom relates directly and properly only to actions, despite the fact that linguistic usage has made the distinction that we too have accepted, we shall begin with the kind of freedom for which we least need to go beyond this concept [340] and for which the actions under consideration must least be determined by something else. Even in this kind of freedom there is still an essential distinction which ought not to be ignored, since it designates two quite different types constituting the content of this kind. Either the law, to which the free action is not supposed to be subordinate, is discovered purely from the concept of an action in general; or it can be known only from certain individual determinations, which, since they are supposed to be characteristic of a particular type, have to be subsumable under a concept but are no longer the concept of mere action, since they add something to that concept through which certain other actions must be excluded.

In the first of these cases this law can be none other than the general law of all that occurs, namely, the law of causality[191], for in the pure concept of action nothing is posited except an effect of one subject upon another. However, since initiation of the effect necessarily presupposes a change in an enduring subject, it is itself an occurrence, albeit related to the subject in a preeminent way. The series we represent through this law as including the action can only be thought of as infinite, since we can think of no change that would not in turn be the cause of another change.

In the other case, individual determinations of the actions *in concreto* upon which the formula of a law is grounded can be either real or ideal. If they are real, they relate to the various ways something occurs (for a real dis-

---

188. **Handlungen.**
189. **Zustände.**
190. **Vermögen.**
191. **Causalität.**

tinction concerning changeable subjects made from some point of view other than this one – that is, other than from the subjects' relation to various kinds of occurrences – would be altogether unsuitable for deriving such a law, unless we should wish to jump ahead to the other two kinds of concept that are to follow). Moreover, the series represented through such a law must then be thought of as undetermined and yet certainly as arbitrarily bounded somewhere – namely, by its termination in a subject who no longer permits this kind of occurrence and, according to this law, cannot either be changed or produce change. If the individual determinations are ideal, they are based upon a certain definite way of thinking about the interconnection of occurrences. Further, since this way of thinking must in turn rest upon an idea, the series [341] represented along with such a law must also be regarded as finite and as terminated in this idea, in that what occurs no longer belongs to that series once the idea of this interconnection is satisfied. In the meantime, these determinations result from the various formulas of the laws that are possible for this kind of freedom, and it will be easy to delineate the types included if we now bring our general explanation of freedom to bear on these determinations.

Freedom As a Predicate of Action in General

Applying the Generic Concept of Freedom to Action in General Leads Back to Equilibrism

If we apply the preceding explanation to the law of actions in general or to the law of causality, specifically with the restriction that the absence of that law *a parte ante* is to apply to all actions of human subjects (for this restriction in itself by no means carries us into the realm of the third or fourth sections below, since the idea of this kind of freedom is not derived from the concept of the subject or from special determinations of the subject's particular features, nor is the legitimacy of this idea's application documented from the concept of the subject, but rather the concept of the subject merely serves to define the perimeter of this kind of freedom), then we have the *equilibristic concept of freedom*. By this we mean that we take human actions in general and considered in a series of events, with respect to the law of this series of occurrences, to be free. Accordingly, *in progressu* these actions produce changes according to the law of the series and thus belong to the series; but *in regressu* they have not themselves been produced by any temporally prior change according to the law of the series. Since nothing in its series can precede it, each action therefore initiates such a series absolutely.

All of this account agrees quite precisely with our earlier explanation of the equilibristic idea of freedom. That is, since that idea ensures the human faculty of acting without dependence upon anything temporally prior for the determination of its causality, it regards human actions in general in this same way, without more particular determination of their relation to temporal necessity or to the law of all occurrences. Moreover, the equilibristic idea asserts this relation with full respect for the subject's distinctive character as an exception to the rule, though it otherwise acknowledges the universality of this law. It therefore thinks of every action in itself as part of a series in itself determined by this law and infinite, also predicating of human actions that they do not originate according to the law of this series, and it must therefore add that each of them initiates such a series from itself.

Since [342] it has been said from the outset that this type of freedom contains the defining character of the entire concept in a preeminent way, and since the general explanation is to a certain extent taken from an explanation of this particular kind, I would not be able to bring up the harmony that exists between the usual concept and the application of the general explanation in this example as something very important in proving the general appropriateness of this general explanation. Still, there enters into the picture a circumstance peculiar to this case which speaks to its advantage even here, a circumstance that I cannot neglect to bring to the reader's attention. Namely, it is clear that our explanation very definitely gives a *place* for this concept, but if we follow the issue just a bit further we can see from the same explanation that this place must necessarily be completely empty of content. I remind once again that I do not want to go against my promise and use my explanation to prove something against the concepts to which I have adapted it (not even after its harmony with the customary concept is shown). I do not pursue this circumstance to damage the equilibristic concept. I am convinced that its nullity has already been shown clearly enough above[192] and shall content myself with that. Rather, I pursue this circumstance solely to benefit my explanation, which by itself could have brought us to what we have recognized on other grounds.

---

192. See pp. 98-109.

The Equilibristic Idea of Freedom Is Shown to Be Self-Negating

The issue at hand has the following structure. We could simply say that in the law by which we here conceive of a series there is no basis for thinking of the series as limited. However, the idea of freedom, which is really supposed to have an influence upon only the beginning of the series, entails that one could also think of an end to the series and of the entire series as limited. The reason is that if every human action can be thought of only as the beginning of such a series, then no action can be a middle member in the series, and the series must terminate as soon as a member's action encounters a subject, who is an exception to the law's rule. It thus appears that the concept of freedom here annuls something that does not really lie within its power, since the finitude or infinitude of a series must depend solely upon the law that determines it. It also appears that henceforth no law at all can exist for that which occurs, since its efficacy in every possible function may be thought of as interrupted.

This contradiction [343] is more apparent than real, however, since it rests merely upon the fact that we had previously formed too extensive an idea of the law's universality, without respect to the concept of freedom. Had it occurred to us only that some type of subject could well be an exception, then we would immediately have thought of the series as limitable. Yet, this must be added: it appears that the exceptions would be at least as numerous as the rule, and the rule would thus be completely lost. So this says something further against the concept, but at least it cannot be charged to our explanation.

The advantage of our explanation, however, is the following. Humanity includes not just one subject but many individual subjects. Thus, if restriction of the law is granted, no series is thinkable that would include those actions relating one of these individuals to another, and that is a great many actions. What is more, before an action of one person upon another can occur, a multitude of purely internal actions have preceded which accordingly lie outside of any series[193] because they are not included under the law of all that occurs. This meaning of freedom, then, does not apply to any of these actions included in no series – not as a first, middle or final member – because belonging to a series is an essential feature in the definition of freedom.

---

193. Ed. note: Reading from the Ms. "**die also Handlungen aus gar keiner Reihe sind**" instead of the KGA's "**die also als Handlungen aus gar keiner Reihe sind.**"

Here, therefore, our definition reveals that this kind of freedom negates itself in that it fulfills nothing of what it promised, since most human actions, all of which ought to be included, abnegate its realm altogether. This is a genuine self-contradiction in the idea, revealed by our explanation without any outside assistance. One might wish to rescue this contradiction as we rescued the one above, saying that we must make another restriction and include under the idea only those actions relating to another subject and thus belonging to a series, albeit a limited and truncated one. By this means, however, one would destroy the entire purpose for which this idea is constructed – as anyone can be convinced who remembers what has been said about this in earlier sections. Not only that: one would no longer have the same kind of freedom but would rather have quite a different concept, and human actions as actions could no longer be the issue (because in order to justify their relationships *a parte ante*, one must classify them according to their relationships *a parte post* [344] and according to the subjects to which they relate in this respect). One would therefore have to express the law in such a way as to justify and indicate this restriction, and thus all the concept's defining features would be altered and the issue would no longer be the same.

Freedom of Action in General Applies Only to the Deity As the Undetermined Cause of All Determined Things

In contrast, one might wish to oppose this advantage of our consideration of the issue on the basis of a general explanation, countering that while it had indeed assigned a place to this concept of freedom subsequently found to be empty, it was thus consequently in conflict with itself to a certain degree in that it denied on the one hand what it had granted on the other. This explanation too will serve more to defend our consideration than to constitute a well-grounded complaint against it. It is not at all the same thing that our consideration has granted and denied. It has approved the idea and rejected its object. This would not be called a contradiction even if among all known or knowable things there were none corresponding to our explanation of this idea, for even in this case the idea would be *left empty* but would not be in itself an empty or *nullified* concept. Our consideration is far removed from this assertion, however. It has rejected only the application of the idea of such freedom to a certain subject, namely to human beings, without questioning the possibility of some other more appropriate subject.

Indeed, perhaps from the grounds of the judgment rejecting this application something may be more precisely determined in this connection. Human beings were judged inappropriate subjects of this freedom because (1) there are many individuals of this kind, whose actions in relation to each other are something that occurs, and since the actions occur in human beings this freedom would also have to be predicated of them, yet on the other hand, due to the complete lack of a series of events, those actions lie entirely outside the realm of freedom; and because (2) there have been inner actions within each individual to which this same state of affairs applies. Now if we could find an object for whom this would not be the case, an object for whom (1) its general concept would be exhausted in a single individual and would not allow any others, and for whom (2) no inner action could be conceived, either not at all or not as something that occurs, then a possible application of this idea would be found.

It is clear that the concept of the deity, which whether its reality be known or problematic still has the reality of possibility, has fulfilled all of these conditions and therefore appears to be the true object for this kind of freedom. In [345] such an application the inconvenience from which the apparent contradiction arises that we previously[194] ascertained for its true worth falls away. Even the deity does not perform many actions upon outward things, interrupting a series of occurrences in itself infinite and subject to the law. Rather, we can think in an absolutely natural way of only one action of the deity belonging *a parte post* to the series of occurrences, namely the action through which all occurrences in general began and by virtue of which alone, in a cosmological respect, the concept of the deity as the undetermined cause of all determined things is accepted.

Freedom As a Predicate of Particular Determinate Actions

Freedom As a Predicate of Real Particular Actions: Passage of A Succession of Ideas into a Mechanical Succession of Motion

The second type treated in this section's principal kind of freedom has had this preliminary defining feature: that instead of beginning from the concept of mere action, people have rather restricted this action by certain special determinations, upon which the law of the series was then seen to rest, and thus this law applies to only certain kinds of actions. The basis upon

---

194. See pp. 127-128.

which these kinds of actions can be classified, insofar as it is supposed to be general, can relate either to the ways in which actions occur – that is, to the ways we perceive what occurs – and then I would like to call it *real*, or to the way we think of occurrences in relation and subordination to each other according to some arbitrary ground, and then I would like to call it *ideal*.

The first basis seems to entail two kinds of actions: those we perceive by means of outward and inward sense alike, and those we perceive by means of inward sense alone. The former actions stand under the law of change governing all objects of outward sense, namely the law of motion in time; the latter actions occur according to the law of objects of inward sense, namely the law of succession of ideas in time.

From these two kinds of actions come two different kinds of series and related to these, two subordinate kinds of freedom. That is, when we apply the present idea of freedom to actions defined in this way, we will label as free those actions belonging *a parte post* to a series of changes which are interconnected according to the law of motion but which cannot themselves have proceeded *a parte ante* from another series, according to this law. Now it in no way follows that these actions have arisen according to no law at all, and thus from no preceding changes, for that would again be the sort of equilibristic freedom [346] we rejected above[195] and would also be completely inconsistent with the idea that now concerns us. We leave completely indefinite whether or not the action, as mere action, is generally a middle member of a series and is thus subject to the law in every respect. Rather we say only that the action is free with respect to this law and therefore could only initiate a series that relates to it.

We cannot lack for applicable objects with this idea of freedom, since its true seat is undeniably our own *ego* – the very subject that revealed the first type of freedom to be an empty concept when we tried to apply it there. Here we have nothing of the kind to fear. All outward actions of our soul, all effects of our faculty of causation upon external objects are exemplary advocates of this freedom. When we want to change something in the material world, that cannot happen except by motion. Motion is at our disposal in only the outward organ[196] of our soul. Here again we must not regard all motions relating to the soul's volition *a parte ante* as effects of motion, because we would again arrive at an effective cause of these motions outside our organ, and then the relation of motion to the soul's volition would com-

---

195. See pp. 98-109.
196. **Organ.**

pletely end. Rather we must regard those motions as free from this law, and *a parte ante* as effects according to the law of the succession of ideas.

This view becomes the more necessary when we think of ourselves as moral beings. The reason is that since these outward effects of our soul, possible only through motion, are the only means by which our effects upon others of our species are possible – that is, the only means for exercising our duty – all relation of these actions to the purely inward according to the law of morality would cease if this intermediating series did not originally depend upon those inner actions. Even more clear is the necessity of such freedom for the theoretical unity of our knowledge, and it would be a poor compliment to my readers if I had a mind to work this notion out for the first time.

In *one* world, in a system of appearances and changes, we are absolutely compelled to distinguish these *two* laws, the mechanical law of motion and the psychological law of the succession of ideas (and the diversity of our receptivity[197] itself forces this distinction upon us, if we assume that the persevering ground of the objects of both senses is not essentially diverse). So long as this is the case, this idea of freedom is the only conceivable means for combining the effects of the two laws into a whole, since it provides a kind of passage from one of these laws to the other.

For this reason we find [347] everywhere nothing but confirmations of this idea, and if we trace what takes place from beginning to end, none of the objections to the previous kind of freedom are applicable to this idea, nor does any new objection peculiar to it come to light. The motion of the organ through which a person produces change in the material world is just as we perceive it: not the first free member of the series but only the final stage of the organic motions belonging to this action. If, moreover, we go back to the nerves or whatever else is the first ground and seat of motions in the human body, we must hit upon a first that has not arisen from any earlier, according to the law of motion, but that rather relates to a volition determined by the succession of ideas in the soul. The freedom of which we are speaking properly corresponds then to this first motion.

Interchange of Ideas and Motion As a Complex, Reciprocal Process

Several doubts might arise concerning the extension of the series following upon free action, but these likewise do not work to the detriment of the idea of freedom itself. That is, if we think of this extension as possibly

---

197. **Receptivität.**

limited by the chance intervention of subjects who are subject only to the other law, this does not contradict the formula of the law; rather the law can very well coexist with such limitation, as we have adduced above[198] in the case of general, preliminary determinations. Whether or not this limitation exists depends altogether upon how we conceive the nature of the matter: with greater restriction we have to take it into consideration, with greater generality this is unnecessary. If we consider changes in such a series only *in abstracto*, and think of their effects in turn as isolated from all alien influence, then in such a series an effect can impinge upon a subject who can be active only according to the law of the succession of ideas, and then the series according to the law of motion comes to an end. Likewise with a similarly restricted series governed by the law of the succession of ideas: it may lead to an action upon the body, which then transmits changes only according to the law of motion but terminates the former series. In this sense we can thus say *that series*, according to the diverse laws governing alterations, *interrupt themselves through freedom* and interchange[199] with each other.

This way of thinking strays almost too far from the nature of things, however. [348] Changes exist not abstractly but rather in subjects. These subjects all stand in nearer or more distant reciprocity with each other and thus belong not to one but to many series – indeed, to speak more precisely, to all series proceeding simultaneously. In fact, even their participation in these various series is not something separate. Rather, the changes within them relative to these various series are themselves related to one another through the law of reciprocity and are changed by one another. Thus, a change in some object of outward sense – arising according to the law of motion and regarded solely as a part of the series to which it belongs by virtue of a certain determination – may now effect a change in an object belonging solely to inner sense, and will accordingly terminate the series; yet even so, this same change – by means of some other determination or regarded from some other point of view – will also have an effect upon external objects. Moreover, if we thus consider that change's entire, overall effect as a unity, the series will, according to the law of motion, likewise continue, despite the fact that the other has commenced alongside it. In the same way, if a change in an object of inner sense effects an outward action that then proceeds according to the system of motion, this same change – regarded from

---

198. See p. 125.
199. **Abwechseln.**

another point of view and in another relationship – will always continue to affect the object of inner sense, and the series, according to the law of the succession of ideas, will have to be regarded as continuous, provided that we take all the effects of the change together, as is actually the nature of the case. In this sense we can say that the series, according to both laws of change, continue uninterrupted alongside one another, but *through freedom* reciprocally *intermesh*[200] and are brought into connection.

Thus this appearance of ambiguity – that we are equally justified in regarding series as limited or as infinite – which could have been detrimental to our idea of freedom, portraying it as uncertain, disappears with the conviction that it relates to two clearly distinguishable concepts of series. This distinction could not contribute to the rescue of equilibristic freedom, however, since that idea involves a complete absence of series in general. Indeed, if we consider the conditions under which (as we have already shown)[201] that kind [349] of freedom would be possible, we shall find that the equilibristic idea would have been changed into our own concept. Namely, it would have had to be restricted to those actions related to external objects arising in accordance with the law of the succession of ideas, and initiating a series, according to the law of motion, as its first and free member. Yet, in order to justify this restriction, it would have had to be inserted into the law's formula, and then the issue would not be merely action and its law but rather the law of changes in objects of outward sense and actions related to that law. This need confirms our present concept exactly and makes it quite clear that this is really the principal concept of freedom, as regarded under our first basic classification: freedom as a predicate of action.

Before we leave this kind of freedom, where determinations from the real principle of classification are added to the concept of pure action, we still have to note that this kind has included two subclassifications, of which we have named only one explicitly, since only it really concerned us. Specifically, just as we are justified in calling an action free that arises according to the law of the succession of ideas and initiates a series according to the law of motion, so too we are correct in calling an action free that arises according to the law of motion and initiates a series according to the law of the succession of ideas. To what extent and under what restrictions this latter case may be conceived as possible can be judged from the previous discussion and cannot be further developed here. Insofar as we think of the two kinds of series as

---

200. **Eingreifen.**
201. See pp. 125-126.

mutually interrupting, there must be actions that terminate a series according to the law of motion and at the same time initiate one according to the law of the succession of ideas. Among such actions we may include those linkages that without any apparent connection with[202] their antecedents arise from the influence of an external object and that often seem to initiate in us a completely new series appearing to have nothing at all in common with the series that preceded. Here linguistic usage does not keep pace with actuality, however. Either one makes a leap and on the basis of these representations predicates equilibristic freedom, or one grants validity to none of these representations, on grounds that will perhaps appear below.

Freedom As a Predicate of Ideal Particular Actions: Understanding Initiates a Succession of Appearances by a Rule of Will

We come now to a kind of freedom that is also related immediately to actions but whose concept is supplemented by stipulations suggesting an ideal interconnection among them. We do not at all understand this to mean interconnection [350] as the work of fantasy, however. Acting according to laws peculiar to itself, fantasy constantly connects appearances that in themselves cannot belong together in this manner. Such connection can have no place here, since fantasy does not extend its associations beyond itself, unless through an error of understanding it is presumedly authorized to do so, and thus those series it creates have no existence or meaning outside itself; they consist not even of actual appearances but only of images of appearances. Rather we are speaking only of interconnection provided by the understanding, which here as everywhere demands of nature the realization of its idea and comprehends every connection of appearances only according to such rules as it has conceived for the purpose.

Here this rule should not be taken from the concept of universal nature and its related laws, where whatever in the sensible world that accords with those laws follows from itself. It must be taken from a rule of the will for the nature of its own subject, specifically insofar as that subject is distinct from universal nature and is subject to other laws. Here we find ourselves on the boundary, so to speak, between this kind of freedom and those kinds that can first be developed only in the following two sections. That is, if this rule were

---

202. Ed. note: Reading from the Ms. "**ohne allen scheinbaren Zusammenhang mit den vorhergehenden bei der Einwirkung**" instead of the KGA's "**ohne allen scheinbaren Zusammenhang aus den vorhergehenden Begriffen der Einwirkung.**"

so extensive that it related to the function of some faculty of the soul in general, or at least to some entire state of the subject, then it would not belong here. Our present discussion can deal only with a rule of the will insofar as it is in relation to particular actions and with whatever may be thought of as akin to this rule. On the other hand, this rule and its sphere must be extensive enough for a series to arise from it, upon which we must base the application of our idea of freedom.

Already we see that this idea of freedom cannot relate only to the sum of all ethical actions, because this sum cannot be regarded as a series in which the next member always depends upon the preceding; later we shall provide even more reasons why this relation is prohibited. This kind of freedom, then, has to do with a series of appearances that may be thought of as interconnected only through the realization of a rule of will[203].

Freedom Operative in Every Action, Not Merely at the Beginning Of a Sequence of Actions

It would appear that another significant distinction is to be made here as to whether the realization of this idea of freedom relates to the interconnected appearances as ground or as consequence. In [351] the former case the realization has preceded, and the appearances that are supposed to flow dynamically from it must be thought of as morally dependent upon that idea and therefore must be thought of likewise as actions. This series of actions thus coheres through the law which expresses a conditioned "ought" depending upon that first action of the will; but the series itself is not subject to this law, since the law relates solely to the initial action.

Now it may be that this first action, considered purely in itself, is not known from the moral law but is rather one of those actions whose morality cannot be judged in comparison with other equally possible actions and only as it is determined by our choice will have become the basis of a series of actions to which a definite and generally knowable morality belongs. Or it may be that this first action can be known completely from the moral law – as in accord with it, or, as is also sometimes the case, as opposed to it. In either case, we call the first action *free* with respect to the law, first revealed through that action; those actions that follow according to this law, however, we call *not free*.

---

203. **Mit der Realisirung einer Regel des Willens.**

We often hear these expressions used in this sense. When people have undertaken something, let its morality be what it will, these expressions are applied to all those dubious steps into which they are led but upon which they had not originally reckoned – namely, at the time when they believed they ought not to neglect these steps because of their ethical relation to the first action, the point of entry into this process. We then hear them say that they were truly free at the outset and that with the first step they could have avoided all of these consequences, but they then complain that they are no longer free.

This usage of "free" and "not free" is based on a self-delusion, best exposed by viewing the issue in light of our explanation of freedom. That is, the necessity that orders the members of the series brought forth by the law is none other than the necessity under which the first member also stands, so that in the sense of our explanation we cannot properly say of that first member that it ordains the series. This position becomes quite clear when we reflect that what is morally necessary is in practice never so necessary that we could not omit it, since it becomes actual only if the moral impulse prevails over all other inclinations. Thus these moral consequences – allegedly unavoidable – really become actual only through this psychological necessity resulting from the predominance of one of the competing inclinations. However, the first member stood under this same necessity, whether it was moral [352] or not, for if it was not moral, motivating grounds certainly came into play, both in favor of morality and opposed to it, and a competition of inclinations resulted.

We thus convince ourselves that the ideal interconnection[204] of obligation in the deduction of maxims possesses, at the same time, all the necessity that the real interconnection within the succession of ideas effecting actions does. This conclusion would then entail that the moral impulse, wherever it saw an object before it, would inevitably prevail over other impulses in realizing that object. Accordingly, we often persuade ourselves that actions are justified in which the moral impulse in fact takes no part, though we would like to lay the actions to its charge. Strictly speaking this line of reasoning is completely empty. The reason is that the understanding is in a position to realize the results of its ideal interconnection in the realm of appearances only when it finds among the effects of natural law within its subject data through which its ideas can be executed – thus, only when a real interconnection is present, in step with the ideal interconnection but never against all real interconnection. This interpretation is only apparently correct if the initial action really has no knowable morality, but its basis is still the basis of

---

204. **Der ideale Zusammenhang.**

obligation that renders moral actions morally necessary. Yet, therein there is never any relation to the *actual* actions we have nonetheless required; rather, there is a relation merely to required actions without regard to whether they become actual or not.

Freedom Operative in Every Action, Not Merely in the Choice of Purpose for a Sequence of Actions

Now it remains for us to see whether a better state of affairs exists for the other case, where the realization of volition according to a rule is a consequence of connected changes. In this case the entire series of changes, which is thought to stand connected only by virtue of the idea and through it, precedes the realization of that idea. The idea is thus the final cause of the series, and the series is the effective cause of the idea's realization. With this realization of the idea, the series ceases entirely, just as it began with the first action relating to the idea. This first action we call *free*, because it occurred in relation to a final cause; the other actions, in contrast – insofar as they follow from this first one according to the law of natural necessity, without relating immediately to this final cause – we call not free. These succeeding members of the series, precisely because they lack this relation, will not be within the subject of the first free action, but will rather have been externally effected by the subject.

It is not difficult to discover the great illusion upon which this usage of the words *free* and *not free* is based. Namely, the action that relates immediately to the final cause [353] is incorrectly regarded as the same as an action that initiates a series. If we regard the law of this series simply as that of natural efficient causality, it is incorrect to consider the first member an exception. If by final cause we understand simply the representation of a future object which becomes a motive for action, then it is true that the origin of this motive is other than an efficient cause. However, if something is supposed to become actual through a final cause, then that final cause must operate according to the law of causality concerning all objects of inner sense. Moreover, at this point we thus have two different viewpoints for the same thing, and they must not be confused. The first thing that occurs in immediate relationship to this final cause has occurred just as much according to the law of causality as every subsequent member in the series of means; the necessity of the series is the same as that which we abstracted from the first member.

If one wished to help in this difficulty by giving the law another expression, including the idea of means in its formula, then one would have to go one member farther back and conceive the free action initiating the series not as the first bringing forth of a means but rather as the resolution "to realize the object of the will through a series of means," by which the representation of a future object can for the first time be subsumed under the idea of a final cause. To this extent, moreover, the difference between this first member and the consequent members would be preserved. However, one would also have given the entire subsequent series a false character, since this law in which the idea of the means is included as a part of the formula is no longer suitable for the series and no longer strongly necessitates it.

True, in this idea we think of every means as necessarily producing its goal in the realm of actual appearances, but *in concreto* that is not the case, since through the general interconnection of all series of changes this production is now hindered, now furthered, in a way different from our idea. Nevertheless we usually regard the series as if it were actual through this law and also fully satisfies it, and the misuse promulgated with this idea of freedom in this manner is very extensive. We commonly regard the entire series exactly as it was conceived to achieve its goal, and also as necessarily given through its first action; thus if the universal interconnection of things – given that we failed to take it into consideration – makes some alterations in the series, we regard it as disruptive of the entire series. Indeed, we speak as if the universal interconnection even negated the freedom of the first action, since the efficacy of the law according to which this action [354] was supposed to initiate a series has suffered.

Nor do we exempt the actions of choosing subjects from this necessity of the series – actions that follow the highly complicated law of the succession of ideas and always belong to many series. We deny freedom to actions included in a series of means – even that freedom accompanying every outward human action. Further, we regard those actions as if they were necessitated directly and solely through the beginning of the series. This we do, not only when we have initiated a series, glad for the superiority that we thereby establish over others of our kind, but also to excuse or lament those of our own actions that are part of a series initiated by others. That is, since, as was previously shown,[205] we were justified in calling free those changes in ourselves – whether in representations or actions – that initiate in us a new series according to the law of the succession of ideas, and since this series itself has arisen according to the law of motion occasioned by some external

---

205. See pp. 129ff.

object, so we are in this case strongly inclined to give up our right and deny the freedom of such a change. We do this under the pretext that this change and the entire consequent series have not occurred in the natural series of our own representations, as that series would have developed in and by itself, in that at the beginning of the series the occasioning object, with which our lot was already cast, was deliberately laid in our way and we were therefore actually necessitated by the originator of the series.

Everyone may easily see that, according to our explanation, none of this account hinders the application of the idea of freedom to such actions and that all the related conflicts so often waged in particular cases rest upon no real grounds. A great many of these confused misunderstandings and false consequences are incontestably the fault of linguistic usage, which does not come close to making the distinctions here that we have made. All the different cases that we have comprehended in our second type – so dissimilar with respect to the way the idea of freedom is applied, in relation to both practical worth and the validity of the whole concept – usage lumps under the name of *outward freedom*. No wonder, then, that in this way what [355] bears the same name is credited with the same worth and validity and that it even frequently happens that we completely exchange one of these concepts for the other. It is evident that only a general explanation of the principal concept, together with a well regulated application of it, can lead us securely here and show us the distinctions we usually overlook.

Section 3. Concerning Freedom As a Predicate of a Situation

Convinced of these advantages, we wish to follow the same course here, so that first we shall employ the concept of a situation that we presented above,[206] seeking to determine the content of this rubric in general. The laws that are to circumscribe the magnitude and direction of a situation's power to influence such a series in its actions could never come from anywhere else than from the things with which the situation stands in reciprocity – thus either from the natural things outside the situation or from human beings, insofar as we are viewed not merely as things of nature but as law-giving[207].

---

206. See p. 123.
207. **Gesezgebend.**

In connection with the former of these, it is certainly true that we are subject in many ways to the things of outer nature, which by their character and influence very often restrict our actions and set limits to our intentions. Yet there are various causes why these restrictions cannot be thought of as a situation, and least of all as a situation in relation to freedom. First, the laws by which this influence is regulated are laws by which a particular situation is formulated only for natural things and for our bodies. Our souls, however, are almost always regulated only by singular, accidental influences, produced not by simple laws easy to understand but rather by an externally compounded – and for this reason difficult to determine and constantly changing – complexion of circumstances. Furthermore, these restrictions do not really affect our will immediately but only our faculty of causation with respect to external objects, which relates to action that actually occurs. In this way two divisions are defined, distinguishing between actively desiring and wishing – the latter being the proper field for the well-known rule, "will nothing except what [356] you can do." However, this outward influence cannot be thought of as a situation in relation to freedom. True, such influence very often enters our path, but it always impinges upon our actions only in their particular parts and ancillary circumstances, never determining entire series of our actions.

Thus there remain only the restrictions which we cause, insofar as we are not regarded as things of outer nature, through the influence of our will and actions upon the wills and actions of others. The community of people with other people, as choosing, acting beings, is called *sociality*[208]. Now if we should think of sociality and its consequences also as something merely accidental, not existing under rules that pertain to and are derived from it alone, then it would likewise not belong here. Only insofar as this community exists under distinctively characteristic laws as conditions of its possibility do people live in a *social situation*[209]. Laws for every betterment and extension of community must often be modified in response to particular significant circumstances, however, and therefore they are not permanent but are rather constantly changing. Thus the social situation can be regarded from two points of view: with respect to effects the social situation's laws have upon actions, or the *civic situation*[210]; and with respect to the direct effects

---

208. **Geselligkeit.**
209. **Geselligen Zustand.**
210. **Bürgerlichen Zustand.**

the combined actions have upon the community's laws themselves, or the *political situation*[211].

With reference therefore to the applicability and meaning of the common expressions civic freedom and political freedom, in order to decide in light of our explanation whether and to what extent actions determined through the law of these situations can be thought of within a series and as initiating a series[212]

---

211. **Politischen Zustand.**
212. Ed. note: Here the manuscript breaks off. Schleiermacher did not complete this third section or his planned fourth section on freedom as a predicate of human faculties.

SELECTED BIBLIOGRAPHY

Works Cited

Blackwell, Albert. *Schleiermacher's Early Philosophy of Life: Determinism, Freedom, and Phantasy*. Chico, CA: Scholars Press, 1982.

Dilthey, Wilhelm. *Leben Schleiermachers*. Berlin: Georg Reimer, 1870.

Fawcett, Joseph. *Sermons Delivered at the Sunday-Evening Lecture, for the Winter Season, at the Old Jewry*. 2 vols. 2d ed. London: J. Johnson, 1801.

Gamwell, Franklin I. *The Divine Good: Modern Moral Theory and the Necessity of God*. New York: Harper Collins, 1990.

Grommelt, Carl, and Christine von Mertens. *Das Dohnasche Schloß Schlobitten in Ostpreußen*. Stuttgart: W. Kohlhammer, 1962.

Kant, Immanuel. *Critik der practischen Vernunft*. Riga: Johann Friedrich Hartknoch, 1788.

Kant, Immanuel. *Critik der reinen Vernunft*. 2d ed. Riga: Johann Friedrich Hartknoch, 1787.

Kant, Immanuel. *Critique of Practical Reason*. Tr. Lewis White Beck. Indianapolis and New York: Bobbs-Merrill, 1956.

Kant, Immanuel. *Kritik der praktischen Vernunft. Kant's gesämmelte Schriften* I/5. Ed. Königlich Preußischen Akademie der Wissenschaften. Berlin: Georg Reimer, 1908.

Kant, Immanuel. *Kritik der reinen Vernunft. Kant's gesämmelte Schriften* I/3. Ed. Königlich Preußischen Akademie der Wissenschaften. Berlin: Georg Reimer, 1905.

Meckenstock, Günter. *Deterministische Ethik und kritische Theologie: Die Auseinandersetzung des frühen Schleiermacher mit Kant und Spinoza 1789-1794*. Berlin and New York: Walter de Gruyter, 1988.

Meisner, Heinrich. *Schleiermachers Lehrjahre.* Ed. Hermann Mulert. Berlin and Leipzig: Walter de Gruyter, 1934.

Meyer, E. R. *Schleiermachers und C. G. Brinkmanns Gang durch die Brüdergemeine.* Leipzig: Friedrich Jansa, 1905.

[Müller, Adolph.] *Aus dem Nachlaß Varnhagens von Ense: Briefe von der Universität in die Heimath.* Leipzig: F. A. Brockhaus, 1874.

Schleiermacher, Friedrich. *Die christliche Sitte.* Ed. L. Jonas. 2d ed. Berlin: Georg Reimer, 1884.

Schleiermacher, Friedrich. *Friedrich Daniel Ernst Schleiermacher: Kritische Gesamtausgabe.* Ed. Hans-Joachim Birkner et al. 5 divisions in multiple vols. Berlin and New York: Walter de Gruyter, 1980-

Schleiermacher, Friedrich. *Grundlinien einer Kritik der bisherigen Sittenlehre. Sämmtliche Werke* III.1. Berlin: Georg Reimer, 1846, 1-344.

Schleiermacher, Friedrich. *Predigten. Erste Sammlung. Sämmtliche Werke* II.1. Berlin: Georg Reimer, 1834, 5-184.

Schleiermacher, Friedrich. *Psychologie.* Ed. L. George. *Sämmtliche Werke* III.6. Berlin: George Reimer, 1862.

Schleiermacher, Friedrich. *Schleiermacher als Mensch. Sein Werden. Familien- und Freundesbriefe 1783 bis 1804.* Ed. Heinrich Meisner. Gotha: Friedrich Andreas Perthes, 1922.

Schleiermacher, Friedrich. "Schleiermachers Briefwechsel mit Friedrich Heinrich Christian Schwarz." Ed. H. Mulert and H. Meisner. *Zeitschrift für Kirchengeschichte* 53 (1934), 255-294.

Schleiermacher, Friedrich. *Versuch einer Theorie des geselligen Betragens.* Ed. Herman Nohl. *Schleiermachers Werke,* II. Ed. Otto Braun and D. Joh. Bauer. Leipzig: Felix Meiner, 1913, 1-31.

Other Works

Adams, Norman Ratcliff. "Schleiermacher's Philosophy of Freedom and His Relation to the Leibnizian Tradition." Diss. Syracuse University, 1941.

Allison, Henry E. *The Kant-Eberhard Controversy.* Baltimore: The Johns Hopkins University Press, 1973.

Brandt, Richard B. *The Philosophy of Schleiermacher.* New York: Harper and Brothers, 1941.

Creuzer, Leonhard. *Skeptische Betrachtungen über die Freyheit des Willens mit Hinsicht auf die neuesten Theorien über dieselbe.* Giessen: Georg Friedrich Heyer, 1793.

Dorner, August. *Schleiermachers Verhältnis zu Kant. Theologische Studien und Kritiken* 74 (1901), 5-75.

Dunkmann, Karl. *Der Religionsbegriff Schleiermachers in seiner Abhängigkeit von Kant. Zeitschrift für Philosophie und philosophische Kritik* 151 (1913), 79-101.

Esselborn, Friedrich Wilhelm. *Die philosophischen Voraussetzungen von Schleiermachers Determinismus.* Ludwigshafen: J. G. Biller, 1897.

Hering, Hermann. *Samuel Ernst Timotheus Stubenrauch und sein Neffe Friedrich Schleiermacher.* Gütersloh: C. Bertelsmann, 1919.

Herms, Eilert. *Herkunft, Entfaltung und erste Gestalt des Systems der Wissenschaften bei Schleiermacher.* Gütersloh: Gerd Mohn, 1974.

Kimmerle, Heinz. *Das Verhältnis Schleiermachers zum transzendentalen Idealismus. Kant-Studien* 51 (1959/60), 410-26.

Loew, Wilhelm. *Das Grundproblem der Ethik Schleiermachers in seiner Beziehung zu Kants Ethik. Kantstudien* 31 (1914), 113 pp. Reprint ed., Würzburg, 1971.

Meding, Wichmann von, "Schleiermacher als Zeuge gegen die Todesstrafe." *New Athenaeum/Neues Athenaeum* II (1991), 60-68.

Seifert, Paul. *Die Theologie des jungen Schleiermacher.* Gütersloh: Gerd Mohn, 1960.

Weber, Fritz. *Schleiermachers Wissenschaftsbegriff. Eine Studie aufgrund seiner frühesten Abhandlungen.* Gütersloh: Gerd Mohn, 1973.

Wehrung, Georg. *Schleiermacher in der Zeit seines Werdens.* Gütersloh: C. Bertelsmann, 1927.

INDEX

Names, Places, and Titles

SCHLEIERMACHER: STUDIES-AND-TRANSLATIONS

1. Friedrich Schleiermacher, **Brief Outline of Theology as a Field of Study**, Terrence N. Tice (trans.)

2. Friedrich Schleiermacher, **On the Academy**, Terrence N. Tice and Edwina Lawler (trans.)

3. Friedrich Schleiermacher, **Sermons on The Christian Household**, Dietrich Seidel and Terrence N. Tice (trans.)

4. Friedrich Schleiermacher, **On Music**, Albert L. Blackwell (trans. and introduction)

5. Herbert W. Richardson (ed.), **Friedrich Schleiermacher and the Founding of the University Of Berlin: The Study of Religion as a Scientific Discipline**

6. Ruth Drucilla Richardson (ed.), **Schleiermacher in Context: Papers from the 1988 International Symposium on Schleiermacher at Herrnhut, the German Democratic Republic**

7. Ruth Drucilla Richardson, **The Role of Women in the Life and Thought of the Early Schleiermacher (1768-1806): An Historical Overview**

8. Friedrich Schleiermacher, **Occasional Thoughts on Universities in the German Sense, With an Appendix Regarding a University Soon to Be Established (1808)**, Terrence N. Tice and Edwina Lawler (trans.)

9. Friedrich Schleiermacher, **On Freedom**, Albert L. Blackwell (trans., annotation and introduction)